Sound and Form in Modern Poetry

Sound and Form in Modern Poetry

A Study of Prosody from Thomas Hardy to Robert Lowell

—

Harvey Gross

Ann Arbor Paperbacks
The University of Michigan Press

First edition as an Ann Arbor Paperback 1968

Published in the United States of America by
The University of Michigan Press and simultaneously
in Rexdale, Canada, by Ambassador Books Limited
United Kingdom agent: The Cresset Press
Manufactured in the United States of America

TO MY MOTHER AND FATHER

sine quibus hic liber . . .

Acknowledgments

The writing of this book has been aided by grants of money and time from the Graduate College of the University of Denver and from the Chancellor's Venture Fund. I am indebted to Vice-Chancellor Edward K. Graham and Chancellor Chester M. Alter, the former for suggesting, the latter for securing, a quarter's leave and a generous allotment of money.

Friends and colleagues have read portions of the manuscript and saved me from both error and arrogance. Florence Howe, of Goucher College, John F. Adams and Robert D. Richardson, of the University of Denver, and Myron Simon, of the University of Michigan, have made valuable comments on style and content. My brother-in-law, Jan La Rue, of New York University, has made helpful suggestions on musical matters; John N. Hough, of the University of Colorado, and Stephanie Benton, of the University of Denver corrected my Latin scansions. Sonia Bronstein typed and retyped the manuscript; Jeanette McGovern conscientiously checked it; Virginia McGehee helped with bibliographical problems. My wife, Virginia La Rue Gross, has taken the advice of that great "master of the meters," John Donne, and studied, to its infinite improvement, "this all-graved tome/ In cypher writ."

I owe special thanks to my friend William B. Goodman whose interest and enthusiasm persuaded me to undertake this book.

I am grateful to the Department of Special Collections of the library of the University of California at Los Angeles for permission to reproduce the manuscript of Ezra Pound's *Canto XIII.*

Portions of this book have appeared in *The Centennial Review* and *The Bucknell Review;* their editors, Herbert Weisinger and Harry Garvin, have graciously allowed me to rework my material here.

H. G.

Denver, Colorado
January 1964

Acknowledgments are extended to the following authors, publishers, and agents for kind permission to quote copyrighted materials.

To the Estate of Richard Aldington for "The Faun Sees Snow for the First Time," from *Collected Poems,* 1949.

To Random House, Inc. and Faber and Faber Ltd.:

for "Doom Is Dark and Deeper" (excerpt):
From "Doom is dark and deeper," Copyright 1934 and renewed 1961 by W. H. Auden. Reprinted from *The Collected Poetry of W. H. Auden.*

for "Hearing of Harvest Rotting" (excerpt):
From "Hearing of Harvest Rotting." Copyright 1937 by W. H. Auden. Reprinted from *On This Island,* by W. H. Auden.

for "Look, Stranger, on This Island Now":
Copyright 1937 by W. H. Auden. Reprinted from *The Collected Poetry of W. H. Auden.*

for "May with Its Light Behaving" (excerpt) and "Now the Leaves Are Falling Fast" (excerpt):
From "May with Its Light Behaving" and "Now the Leaves Are Falling Fast." Copyright 1937 by W. H. Auden. Reprinted from *The Collected Poetry of W. H. Auden.*

for "Musee des Beaux Arts" (excerpt) and "The Unknown Citizen" (excerpt) and "In Memory of W. B. Yeats" (excerpt):
From "Musee des Beaux Arts," "The Unknown Citizen," and "In Memory of W. B. Yeats." Copyright 1940 by W. H. Auden. Reprinted from *The Collected Poetry of W. H. Auden.*

for specified lines from *For the Time Being:*
From "For the Time Being." Copyright 1944 by W. H. Auden. Reprinted from *The Collected Poetry of W. H. Auden.*

for "Dame Kind" (excerpt):
From "Dame Kind," © Copyright 1960 by W. H. Auden. Reprinted from *Homage To Clio,* by W. H. Auden.

for *The Age of Anxiety* (excerpt):
From *The Age of Anxiety,* by W. H. Auden. Copyright 1946, 1947 by W. H. Auden.

for "Under Which Lyre" (excerpt):
From "Under Which Lyre," Copyright 1946 by W. H. Auden. Reprinted from *Nones,* by W. H. Auden.

for "The Shield of Achilles" (excerpt):
From "The Shield of Achilles," Copyright 1952 by W. H. Auden. Reprinted from *The Shield of Achilles,* by W. H. Auden.

To the Clarendon Press Oxford for *Poetical Works of Robert Bridges,* 1953.

To Liveright Publishing Corporation for *The Collected Poems of Hart Crane,* copyright © 1933, 1958 by the Liveright Publishing Corporation.

To Harcourt, Brace & World, Inc., for 1 and 13 from E. E. Cumming's *No Thanks;* for 13 and 40 from *XAIPE;* for 1 from *95 Poems;* from *Poems,* 1923–1954, copyright 1935, 1950 by E. E. Cummings; *95 Poems,* copyright 1958 by E. E. Cummings.

To Little, Brown and Company for Emily Dickinson's "After Great Pain, a Formal Feeling Comes."

To Harcourt, Brace, and World, Inc., and Faber and Faber Ltd. for excerpts from T. S. Eliot's *Collected Poems* 1909–1962, copyright 1963 by T. S. Eliot; from *Selected Essays,* copyright Harcourt, Brace, and Co., 1932, 1936, 1950; from *The Family Reunion,* copyright 1939 by T. S. Eliot; from *The Cocktail Party,* copyright 1950 by T. S. Eliot.

To Farrar, Straus & Company and Faber and Faber Ltd. for excerpts from T. S. Eliot's *On Poetry and Poets,* copyright © 1943, 1945, 1951, 1954, 1956, 1957 by T. S. Eliot; from *The Elder Statesman,* copyright © 1959 by T. S. Eliot.

To Harcourt, Brace, and World, Inc. and Chatto & Windus Ltd. for excerpts from William Empson's *Collected Poems,* copyright 1935, 1940, 1949, 1955 by William Empson.

To Charlie May Fletcher (Mrs. John Gould Fletcher) for excerpts from John Gould Fletcher's "The Green Symphony" and "The Skaters."

To Holt, Rinehart and Winston, Inc., Jonathan Cape Ltd., and Laurence Pollinger Ltd. for excerpts from Robert Frost's *Collected Poems of Robert Frost,* copyright 1930 by Henry Holt & Co.; copyright 1936 by Robert Frost.

To The University of Chicago Press and Faber and Faber Ltd. for "My Sad Captains" from Thom Gunn's *My Sad Captains,* © 1961 by Thom Gunn.

To The Macmillan Company (United States), The Macmillan Company of Canada Limited, and St. Martin's Press for excerpts from *Collected Poems of Thomas Hardy;* by permission of the Trustees of the Hardy Estate, Macmillan & Co. Ltd., London, and The Macmillan Company of Canada Limited.

To the Grove Press, Inc. for excerpts from H. D.'s *Selected Poems,* copyright © 1957 by Norman Holmes Pearson; from *Helen in Egypt* by H. D., copyright © 1961 by Norman Holmes Pearson.

To the Oxford University Press for excerpts from *Poems of Gerard Manley Hopkins,* Third Edition, copyright 1948 by Oxford University Press, Inc.

To the Viking Press, Inc. and The Society of Authors (London) for a passage from James Joyce's *Finnegans Wake,* copyright 1939 by James Joyce.

To Little, Brown and Company for excerpts from *Selected Poems, 1928–1958* by Stanley Kunitz, copyright © 1929, 1930, 1944, 1951, 1953, 1954, 1956, 1957, 1958 by Stanley Kunitz.

To The University of Chicago Press for excerpts from Richmond Lattimore's *Greek Lyrics,* copyright 1949 and 1955 by Richmond Lattimore; all rights reserved; copyright International Copyright Union, 1955.

To Houghton Mifflin Company for excerpts from *Selected Poems by Amy Lowell,* copyright 1922, 1925, 1926, 1927.

To Harcourt, Brace, and World, Inc. and Faber and Faber Ltd. for excerpts from Robert Lowell's *Lord Weary's Castle,* copyright 1944, 1946 by Robert Lowell.

To Farrar, Straus & Company, Inc. and Faber and Faber Ltd. for excerpts from Robert Lowell's *Life Studies,* copyright © 1956, 1959 by Robert Lowell.

To Houghton Mifflin Company for Archibald MacLeish's "Frescoes for Mr. Rockefeller's City," from Archibald MacLeish's *Collected Poems,* 1917–1952, copyright 1952 by Archibald MacLeish.

To Faber and Faber Ltd. for excerpts from Louis MacNeice's *Collected Poems 1925–1948,* all rights reserved.

To The Macmillan Company and Faber and Faber Ltd. for "The Monkeys" and excerpts from Marianne Moore's *Selected Poems,* copyright 1935 by Marianne Moore; for excerpts from *What Are Years,* copyright 1941 by Marianne Moore. To the Viking Press for "In the Public Garden" from *O To Be a Dragon,* copyright © 1956, 1957, 1958, 1959; copyright © 1958 by The Curtis Publishing Company.

To Grove Press, Inc. and Faber and Faber Ltd. for excerpts from Edwin Muir's *Collected Poems 1921–1951,* copyright © 1957 by Edwin Muir.

To New Directions and Chatto & Windus Ltd. for excerpts from *Poems of Wilfred Owen,* all rights reserved.

To New Directions, to Mr. Arthur V. Moore (agent), and to Mr. Ezra Pound for excerpts from *Personae, the Collected Poems of Ezra Pound,* copyright 1926 by Ezra Pound; *The Cantos of Ezra Pound,* copyright 1934, 1937, 1940, 1948 by Ezra Pound; from *Section: Rock-Drill,* copyright 1956 by Ezra Pound; from *Thrones* © 1959 by Ezra Pound.

To Alfred A. Knopf, Inc., Laurence Pollinger Ltd., and Eyre & Spotteswoode Ltd. for excerpts from *Selected Poems by John Crowe Ransom,* copyright 1924, 1927, 1934, 1939, 1945 by Alfred A. Knopf, Inc.

To Harcourt, Brace, and World, Inc. and Jonathan Cape Limited for excerpts from Henry Reed's *A Map of Verona and Other Poems,* copyright 1947 by Henry Reed. To Mr. Henry Reed for excerpts from "The Auction Sale" published in *Encounter,* October 1958.

To The Macmillan Company for excerpts from *Tilbury Town: Selected Poems of Edward Arlington Robinson,* copyright 1925, 1953 by The Macmillan Company.

To Doubleday & Company, Inc. for excerpts from *Words for the Wind* (*The Collected Verse of Theodore Roethke*), copyright 1958 by Theodore Roethke.

To Doubleday & Company for excerpts from Delmore Schwartz's *Summer Knowledge,* copyright 1959 by Delmore Schwartz.

To Random House, Inc.

for *Essay On Rime* (excerpt):

From *Essay On Rime,* by Karl Shapiro. Copyright 1945 by Karl Shapiro.

To Random House, Inc. and Faber and Faber Ltd.

for "I Think Continually of Those" (excerpt):

From "I Think Continually of Those." Copyright 1934 and reprinted 1961 by Stephen Spender. Reprinted from *Collected Poems 1928–1953,* by Stephen Spender.

for "An Elementary School Classroom" (excerpt):

From "An Elementary School Classroom." Copyright 1942 by Stephen Spender. Reprinted from *Collected Poems, 1928–1953,* by Stephen Spender.

for *Vienna* (excerpt):

From *Vienna* by Stephen Spender, all rights reserved; copyright 1935 by the Modern Library, Inc.

To Alfred A. Knopf, Inc. and Faber and Faber Ltd. for excerpts from *The Collected Poems of Wallace Stevens,* copyright 1923, 1931, 1942, 1947, 1954 by Wallace Stevens.

To Harcourt, Brace, and World, Inc. for excerpts from Ruth Stone's *In an Iridescent Time,* © 1959 by Ruth Stone.

To New Directions, J. M. Dent & Sons, Ltd. and the Executors of the Dylan Thomas Estate, for "What Is the Meter of the Dictionary," and other excerpts from Dylan Thomas' *Collected Poems,* copyright 1953 by Dylan Thomas.

To New Directions and Faber and Faber Ltd. for excerpts from Vernon Watkins' *Selected Poems,* 1948, all rights reserved; from Vernon Watkins' *The Death Bell,* all rights reserved.

To New Directions and MacGibbon & Kee Ltd. for excerpts from *The Collected Earlier Poems of William Carlos Williams,* copyright 1951 by William Carlos Williams; from *Paterson, Book II,* copyright 1948 by William Carlos Williams.

To The Macmillan Company, The Macmillan Company of Canada, A. P. Watt & Son (agent), Messrs Macmillan, and Mrs. W. B. Yeats for excerpts from *Collected Poems of W. B. Yeats* and *Collected Plays of W. B. Yeats.*

Contents

Sound and Form in Modern Poetry

A NOTE ON SCANSION

I scan syllable-stress or traditional meter as follows: all unmarked syllables count as unstressed; all syllables marked with an acute accent (/) count as stressed. A grave accent (\) marks syllables metrically unstressed but which carry a weight of rhetorical stress heavier than normal unstressed syllables. A vertical line (|) marks the division between feet; a double vertical line (||) marks the caesura. For the scansion of strong-stress or Old English accentual meter, see the principles outlined in Chapter II.

Prologue: In the Dark Wood

The prosodist attempting the hazards of modern poetry finds his way blocked by the beasts of confusion. Like Dante he wavers at the very outset of his journey. He finds four beasts: no general agreement on what *prosody* means and what subject matter properly belongs to it; no apparent dominant metrical convention such as obtained in the centuries previous to this one; no accepted theory about how prosody functions in a poem; and no critical agreement about the scansion of the English meters.

We must first brave the Terminological Menace. Classically understood, prosody was part of grammar and, like grammar, concerned itself with rules and paradigms. Schoolboys set to scan their Virgil and Horace had to learn the rules and the exceptions, the exceptions to the exceptions, and the other minutiae which determined the short and long of Latin versification. Prosody explained the classical meters, their nature and structure. Prosody was the grammar of metrics; its precision was such that dictionaries still give as its first meaning *that science which treats of versification*. Far from naming a science or being subsumed under grammar, prosody has now a number of descriptive and evaluative meanings.

The word denotes not only the study of a poet's versification, but that which is studied, the versification itself. This is an accepted meaning of the word. When Saintsbury came to title his *History,* he called it a *History of English Prosody*. He did not intend it as a history of the theory of versification; he meant it primarily as an account of the poetry itself. Thus I speak here of "Yeats' prosody" or "Eliot's prosody." Perhaps it would be clearer if we relinquished this use of *prosody* to describe the technical abilities a poet shows in versification, and speak only of a poet's *metric*. Unfortunately *metric* suggests meter, and it seems absurd to discuss the *metric* of lines like these:

(im)c-a-t(mo)
b,i;l:e

FallleA
ps!fl
OattumblI

sh?dr
IftwhirlF
(Ul)(lY)
&&&

away wanders: exact
ly;as if
not
hing had, ever happ
ene

D

Cummings, 57 from XAIPE

Here is our second beast: the "prosody" of nonmetrical verse. The lines above are an extreme example, even for Cummings, but the rhythmic structure of much modern poetry is seemingly without metrical bases. I say *seemingly* because a true nonmetrical prosody is difficult to sustain in English: Whitman again and again falls into "English hexameter"; Eliot often writes in strong-stress meter. But we must recognize the typographic rhythms of Cummings as characteristic nonmetrical prosody. In the poem above prosodic shape exists for the eye alone; the poem's rhythms are visual rather than aural. We cannot, however, write a grammar of Cummings' visual prosody; we can locate the ground of his rhythm, but not the measure by which it moves.

Our third beast twins with the first: understanding what prosody *is* depends on how we conceive its function. My first chapter describes the way rhythmic structure works in a poem. I venture that rhythmic structure neither ornaments conceptual meaning nor provides a sensuous element extraneous to meaning; prosody is a symbolic structure like metaphor and carries its own weight of meaning. This concept of prosody is possibly too broad; it might be the cannier strategy to restrict *prosody* to exclusively metrical matters. But I would have to discard, as being without rhythmic structure, the unmetered sections of *The Bridge* and

Four Quartets, the *Song of Myself,* and nearly all the poems of D. H. Lawrence.

Prosody is an evaluative as well as a technical term. We tend to use the word qualitatively: if not precisely as an honorific, certainly with a charge of special meaning. A prosody is something a poet achieves—distinction in the movement of his language, rhythmic style. And perhaps the title of this book should be *Examples of Style in Modern Prosody.* Style in art, as Whitehead remarks, "is the fashioning of power, the restraining of power"—in other words, control. Such control is always the result of an equilibrium: the balancing of idiosyncracy with tradition, personal freedom with restraint, revolt with conformity. To be idiosyncratic, however, presupposes the existence of tradition; to revolt presupposes the presence of a conformity, a convention, against which revolt is possible.

In English verse syllable-stress (frequently called accentual-syllabic) meters establish the normative convention. Against this convention, or against the memory of it, poets achieve distinguished prosodies. Mere metrical regularity, of course, does not produce distinctive prosody; it is more apt to produce doggerel. But when we turn to the poetry that evokes the deepest feelings, we often find metrical structures controlling the rhythms, making thought clear and emotion precise. This is even true of the many varieties of nonmetrical prosody—where rhythm hardly runs down the "metalled ways" of iambs or anapests. Whitman's prosody is largely a matter of syntactical parallelism, but many memorable lines move to a hexameter lilt:

> O how shall I warble myself for the dead one there I loved?
> And how shall I deck my song for the large sweet soul that
> has gone?
> And what shall my perfume be for the grave of him I love?

Those often-quoted passages from Pound's *Cantos,* which disentangle themselves from the encumbering wreckage of the rest of the poem, reveal the smoothest, most limpid meters:

> Hast 'ou seen the rose in the steel dust
> (or swansdown ever?)
> so light is the urging, so ordered the dark petals of iron
> we who have passed over Lethe.
>
> from *Canto LXXIV*

We now encounter the Lion In Our Path: the scansion of the English meters. "Very few can mark the scansion from a line of Shakespeare's sonnets," Yvor Winters gloomily remarks.[1] Handy proof of his observation is offered in a recent book on "the enjoyment of poetry":

And tróu | ble deaf héav | en wíth | my bóot | less críes . . .[2]

This scansion compounds insensitivity with ignorance. *Heaven* is monosyllabic in Elizabethan verse; to scan the second foot as trisyllabic, placing a heavy stress on *with,* distorts the rhythmical beauty of the line. The trisyllabic foot is conspicuously absent in the Shakespearean sonnet line; but the inverted foot, at strategic points of rhythmical tension, is often very much present. The line scans:

And tróu | ble déaf | héaven with | my bóot | less críes . . .

We might expect to find metrical ineptness in popular books of appreciation. However, when a scholar with the stature of Sir Herbert Grierson scans the final line of Donne's "A Nocturnall upon S. Lucies Day,"

Bŏth thĕ yēars | ănd thĕ dāys | dēep mīd | nĭght ĭs . . .[3]

we wonder if anyone understands the nature of English syllable-stress metric. Grierson uses the inappropriate macron (—) and breve (⌣) of classical prosody, and marks approximate speech stress rather than the metrical pattern. He is phrasing the poem, not scanning it. Our reading of the meter is:

Bóth the | yéars and | the dáys | deep míd | night ís . . .

Grierson's scansion, following as it does his own performance of the line, does not discover the crucial variation from the metrical norm: the inversion of the rhythmically sensitive second foot.

Since polemic is not our intention, we need not multiply examples of the mistakes and misconceptions which plague metrical theory. It is enough to say that generations of scholars, critics, and cranks obscured simple but basic principles. Men of otherwise sound minds and good breeding forsook their wits and exhibited the most appalling manners when they discussed prosody. From about the middle of the nineteenth century to the publication of Saintsbury's *History* (1906–1910), prosody developed into a bloody war of contending theories. The results of the controversy were desultory and inconclusive. No one ever knew whose side he was on; no one ever found out who won.

The various "revolutionary ideas" developed and promulgated now seem so wrongheaded that we wonder how anyone could have seriously entertained them. The musical scansion of Sidney Lanier's *The Science of English Verse,* praised by T. S. Omond, Harriet Monroe, and others, remains a dismaying example of a theory ridden sadly beyond the limits of good sense. A "scansion" which gives this sort of thing is worse than useless; it scatters sand in the eyes and pours wax in the ears:

3/8 To be | or not | to be: | that is | the ques-tion . . .[4]

We might, for the moment, oppose Saintsbury to Lanier. *The History of English Prosody* is in the great tradition of three-volume scholarship; it is still, after fifty years, the only complete treatment of its subject. But Saintsbury dodges fundamental theoretical questions, talks about "long" and "short" syllables, and heroically resists the idea that stress has the crucial role in determining the English metrical foot. We are, of course, impressed by Saintsbury's vast acquaintance with the texts of English poetry; we may be charmed or irritated by his chauvinism, and sometimes appalled by what can be only deliberate or convenient ignorance in elementary matters:

> Is it not a rather more reasonable theory that we Englishmen talk very much as our ancestors talked when first the blend of 'Saxon and Norman and Dane' historically established itself in our race and, to say the very least, historically coincided with these first appearances of our poetry?[5]

This in the face of the philological and linguistic evidence painstakenly gathered by Saintsbury's contemporaries!

His faults are also his virtues. To modern scholarship his lack of method may seem frivolous and irresponsible; in an age equipped with oscillographs, tape recorders, metalinguistics, and the newest criticism, he seems naive and unprofessional—an English don who relishes poetry. Yet carrying no great burden of theoretical preconceptions, he rarely stumbles into self-contradiction. He relies on his ear to tell him what is good or bad prosody. Unhindered by set formulas, he can approve of Walt Whitman's "versicles" and acknowledge that the prosodical ideas of a yet unpublished poet, Father Gerard Hopkins, deserve special notice.

An ideal prosodist would combine Saintsbury's taste and enthusiasm with a comprehensive theory of English metric. But what theory? The old battle about the nature of the English meters is being fought with new weapons and renewed fury. The issues are all familiar: quantity versus stress; foot-prosody versus musical scansion; the linguists versus the aestheticians. The strategies are, however, more refined; the prosodist has at his disposal the analytic techniques of the New Criticism and the methodological machinery of the phoneticians. Although it may be still too early to make accurate predictions, this new war may end in a definite victory. A clear and unequivocal point of view is emerging.

Two recent studies have helped clear the battlefield of prosodical inquiry. One is Wimsatt and Beardsley's "The Concept of Meter"; the other, C. S. Lewis's "Metre." Both studies affirm the paradigmatic nature of meter: "When we ask for the metre of a poem we are asking for the paradigm"[6]; ". . . meter is something which for the most part inheres in language precisely at that level of linguistic organization which grammars and dictionaries and elementary rhetoric can successfully cope with."[7] Wimsatt and Beardsley and Lewis would return metrical study to its classical concerns with law, with figures of grammar—not matters of taste or of interpretation—on which general agreement can be reached. Consequently, these authors recommend the traditional foot prosody and its traditional nomenclature for scanning syllable-stress meter.

These views, which I believe correct, have no general currency. The journals re-echo with noisy polemics and learned confusion; the writer on prosody can take nothing for granted. A lion and a leopard still block our path; to drive them away means returning to basic facts and elementary principles. The beast of terminology can be best handled by a few clear statements about *prosody, metric,* and *versification,* and the consistent use of these words in similar contexts. The prosodical nature of modern poetry will menace us throughout the book; we shall, I hope, bring this beast into the house for domestication. It is the whole intention of this study. But the howling disagreements about the function of prosody and the nature of the English meters must be put down before we can proceed.

I

Prosody as Rhythmic Cognition

I

Our understanding of prosody's function is based on what a poem is, and how we conceive the nature of rhythm. Without launching into extended aesthetic theory, let us scrutinize briefly the ontological terrain. A poem is not an "idea" or an "experience" rendered into metrical language; still less is it an attitude toward an experience. A poem is a symbol in which idea, experience, and attitude are transmuted into feelings; these feelings move in significant arrangements: rhythmically. It is prosody and its structures which articulate the movement of feeling in a poem, and render to our understanding meanings which are not paraphrasable. Prosody enables the poet to communicate states of awareness, tensions, emotions, all of man's inner life which the helter-skelter of ordinary propositional language cannot express.

Rhythmic structure, like all aesthetic structure, is a symbolic form, signifying the ways we experience organic processes and the phenomena of nature. We speak of the rhythm of life: the curve of human development up from birth, through growth, and down to decay and death. These are not elements in a pattern of simple recurrence. They form patterns of expectation and fulfillment; birth prepares us for each succeeding stage of human development, but no stage merely repeats the stage which precedes it. All process, human or natural, thus has characteristic rhythm. We experience life not only by clock and calendar; we live by another kind of awareness. We shall, let us say, be taking a trip in a few months. We chafe with expectation; the day comes to leave and the tensions of expectation disappear. Our calendar has told us a certain period in time has been traversed; our "other awareness" has told us a certain passage of time has been experienced. The period is a series of separate events, which we can measure and date; the passage of time itself is experienced as a continuum; a mounting tension and its resolution, a rhythm.

It is rhythm that gives time a meaningful definition, a "form." "[If] the feeling of rhythm must be granted the status of a genuine experience, perhaps even of a cognition, then what is experienced in rhythm can only be time itself."[1] In the arts of time, music and literature, rhythmic forms transmit certain kinds of information about the nature of our inner life. This is the life of feeling which includes physiological response as well as what psychologists term affect. There is often difficulty in distinguishing between affect, or emotion, and certain kinds of physical sensation. Those who attempt the neurological explanation of human experience see the difference between physiological and emotive behavior as one of degree and not one of kind. Wild anger or mild irritation depends on how much current flows along the nerves and across the synapses.

Rhythmic sound has the ability to imitate the forms of physical behavior as well as express the highly complex, continually shifting nature of human emotion. The rhythmic form of the following lines is imitative; we hear the rise and fall of feet keeping time to the beat of a drum:

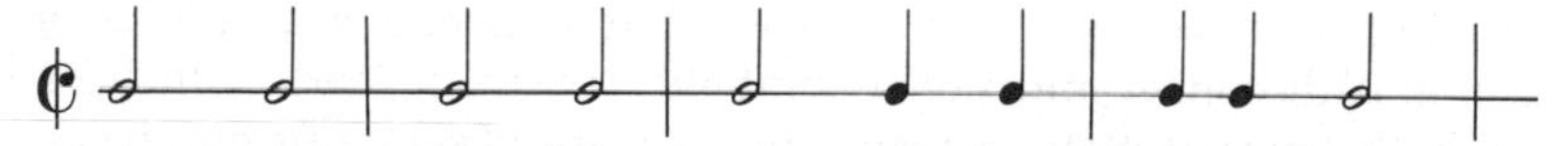

Stone, bronze, stone, steel, stone, oakleaves, horses' heels . . .

T. S. Eliot, "Coriolan"

Prosody here is onomatopoeic, or nearly so. It sounds and "feels like" bodily movement, the flexing and unflexing of muscle and bone. Prosody functions more subtly in these lines:

> Daughters, in the wind's boisterous roughing,
> Pray the tickle's equal to the coat tearing,
> And the wearing equal to the puffing . . .

Ruth Stone, "Vernal Equinox"

Prosody does not imitate the noise of the wind, but gives a curve of feeling, the shape of an emotion. Prosodic elements include the formal patterning of syntax and stress, the quantities of the vowels, and the alliteration of consonants.

As I see it, then, prosody—rhythmic form in poetry—has a more crucial role to play than most theoreticians have previously discerned. The function of rhythmic form in poetry has been treated almost exclusively as a matter of meter and meaning. Ransom believes that meter offers a phonetic surface independent of meaning; we enjoy metrical textures for their own sake. Winters agrees that meter has an expressive function, and in a highly suggestive passage points out the possible relationship between emotion and rhythmic structure:

> In the first place, music is expressive of emotion. I do not understand the relationship between sound and emotion, but it is unquestionably very real: the devotional feeling of Byrd or of Bach, the wit and gaiety of much of Mozart and Haydn, the disillusioned romantic nostalgia of Franck, these are perfectly real, and it is not profitable to argue the point. The correlation between sound and feeling may have its origin in some historical relationship between music and language, or it may, like the capacity to form ideas, have its origin simply in human nature as that is given to us.[2]

But Winters shies away from what might have been a theory of rhythm and feeling; his insistence that a poem is a species of rational discourse and not a symbolic construct leads him back to the belief that meter is primarily a means of semantic emphasis. Regular or irregular metrical structure, in continual interaction with the poem's propositional sense, points up or submerges words, ideas, and attitudes.

The view I take is that meter, and prosody in general, is itself meaning. Rhythm is neither outside of a poem's meaning nor an ornament to it. Rhythmic structures are expressive forms, cognitive elements, communicating those experiences which rhythmic consciousness can alone communicate: empathic human responses to time in its passage. My view does not contradict the theories of Ransom and Winters but supplements them. Prosody, as meter, does offer a texture, an "aesthetic surface"; meter unquestionably brings into special prominence words and ideas. But neither theory stresses that it is through rhythmic structure that the infinite subtleties of human feeling can be most successfully expressed.

The theories of Ransom and Winters, restricted as they are

to metered verse, cannot account for the function of rhythmic structures in nonmetrical verse or in well-written prose. Rhythmic structure offers the means by which a work of literature achieves its peculiar reality, the illusion that what we are reading is quickened with a life of its own. This life is perceived in mental performance as well as in oral recitation; any good prose written for silent reading has significant movement, a "prosody." We do not ordinarily speak of the "prosody of prose," but certainly the rhythmical elements of well-wrought prose offer themselves to aesthetic analysis. Two novelists, far apart in technique and point of view, reveal themselves masters of prosody:

> It is a truth universally acknowledged, that a single man in possession of a good fortune, must be in want of a wife.
>
> Stately, plump Buck Mulligan came from the stairhead, bearing a bowl of lather on which a mirror and a razor lay crossed.

Jane Austen creates "a motion of meaning" by exercising the most loving care for grammatical arrangement. By dispossessing the adjective from its normal position ("truth universally *acknowledged*"), and delaying the predicate of the modifier group with information of crucial interest to middle-class mommas ("in possession of a good fortune"), she fashions a prosody of wit. The movement of her language is quick with "the feel of thought"—the powers of abstraction, of generalization, of perceiving and confronting ideas. Joyce's language moves on different principles. His prose is dense with heavy stresses, alliterative effects, and a careful placing of long and short vowels. He is not concerned with the witty presentation of an idea but with *things* and arrangements; and, as we learn from the context, symbols. The rhythm of Joyce's prose is determined by the weight and shape of the words; Jane Austen's rhythm is determined by the shape of her syntax formed by the energy of her mind.

It is clear that Joyce's prosody is achieved by devices characteristic of poetry: stress, alliteration, and quantity. But how can Jane Austen order *by syntax* the sounds of language into rhythmical meanings symbolic of feeling? Precisely because "such syntax is rhythm but soundless."[3] The logic of grammar sets up a pattern of expectation, and the expressive delays, the departures from usual word order, and the surprising repetitions all form an articulating rhythm representing the liveliest intellectual activity. It may be the rhythm existed in Jane Austen's mind even before she fully worked out the ideas; the feeling of a thought may take shape in consciousness even before the thought can be adequately formulated.

All expressive rhythms are variations upon a pattern of expectation. The "prosody of prose" functions first as those departures from the normal grammatical structures of the language which set up lesser or greater impulses of meaning. When phonetic patterning increases, as in the example from Joyce, prose is shocked into verse. We usually think of the difference between prose and verse as a matter of meter; this is partially true. But the difference lies in the ability of poetry, through *all* the organizing devices of prosody, to achieve a higher expressiveness. The overlappings and concurrences of meter, quantity, and syntax can symbolize the movement of many simultaneous physical or psychological tensions. The tensions of life are never felt singly, in a straight line, as it were; they cross and overlap each other. They exist in depth and are felt in many dimensions. As one tension resolves a second begins, and a third or fourth may be in yet another stage of development. Prosody transmits the intricacy of the life of feeling—an organism where systems of bone, blood, muscle, and nerve often work on different frequencies, cross rhythmically.

2

The function of prosody is to image, in a rich and complex way, human process as it moves in time. On the lower level, prosody can be a direct representation of physical activity. Numerous theorists have pointed out that iambic pentameter resembles simple human physiology: the systole and diastole of the heartbeat or the inhalation and exhalation of breathing. But human process, even in its more basic physiological aspects, is enormously complicated. Growth, fruition, decay, stasis; the process of maturation and decay: all have rhythms which prosody can image. Prosody can also trace the curves of psychological process: perception, sensation, and affect move in time and have their characteristic rhythms. The rhythmic structures of prosody reveal the mind and nerves as they grow tense in expectation and stimulation and relax in fulfillment and quiet.

A short poem of Emily Dickinson shows, in a highly dramatic way, prosody's functions; the poem's subject is the very nature of the inner life of feeling:

1 After great pain, a formal feeling comes—
2 The Nerves sit ceremonious, like Tombs—
3 The stiff Heart questions was it He, that bore,
4 And Yesterday, or Centuries before?

5 The Feet, mechanical, go round—
6 Of Ground, or Air, or Ought—
7 A Wooden way
8 Regardless grown,
9 A Quartz contentment, like a stone—

10 This is the Hour of Lead—
11 Remembered, if outlived,
12 As Freezing persons, recollect the Snow—
13 First—Chill—then Stupor—then the letting go—

A prose paraphrase (a deliberate heresy) tells us that profound physical suffering leaves mind and body in a curious state of detachment. The mind sees the body from a great distance; feelings of depression, inadequacy, indifference afflict consciousness but cause no tremor of emotion. Life has been arrested; the soul has crossed over to the country beyond despair.

Our paraphrase is inadequate, of course. The experience is rendered in the movement of the lines, and part of what the poem "means" is the movement itself. Syntax, meter, quantity, and pause articulate feelings of formal detachment, stupefied indifference, and ceremonious numbness. Rhythmic structure conveys these "ideas"; the rhythms or conveyers are forms for the feelings they convey.

The poem opens with an abstract statement of feeling in a syntactically complete proposition. At the fourth line the syntax becomes fragmentary, and the soundless rhythm of meaning falters on an unresolved grammatical ambiguity. A similar ambiguity arrests the meaning of line eight. Metrically, the lines are of uneven length, although iambic movement dominates. In the second stanza the meter beats metronomically:

Of Gróund, | or Aír, | or Óught—

the quantities of the vowels are nearly equal. The poem ends with a slowing down of rhythmic energy as consciousness dwindles into coma: the stupefaction after terrible suffering. We may show the quantitative rhythms created by syllabic length and rhetorical pause in this approximate way.[4]

We have gradual expansion and relaxation, ending not with the final syllable, but continuing into the silence of the final dash—which I read as a held rest. The effect is hesitating; the line slows down and subsides into nothingness. Prosodic movement carries over beyond the final sound in much the same way that a Beethoven adagio slowly progresses into the silence of apparent time:

This *adagio* does not end at the F major chord, but at the held rest. Artur Schnabel, a scrupulous editor, cautions the performer to observe these final *silences:* a reminder that the musical work exists not only in the world of physical sound but in a temporal continuum formed by sound *and* silence.

We approach the crux of the problem, and we can formulate a working definition of what prosody is and how it functions in poetic structure. It comprises those elements in a poem which abstract for perception the flow of time. This time, experienced in a passage of verse, is not chronological time, measured by metronomic pulse, but *felt* time, musical "duration." If we understand this, the widely used term "the music of poetry" becomes more than an empty honorific—a facile way of complimenting a poet for smoothness of texture or skillful use of verbal color. Prosody is the musical element in poetry because it reveals time in its passage and the life of feeling that moves between points *then* and *then.* Prosodic structures are akin to musical structures because phonetic patterning and syntactical expectation constitute a semantic system, a language, as it were. Like music, the language of prosody is abstract: it represents nothing and may suggest everything. But nonverbal "languages" are meaningful; few modern aestheticians are prepared to assert that the abstract art of music is purely formal, devoid of human qualities and human import.

To insist on "prosody as music" neither denies that prosody develops out of, or emphasizes, conceptual meaning nor asserts that rhythmic and phonetic elements are autonomous structures. A poem's prosody cannot exist apart from its propositional sense. Prosodic rhythm and propositional sense work as identities in poetic language. Phonetic patterning creates meaning in language; rhythm in linguistic structure is itself *sense.* I recall lunching with a cultivated, highly literate East Indian who had never been outside of India until a few weeks before this luncheon. I discovered eventually that his grammar was flawless, his vocabulary rich and varied; but I must confess that during the first hour of our conversation I could barely understand him. He spoke English to a rhythm which made no *sense* to my ears. Prosodic structures, which are a heightening of the ordinary rhythms of English, are created by the meanings of words and the logic of syntax. The elements of prosody work in the closest possible way with the poem's propositional sense—even when that sense is ambiguous or seemingly nonsensical.

Lewis Carroll's "Jabberwocky" provides a good example of a poem in which prosody functions in seeming isolation (it does not, really), and hence we can analyze the poem's rhythmic structure somewhat apart from its paraphrasable meaning. "Jabberwocky" is not, however, meaningless. Carroll conceals, parodies, ornaments meaning; there is more "sense" than the mind can handle:

> 'Twas brillig, and the slithy toves
>   Did gyre and gimble in the wabe:
> All mimsy were the borogoves,
>   And the mome raths outgrabe.

Although what is going on is not clear, the controlling rhythms of syntax and meter give an illusion of denotational meaning as well as the tenor of feeling. Precise grammatical structure creates a soundless syntactical rhythm, a skeleton of meaning without lexical sense. Carroll preserves word order, inflectional endings, and empty words; consequently we can diagram the lines without knowing what the words mean. Meter is regular until the fourth line; here trimeter breaks the prevalent tetrameter movement. The feeling is one of hollowness and sinister vacancy; we are reminded of "And no birds sing."

We respond to prosodic structure, to metrical and syntactical rhythm. Because Carroll maintains English syntax we feel that we understand the qualities of *brillig* and *slithy*, the actions of *gyre* and *gimble*. Syntactical rhythm gives the *feeling* of thought, the forms of mental activity. The closely patterned metrical rhythms elicit generalized affective responses: mystery, confusion, pointless activity. Rhythms of syntax and meter articulate relationships among objects, qualities, and actions which are never precisely denoted. Carroll, we remember, was a mathematician; mathematics deals in pure relationships, devoid of "content." Using the rhythmic structures of language to indicate pure relationship is the essence of Carroll's nonsense—and is the "meaning of his meaning."

The full meaning of a poem involves a great deal more than its paraphrasable conceptual content. This is a truism of contemporary poetics, yet little critical attention has been paid to rhythmic structures which are the direct conveyers of feeling. Indeed, Richards, Empson, and their disciples are contemptuous of the "emotive" aspects of language; the party-line New Criticism has largely concerned itself with the poem's paraphrasable content (ambiguity, paradox, semantics) while maintaining a piety toward the notion that poetry is unparaphrasable. The meaning of a poem includes the meanings its rhythmic structures communicate to the nerves and brain. Obviously we must expand our concept of "meaning" to include rhythmic cognition if we admit prosody as an important structural element in poetry. Like metaphor, prosody is a symbolic structure and is not merely perceived in a poem; its meanings are understood through the symbolizing activities of human consciousness. The mind interprets prosody as feeling, whether we name as feeling crude sensation, violent emotion, or the most delicate of responses to the outside world.

We see the futility in using scientific instruments to interpret the phonetic patterns of poetry. It is true, of course, that prosody orders into special patterns phonetic values: the sounds and silences of language. As a formal element in poetry, meter is an immediate perceptual given: we have the demonstrably audible and measurable facts of stress, quantity, pause, and number. But, we insist, the sounds and silences of meter are not perceptual entities as such; we do not respond to metrical texture as we do to fine silk or highly polished wood. The acoustic arrangements of meter are images of time shaped and charged by human feeling. The machines currently used in prosodic analysis show what happens in an arbitrary temporal sequence. The oscillograph knows nothing of *durée,* of time grasped and understood by human awareness; the machine can record but it cannot perceive in psychologic depth. It cannot translate the symbolism of stress and pause, quantity and pitch, into feeling. The results of the machine are a tautology because no machine understands the uniquely human import of symbolic structures; the machine returns a set of symbols still requiring human interpretation.

I object to the linguists' analysis of prosody on the same grounds. To assume that the description and measurement of a poem's phonetic features account for its prosody is to believe that phonetic texture has no symbolic value and consequently no human relevance. Linguistic science can detail every physical minutia in a line of verse; it can show us phonetic structure but not prosodic function. Seymour Chatman believes "that sound symbolism as such—the assumption that individual phonemes have expressive functions in morphemes—is either without objective foundation or is too subliminal to be very useful in linguistics or stylistics."[5] This may be true for individual sounds or words; it is not true for rhythmic structure in poetic contexts. A musical analogy will help here. If we hear these notes played at random or together as a chord, we experience no definable emotional response: only an aura of generalized feeling:

However, if we add rhythmic structure, give the notes a prosody, feelings are immediately brought into sharp focus:

Linguistic analysis ignores the effect of rhythmic structures in poetry; its approach is statistical, counting and measuring phonetic elements isolated from their rhythmic functions. Like the oscillograph, its results are tautological; the symbols of linguistic analysis do not interpret for us the emotional significance of prosodic structures. Like symbolic activity in general, rhythmic cognition is a function of human consciousness.[6]

3

The analysis of poetic structure must show the identity of content or "idea" and the rhythmic conveyers of feeling. But the poet's private experience of the rhythms of nature and human process must be accessible, through the senses, to the reader. The poet makes them accessible by providing a primary "aesthetic surface":[7] an unbroken texture of phonetic values and patterns. Poetry exists in a sensuous realm of sound; we cannot feel a poem's rhythms until our ears have engaged its "aesthetic surface." In most poems this surface is its meter—heard in spoken performance or imagined in silent reading.

Some poems present this surface so obviously that we are aware of little else:

> Before the beginning of years
> There came to the making of man
> Time with a gift of tears;
> Grief with a glass that ran.

Prosody, if it is a valuable part of poetic structure, must create the illusion of experienced or durational time and what we experience in those fictitious intervals—the movement, stress, and tensions of our emotional life. Swinburne's verse creates little more than an illusion of automatic physical activity; we hear marching men or galloping horses.[8] The higher purpose of prosody is not imitation of physical process, though we can, if we like, do sitting-up exercises to

> Strong gongs groaning as the guns boom far,
> Don John of Austria is going to the war . . .

These examples return us to an earlier question: what is the relation of a poem's prosody to its referential meaning, its paraphrasable content? Certainly prosody has, or should have, mimetic value; there should be some correlation of idea and rhythm. If we sense a disparity between thought and movement—if the meter sounds incongruous to the idea—we have valid grounds for making negative judgments about the poem's value. Swinburne's rhythm, with its catchy swing, seems inappropriate to man's making and the tears of time. We should have rhythms expressive of mystery and grief; not a quick march tempo. We feel muscular exhilaration: scarcely what the subject requires.

I do not believe that every emotion has a precise symbolic form, and in the case of poetry, an exact rhythmical equivalent. The rhythms of poetry belong to the "non-discursive forms" of human symbolism.[9] Rhythms are highly connotative structures, and we cannot say the meter of Swinburne's poem denotes anything more than its patterns of stress:

˘ / | ˘ ˘ / | ˘ ˘ /
˘ / | ˘ ˘ / | ˘ ˘ /
/ | ˘ ˘ / | ˘ /
/ | ˘ ˘ / | ˘ /

Swinburne's meter does not fulfill his denotational content. It is as if a composer were to write a funeral march *presto giocoso* in one of the more brilliant major keys. There is no absolute aesthetic demand that funeral marches be written in minor keys or in tempi suited to an actual procession of mourners. We feel, however, that speed and brilliance do not connote dignity and grief; they are not the proper forms for emotions we normally associate with funerals. Swinburne's galloping meter is not an emotional form suitable to his subject.

If prosody is itself meaning, meaning also forms prosody. Rhythmic structures grow out of patterns of rhetorical emphasis: patterns that sometimes move against or across the meter. We find in Donne's poetry many startling instances of expressive rhythms emerging out of ambiguities of emphasis: where meter pulls the propositional sense in one direction, rhetorical emphasis in the other. In *A Valediction: of my name, in the window,* the poet imagines that his mistress might take another lover; he hopes that his name, scratched in the window-glass, will blot out the name of his successor:

And when thy melted maid,
Corrupted by thy Lover's gold, and page,
His letter at thy pillow'hath laid,
Disputed it, and tam'd thy rage,
And thou begin'st to thaw towards him, for this,
May my name step in, and hide his.

The last line presents a metrical crux. If we follow the meter closely, we scan and read:

May mý | name stép | ín and | hide hís . . .

My and *his* are thrown into rhetorical balance; the parallel is between *my name* and *his* [*name*]. The poet feels reasonably secure that his name will cover the name of her new lover. But if we follow the "prose" stresses of the words, we scan:

Máy my | náme step | ín and | híde his . . .

The meter breaks down and we do not even have a regular final foot. *May* is stressed; it now seems highly conditional that the image of the poet's name can keep his mistress faithful. The stressed *hide* tinges the whole line with interrogation—and the poet dissolves in doubts. Although the poet never says he is anxious, his rhythm gives him away.

Whether the patterns of rhythm and meter genetically precede conceptualization; whether they are formed after the idea has been formulated; or whether rhythmic form and conceptual meaning are conceived simultaneously seem matters of individual poetic genius. It is reported that Yeats first wrote his lines out as prose and counted the meters off on his fingers; it is also reported that he always had a "tune in his head" when he composed. Eliot remarks, "I know that a poem, or a passage of a poem, may tend to realize itself first as a particular rhythm before it reaches expression in words, and that this rhythm may bring to birth the idea and the image . . ."[10] However the poet works, the meaningful structures of language can form rhythms and meters. The grammatical function of a word can determine whether it is metrically stressed or unstressed:

Thís is | the énd | of the whále róad | and the whále . . .

Tíme that | with *thís* | stránge ex | cúse . . .

The individual word also has characteristic rhythm, depending on its pattern of stress, and isolated words may form cross-rhythms with basic metrical structure. The opening of *The Waste Land* is written in four-beat strong-stress meter:

> April is the cruellest month, breeding
> Lilacs out of the dead land, mixing
> Memory and desire, stirring
> Dull roots with spring rain.

Words in trochaic form (*April, cruellest, breeding, Lilacs, mixing, stirring*) predominate, and the falling rhythm they create weaves itself about the underlying four-stress beat.

The manifold ways in which sound and meaning coalesce in poetry are, of course, the subjects of our inquiry. It is perhaps sufficient, at this point, to say neither meaning nor sound can operate independently. It is also important to distinguish between what we term the primary and secondary devices of prosody. The articulations of sound in temporal sequences, rhythms and meters, present us with "aesthetic surface"; it is this surface which our perception immediately engages. Prosody is an aural symbolism, a significant arrangement of acoustical phenomena. But since poetry has been written, and more importantly, *printed,* visual qualities have contributed to prosodical arrangement. Line endings, stanzaic shape, the general appearance of the poem on the page—all contribute to rhythmic effect. These visual elements, however, are, and *should be* secondary—in the way that written directions in a musical score are in no sense the music but only useful guides to realizing a correct performance. Visual elements are aids to performance—remembering that "performance" includes the mind's silent re-creation of a poem as we read to ourselves.

To multiply the visual elements in a poem reduces for perception the available "aesthetic surface." Through the agency of sound, poetry makes imaginative facts out of the deepest, most elusive feeling. The poet who substitutes visual tricks for a surface of articulated sound limits his range of feeling; he gives up the primary means by which feelings can be symbolized and apprehended. A poem must sound; it is sound that we first experience as pleasure in the reading of poetry. Nursery rhymes, children's game verses, primitive charms: all appeal through the movement of sound. Prosody offers in the basic forms of metrical structure a continuous articulating surface which makes rhythmic cognition possible. It is to these forms that we now turn.

II

The Scansion of the English Meters

1 *Strong-stress and Syllable-stress Meter*

I should say, of course, the *scansions* of the English meters. The curse of metrical theory has been prosodical monism: the notion that there is a single law governing the behavior of all English verse, from *Beowulf* to Marianne Moore. My historical examples are deliberately chosen. *Beowulf* is composed in the old Germanic strong-stress meter; Marianne Moore counts syllables as the French do. No one "law" of English metric controls the prosody of *Beowulf* and, say, Miss Moore's "The Fish." My basic policy in scansion is to scan the verse according to the system of metric it is written in.

A metrical system, or simply *meter,* singles out and then organizes, in a pattern of regular recurrence, a normative feature of language. The linguistic feature must be an obvious one; no meter can be based on features too faint or too indefinite for the ear to recognize easily. The two dominant English meters are based on the principle of recurring stress. The simplest and oldest English meter maintains a more or less regular number of stresses within the line; there is no fixed number of unstressed syllables. This is the *strong-stress meter* of Old English poetry—and of T. S. Eliot's *Four Quartets:*

> Hére is a pláce || of dís af féc tion
>
> Tíme be fóre || and tíme áf ter
>
> In a dím líght: || nei ther dáy líght

In ves ting form || with lu cid still ness
Turn ing shad ow || into tran sient beau ty
With slow ro ta tion || sug ges ting per ma nence
Nor dark ness || to pu ri fy the soul
Emp ty ing the sen su al || with dep ri va tion
Cleans ing af fec tion || from the tem por al.

III from *Burnt Norton*

The opening of Pound's *Canto I* is also strong-stress meter. Pound maintains the alliterative pattern of Old English verse which gives a characteristic archaism to the lines:

And then went down to the ship,
Set keel to break ers, || forth on the god ly sea, and
We set up mast and sail || on that swart ship,
Bore sheep a board her, || and our bo dies also
Heavy with weep ing, || and winds from stern ward
Bore us out on ward || with bel ly ing canvas,
Cir ce's this craft, || the trim-coifed god dess.

In scanning strong-stress meter we mark the main stresses and the position of the medial pause, or caesura. It is also useful to underline the alliterated syllables. The norm of strong-stress meter is two stresses on either side of the caesura, but even in Old English verse we encounter lines of three or five stresses.

Modern poets have revived strong-stress meter. Pound, Auden, the later Eliot, all have made deliberate use of it. Occasionally what at first might seem free verse (or "cadenced prose") is the older meter:

Miss Hel en Slings by || was my maid en aunt,
And lived in a small house || near a fash ion a ble square
Cared for by ser vants || to the num ber of four.

T. S. Eliot, "Aunt Helen"

The appearance of the meter here is probably accidental; the rhythms of the conversational idiom fall "naturally" into the recurrent patterns of strong-stress meter. Hopkins notes that sprung rhythm, his refinement on the native strong-stress meter, ". . . is the rhythm of common speech and of written prose, when rhythm is perceived in them."[1] It is premature, however, to speak of sprung rhythm; Hopkins' theories and practices require detailed comment. Sprung rhythm, while deriving doubtless out of the native meter, exists also in syllable-stress meter; its analysis is a complicated, and needless to say, controversial matter.

Less controversial (one might think) is the scansion of syllable-stress meter. This is the traditional two-valued meter which established itself with Chaucer, was later ignored or misunderstood, and finally fixed as the norm for English poetry by Wyatt, Surrey, and Spenser. Its position as the basic metric for English verse was scarcely challenged until Whitman and Hopkins; and despite the revolution in prosody which accompanied modern poetry, syllable-stress meter carries a significantly large body of twentieth-century verse. The structure of syllable-stress meter is the subject of disagreement among recent theorists, incredible when we realize that poets have clearly understood the meter since Spenser and that historians like Jespersen described it with perfect structural accuracy as early as 1900.[2]

My view on the scansion of syllable-stress meter is the traditional one. I use the conventional markings to indicate the stressed and unstressed syllables, the caesura, and the groupings into feet. Although I agree with the linguists that in English more than two levels of stress exist, a *metrical* foot consists of two values only: stressed and unstressed syllables. In the foot syllables are stressed and unstressed in relation to each other; our *metrical ear* hears only relative stress. In the line

> The Chaír | she sát | in, líke | a búr | nished thróne . . .
>
> T. S. Eliot

the third foot is iambic even though *like* is rhetorically weak. If we mark only the speech stresses we have a four-beat line,

> The Cháir she sát in, like a búrnished thróne . . .

But *like* is slightly more emphatic than *in;* this slight emphasis is enough to define the third foot as iambic. The pressure of meter tends to equalize discrepancies of stress; thus normally (that is, rhetorically) strong syllables become metrically weak when they occur between two other strong syllables:

> The páth | sìck sór | row tóok, | the má | ny páths . . .
>
> Stevens, "Sunday Morning"

The second foot is iambic although it is made up of *sick* and *sor-*, two rhetorically strong syllables. Similarly, a normally weak syllable gains in metrical strength when it occurs between two weak syllables:

> But dríft | in stíll | ness, ás | from Jór | dan's brów . . .
>
> Hart Crane, "The River"

The third foot is iambic, *as* receiving slightly more stress than *-ness*.

In our scansion-notation spondees and pyrrhics are relatively rare. Spondees do occur, however:

> Dówn, dówn | —born pí | o néers | in tíme's | de spíte . . .
>
> Hart Crane

The double foot of two unstressed and two stressed syllables also occurs in iambic verse. This is the syzygy of ancient prosody. These lines from Robert Lowell show examples of the double foot arranged in minor Ionics (˘˘´´):

> Thís is | the énd | of the whále róad | and the whále
> Who spéwed | Nan túck | et bónes | on the thráshed swéll
> And stírred | the tróubl | ed wát | ers to whírl póols
> To sénd | the Pé | quod páck | ing óff | to héll . . .
>
> "Quaker Graveyard"

We must also recognize the monosyllabic foot. It can appear at the beginning of the line, as the stressed half of a catalectic foot:

> ‸Prín | cess Vól | u píne | ex ténds
> A méag | re, blúe- | nàiled, phthí | sic hánd

To climb | the wa | ter stair. | Lights, lights,
She en | ter tains | Sir Fer | di nand
^Klein. | Who clipped | the li | on's wings . . .

T. S. Eliot

The first feet of lines one and five are monosyllabic.

In all other positions but the first, the monosyllabic foot will "spring" or syncopate the line unless it immediately precedes or follows the caesura. In the first of the following lines, the monosyllabic foot precedes the medial pause; in the second, it follows:

The owls | trilled || with tongues | of night | in gale . . .

Robert Graves, "A Love Story"

In her | own hand, || signed | with her | own name . . .

Robert Graves, "The Straw"

This use of the monosyllabic foot does not seriously disturb the rhythmic stability of the line: it can smoothly substitute for iamb or trochee because the preceding or following pause is equivalent to the missing unstressed syllable. Lines are syncopated or "sprung" when the monosyllabic foot, appearing in an otherwise regular metrical context, cannot be counted as catelectic. This line, from Eliot's *Ash Wednesday,* is sprung at the fourth foot:

I no long | er strive | to strive | towards | such things . . .

"Springing" in syllable-stress metric is something other than what Hopkins calls sprung rhythm. It is related, of course; but as a feature of syllable-stress metric, it has its distinctive characteristics and occasions. As we note above, springing disturbs the rhythmic stability of the line; a number of consecutively sprung lines will destroy the sense of the dominant meter. Intrusive monosyllabic feet, the hammering of consecutive spondees,

Bones built | in me, flesh filled, | blood brimmed | the curse . . .

Hopkins, "I wake and feel"

can endanger the base metric so that we actually move toward stress and away from syllable-stress prosody. What Hopkins calls "counterpointing" can also shake the stability of syllable-stress metric. Any line in which a new rhythm bucks against the prevalent meter may be thought of as counterpointed. Counterpointing is a matter of degree. The reversal of the first foot, or of the foot after the caesura, is not likely to disturb the meter; these are the most usual kinds of substitutions in the pentameter line:

Dúnged with | the déad, || drénched by | the dý | ing's blóod . . .

David Gascoyne "Spring MCMXL"

Although the first and third feet are trochees, this is clearly an iambic line—even out of iambic context.

The iambic balance can be disturbed, however, if certain sensitive feet in the line are reversed; or if too many trisyllabic feet (usually anapests) are substituted for iambs. Ransom thus achieves the startling metrical effects of "Captain Carpenter":

Cáp tain | Cár pen | ter róse | úp in | his príme

Pút on | his pís | tols and wént rí | ding óut

Bút had | gót well | nìgh nó | where át | that tíme

Till hé | fell ín | with lá | dies ín | a róut

It wás | a prét | ty lá | dy‿and áll | her tráin

That pláyed | with hím | so swéet | ly bút | be fóre

An hóur | she'd ták | en‿a swórd | with áll | her máin

And twíned | hím of | his nóse | for é | ver móre.

Ransom plays metrical brinkmanship. He reverses the extremely sensitive second foot (lines one and three), and the fourth foot (line one), and allows trisyllabic substitution (line five, fourth foot; line seven, third foot). He also introduces lines which can, in scansion, be rationalized as syllable-stress metric, but which actually move in strong-stress rhythms:

And a bláde shóok || be tween rót ten teeth a láck.

The effect is like that in the popular ballads where naive intrusions of strong-stress metric, still viable in the fifteenth century, gave a characteristic archaic flavor:

When shawes beene sheene, and shrads fyll fayre,
And leeves both large and longe,
Itt is merry, walking in the fayre fforest,
To heare the small birds songe.

The third line must be "wrenched" into syllable-stress metric; if we scan,

Itt ís | mer rý, | wálk ing in | the fáyre | ffo rést

we are forced to distort normal speech stresses. But this is barbarous. The line is a four-beat, strong-stress line:

Itt is mér ry, wálk ing || in the fáyre ffó rest . . .

In "Captain Carpenter" the archaism is calculated, not naive, creating a prosodic irony to complement the pervading ironic tone. The surface roughness conceals Ransom's skill; what on first reading seems inept or baffling is, in fact, a prosodic tour de force.

Scansion is the basic technique of prosodic analysis. Its correct application to syllable-stress metric involves the precise recognition of the kinds of feet, and the ways these feet may be reversed or substituted. A current objection to foot-scansion is its apparent crudity. The linguists recommend a subtler method of scansion, taking into account the four levels of English stress, juncture, and pitch. A linguist's scansion of Yeats' "Speech, after long silence" looks like this:

2 Speech + after + long 2 3 silence; 1 2 it + is + right . . . 3

Each symbol corresponds to a phonetic feature of the line, and most of its aural structure is accounted for. But looking at this scansion we might well ask, "Where is the meter?" If we remove the extraneous symbols, it is clear enough:

Spéech af | ter lóng | sí | lence; ít | is ríght . . .

Our "cruder" and more traditional scansion shows the important metrical feature of the line: it is sprung by the intrusive monosyllabic foot at the third position.

Our belief is that meter *is* a simple, even crude element in poetic structure. An economy—not an abundance—of linguistic features generates metrical patterns. Any scansion, of course, is a convenient fiction, abstracting certain phonetic elements and ignoring others. But the scansion must describe what is without doubt *really there.* It must indeed be descriptive and not interpretive. A prevalent mistake is to base scansions on performance; and then analyze, either by means of musical notation or through acoustic recordings, the individual patterns a reader imposes on the verse. Wellek and Warren have most cogently revealed the fallacies inherent in all such performative scansions: they are either personal variations played on the metrical pattern or worthless tautologies.[4]

Some may argue that in "Captain Carpenter" the first two feet in this line are anapests:

If he riśk | to be wouńd | ed bý | my tongúe . . .

Some may suppress the fourth foot altogether and discover a three-beat line:

If he riśk | to be wouńd | ed by my tońgue . . .

However, if the foot-structure of syllable-stress meter is understood, neither of these scansions is convincing. Both scan speech stress, not metrical stress. Our scansion

If́ he | riśk to | be wouńd | ed bý | my tongúe

shows the counterpointing (reversed second foot) which in this line is the *significant tension* between speech and metrical stress. The first foot, we agree, is probably controversial. Our scansion hears it inverted; it could also be a normal iambic. A similar ambiguity occurs earlier:

Tiĺl he | fell iń | with lá | dies iń | a roút.

But the structure of the initial foot in an iambic line is scarcely important; a quibble here merely confirms the notion that certain variations in syllable-stress metric are so frequent as to be normal.

2 *Quantitative and Syllabic Meters*

Since the days of Gabriel Harvey prosodists and poets have dreamed of an English quantitative meter. The prosodists have tried to discover a quantitative base for English meter and to prove that our verse moves by the same laws that governed Homer and Virgil. Poets have tried to imitate in English the classical meters. Theorists and practitioners have had no remarkable success; indeed, the best of them have realized that a *purely* quantitative meter is impossible in English. Unlike Greek or Latin, English has neither fixed quantities, existing in nature or defined by rules of grammar, nor a metrical convention which, by artificial and traditional means, can create rhythms out of long and short syllables. To scan a single line from Virgil,

con sti tit | atque oc u | lis Phry gi | a ag mi na | cir cum | spex it

means determining which syllables are long or short by nature, which are long and short by position. Latin dictionaries mark the quantities of the vowels; Latin grammars explain the complex circumstances under which syllables may be lengthened or shortened. Our knowledge must also extend to the conventions governing metrical structure. Virgil's line is dactylic hexameter, but the last foot is conventionally a spondee. The fifth foot of the line above is also a spondee; the normally short *-cum* of *circum* is lengthened in scansion.

The scansion of Latin verse is highly artificial and sometimes arbitrary. No one doubts, however, that measured quantities provide the ground rhythm of Latin verse. It requires some absorption of the rules, some ear-training, before we can hear the meter and then scan:

Sunt ge mi | nae Som | ni por | tae, quar (um) | al ter a | fertur
cor ne a, | qua ve | ris fac i | lis da tur | ex i tus | um bris;
al ter a | can den | ti per | fec ta ni | tens e le | phan to,
sed fal | sa ad cae | lum mit | tunt in | som ni a | Ma nes . . .

Aeneid VI, 893–896

We see, in score, the music of the line: the final spondee, the penultimate dactyl, the mixing of spondees and dactyls within the line; and throughout, the steady and subtle conflict between speech stress and prosodic ictus. We may perhaps understand, but not hear, prosodic music in Robert Bridges' translation of these lines into English "quantities":

> Twín be the gates o' the house of sleep: as fable opineth
> One is of horn, and thence for a true dream outlet is easy:
> Fair the other, shining perfected of ivory carven;
> But false are the visions that thereby find passage upward.
>
> "Ibant Obscuri"

According to Bridges' rules, these lines scan exactly as their originals do. But our ears hear no metrical music; English quantity is too faint an element of linguistic structure, and too unstable—so often a matter of individual pronunciation—to set up a pattern of expectation. We must chant these lines, carefully following the Latin scansion and distorting normal syllabic length, to twist them into rhythmical shape. Using a Schönberg type of *Sprechstimme,* we could sing the third line to the meter of the original:

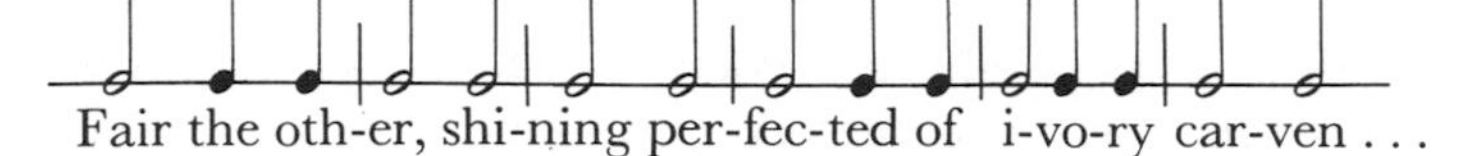

Bridges is not writing quantitative metric; he is setting lines of prose to Virgil's Latin music. It is not true in English that the *i* of *ivory* is exactly double the length of the other two syllables; it *was* true that *-tens* (of *nitens*) was by common poetic convention a long syllable and hence double the length of *e-le* (of *elephanto*). Bridges is trying simultaneously to establish a convention and write in it. The experiment is noble but futile. We are reminded of those primitive flying-machines which flapped and creaked but never got off the ground. They violated a basic law of physics: a man cannot lift himself by his own bootstraps.

Bridges himself doubted the success of his *Poems in Classical Prosody,* observing, "the difficulty of adapting our English syllables to the Greek rules is very great, and even deterrent. . . ."[5] He hoped, however, that his experiments might reveal new and expressive rhythms. Some modern poets have achieved successes in modified or what I call pseudo-quantitative meters. Pound's Sapphics pay close attention to syllabic length, meticulously reproducing the classic pattern:

Gol den | rose the | house, in the | por tal | I saw

thee, a | mar vel, | car ven in | sub tle | stuff, a

por tent. | Life died | down in the | lamp and | flick ered

caught at the | won der.

"Apparuit"

But it is not quantity, as such, which forces our mind into a pattern of expectation. Pound is careful to make each "long" syllable also a stressed syllable; the meter we hear is made up of syllable-stress trochees and dactyls. The rhythms produced by this coincidence of stress and quantity have a limpid and elegiac quality; some may find these lines flaccid. The ear misses those delicate tensions and cross-rhythms produced by an occasional unstressed long syllable:

She slowed | to sigh, | in that | *long* in | ter val . . .

Roethke, "The Dream"

This effect is impossible in Pound's scheme where stress and quantity are never in conflict. And this kind of conflict provides a ground of prosodic interest in English verse.

We find that those reworkings of classical meters which sound metrical to English ears always exhibit strong-stress or syllabic-stress structure. Vernon Watkins' beautiful "Ophelia" is also in the Sapphic stanza. He keeps to the eleven-and-five syllabic structure; the meter is actually a strong-stress pattern:

Stunned in the stone light, || laid among the lilies,

Still in the green wave, || graven in the reed-bed,

Lip-read by clouds || in the language of the shallows,

Lie there, reflected.[6]

The best use of the classical meters has been in adapting them to the stress-based prosody of English, not in trying, as Bridges tried, to write an artificial language which could accommodate the meters. Eliot's absorption of Virgil's hexameter is apparent in these lines:

I do not know much about gods; but I think that the river
Is a strong brown god—sullen, untamed and intractable,
Patient to some degree, at first recognised as a frontier;
Useful, untrustworthy, as a conveyer of commerce;
Then only a problem confronting the builder of bridges.

The Dry Salvages

If we compare them to the thumping dactyls of *Evangeline,* we realize that Eliot "knows everything about Latin versification that an English poet [can] use . . ." [7] and that Longfellow has devised the most narcotic metric in English.

In modern poetry purely syllabic meters are more frequently encountered than quantitative meters. The principle of syllabic meter is simplicity itself. The poet maintains the same number of syllables in every line of the poem; Thom Gunn counts out seven syllables a line for his "My Sad Captains":

MY SAD CAPTAINS

One by one they appear in
the darkness: a few friends, and
a few with historical
names. How late they start to shine!
but before they fade they stand
perfectly embodied, all

the past lapping them like a
cloak of chaos. They were men
who, I thought, lived only to
renew the wasteful force they
spent with each hot convulsion.
They remind me, distant now.

True, they are not at rest yet,
but now that they are indeed
apart, winnowed from failures,
they withdraw to an orbit
and turn with disinterested
hard energy, like the stars.

Count of syllables will not, by itself, provide sufficient rhythmic interest; in Gunn's poem a forceful syntax, a variable number of stresses (from two to four), and the phrasing of the line endings overlay the seven-syllable pattern.

Another syllabic technique, favored by Auden and Marianne Moore, involves the construction of a stanza in which analogous lines have an equal number of syllables. Thus Auden devises for his "In Memory of Sigmund Freud" a stanza of four lines in which the first two lines have eleven, the third line nine, and the fourth line ten syllables. The pattern 11, 11, 9, 10 is kept throughout the poem:

> When there are so many we shall have to mourn,
> When grief has been made so public, and exposed
>   To the critique of a whole epoch
>   The frailty of our conscience and anguish,
>
> Of whom shall we speak? For every day they die
> Among us, those who were doing us some good,
>   And knew it was never enough but
>   Hoped to improve a little by living.

Strong-stress elements overlay the syllabic meter; Auden has four stresses in lines one, two, and four; he changes to three stresses in the third line. The monotony of the old strong-stress meter is avoided by a number of cunning devices. The position of the caesura continually shifts; the third line has no caesura. The stresses do not occupy similar positions in each line, but contract toward or expand away from each other. Iambic feeling is minimized by a prevailing rhythmic pattern of two and three consecutive unstressed syllables:

> Thóse hĕ hăd stú dĭed, thĕ nér vŏus ănd thĕ níghts
>   Ănd shádes thăt stĭll wái tĕd tŏ én tĕr
>   Thĕ bríght cír clĕ ŏf hĭs ré cŏg ní tĭon . . .

The meticulous syllabism of Marianne Moore is another matter. Auden writes a hybrid metric, grafting strong-stress rhythms to a syllabic base. Miss Moore counts syllables and shapes a stanza whose visual appearance has rhythmic function:

>   Pale sand edges England's Old
>   Dominion. The air is soft, warm, hot
> above the cedar-dotted emerald shore
>   known to the red bird, the red-coated musketeer,

the trumpet-flower, the cavalier,
the parson, and the wild parishioner. A deer-
track in a church-floor
brick, and a fine pavement tomb with engraved top,
remain.
The now tremendous vine-encompassed hackberry
starred with the ivy-flower,
shades the church tower;
And a great sinner lyeth here under the sycamore.

"Virginia Britannia"

The appeal to the eye is very great. The stanza emphasizes single words, separating them out of normal word groups: "Old/ Dominion; a deer-/track in a church-floor/brick. . . ." Words, and parts of words, are held up to the eye for special examination; the syllabic meter is analytic and visual. Miss Moore's poetic lineage is through Imagism. The doctrines of Imagism are neither precise nor coherent; however, the effect of the views of Hulme, Pound, and others in modern poetry has led to a prosodical heresy: that visual devices can energize language with significant rhythm. Miss Moore is only mildly heretical; she seldom neglects aural values in her verse. Rhyme, the sound qualities of words, quantity, are carefully balanced against syllabic count and stanzaic shape. But we must describe Miss Moore "a visualist of the imagination" in the speciality of her prosody.

3 *Prosodic Analysis*

We name, as metrical, verse measured by the count of syllable-stress feet; verse measured by the count of strong stresses; verse measured by the count of syllables; and, as far as it can be done in English, verse measured by the count of quantities. Syllable-stress, strong-stress, syllabic, and quantitative: these are the four metrical types basic to English verse. The historically established prosodic norm is, of course, syllable-stress meter; the greatest bulk of our poetry is composed in the familiar iambic, trochaic, or anapestic meters. Our ears, so accustomed to hearing the syllable-stress meters, often fail to recognize the other metrical forms. And occasionally we encounter verse which seems to fall between two metrical types. Scanning the opening lines of *The Waste Land* as syllable-stress meter, we get something like this:

Ap ril | is the | cruel lest | month,^ | breed ing
Li lacs | out of the | dead land, | mix ing
Mem or y | and de sire, | stir ring
Dull | roots with | spring rain.

We can probably rationalize this as trochaic with many exceptions. However, the dominant falling rhythm, the crowding of stresses, and the curious mixture of metrical feet should tip us off. A better scansion reads the lines as strong-stress meter, four beats to the line:

April is the cruellest month, || breeding
Lilacs out of the dead land, || mixing
Memory with desire, || stirring
Dull roots || with spring rain.

Prosodic analysis begins with recognizing the metrical type. In shorter poems we have little difficulty in determining whether we are dealing with one of the other, less frequently encountered, metrical types. The metrical architecture of the significant longer poems of our age requires special scrutiny. Twentieth-century poetry has developed no "carry-all" metric comparable to Elizabethan blank verse or the eighteenth-century couplet; the prosody of *The Waste Land* and *Four Quartets,* of the *Cantos,* of *The Bridge,* and of *Paterson,* is "organic," developed out of the subject and stance of the poem, and not an imposed or adapted style.

Once we have recognized and scanned the meter, we have completed the first step in prosodic analysis. But what of poetic rhythms: the interaction between meter and the other elements of linguistic structure? Scansion does not take into account the *interplay* (Robert Bridges' apt term[8]) between meter and syllabic quantity, meter and syntax, meter and propositional sense. Two passages, which scan exactly alike, may be at opposite prosodic poles:

Not as | a god, | but as | a god | might be,
Na ked | a mong | them, like | a sa | vage source . . .

> Whát are | the roóts | that clútch, | what brán | ches grów
> Oút of | this stó | ny rúb | bish? Són | of mán . . .

The only variations from the blank-verse norm are the inverted initial feet. We have a longer syntactical period before the caesura in the Eliot; the movement of the lines is heavier and slower than the lines from "Sunday Morning." Eliot's rhetoric derives from Ezekiel; we hear the deliberate and solemn thunder of the prophet's voice. The heavy rhythms, which the meter controls, are largely a matter of vowel quantity and consonant orchestration. We could devise a cumbersome notation for quantity and alliteration to supplement our scansion. But I feel it simpler to comment on these matters, pointing out the predominance of stressed *o* and *u* sounds; the consonant clusters *cl-, br-, gr-;* the final *-t* which lengthens the stressed vowel.

We cannot subject rhythm and rhythmic values to the kind of precise analysis that scansion accomplishes for meter. The notation of scansion defines with comfortable accuracy metrical structure; the rhythms of even the simplest poem are too complex to be ever completely analyzed. Every element in poetic structure contributes to rhythmic feeling. Sound effects, the spacing and repetition of images and ideas, diction and vocabulary, matters of texture—these are rhythmic matters, prosodic matters, too. We must talk about them if we wish to give some idea of a poet's prosody. We might occasionally resort to diagrams or mechanical aids; we might occasionally use musical notation to represent quantitative patterns and other rhythmic motifs. The opening of Spender's *Vienna* has certain interior rhythmic melodies:

> Whether the man living or the man dying
> Whether this man's dead life, or that man's life dying
> His real life a fading light his real death a light growing.

We can represent these interior melodies by assigning note-values to significant word-groups:

man living

man dying

The rhythmic motif (♩ ♫) expands as the idea evolves and emotion intensifies. The rhythm returns again and again with melodic persistence.

To show rhythmic patterns in musical notation brings up the much discussed question of isochronism. I have read Spender's word groups as rhythmical sequences and imposed musical pulse on his prosodic structures. My notation may suggest a belief in the basically isochronous nature of English verse, and that "metre is a series of isochronous intervals marked by accents."[9] A pentameter line should contain five "isochronous intervals":

The Rív | er, spréad | ing, flóws || —and spénds | your dréam.

Actual measurement (with the oscillograph) shows that the intervals are far from equal. The third foot, with its *-ing* and *flows,* is considerably longer in temporal value than the other feet. And what of the long pause at the caesura: how much time in the isochronous scheme does it occupy? It depends, of course; it depends on how an individual reader performs the line. And we are back to the old performative fallacy. The meter remains what it has always been, revealed by the traditional method of scanning the stressed and unstressed syllables.

Isochronism is felt, not "real." Meter releases rhythmic potential; it creates an illusion of time, not a chronometric interval. If we measure the feet in the example from Hart Crane, we can show significant differences in actual length. But we have the illusion that the feet occupy units of equal time because the total effect of metrical organization seemingly eliminates temporal discrepancies. Meter is analogous to perspective. If we measure with a ruler the distance between Mona Lisa's nose and her fingertips, and between her nose and one of the rocks she sits among, we may conclude that it is no farther from her nose to her hand than it is from her nose to an imagined point two or three hundred yards distant. What we measure with our ruler is literal space on the canvas, not the illusion of space created by perspective. Perspective creates illusory space; meter creates illusory time. That meter also occupies literal time—the minutes elapsing as we read a poem—is irrelevant just as the measurable dimensions of a painting in perspective are irrelevant.

We must realize that rhythmic analysis is subjective and interpretive; it is not scansion but ancillary to it. The "discovery" of prosodic isochronism is a matter of conviction, not measurement. Scansion, although not devoid of subjective elements, is more objective. Scansion shows the give and take between language and meter; the variations possible within the imposed pattern; the limits between which language may move and still be counted as metrical. Scansion does not, however, tell us everything we need to know about a poem's prosody. We need metaphoric language, phonetic symbols, and musical notation to supplement metrical analysis. We need the basic approaches and techniques of literary criticism to place prosodic analysis in the larger context of humanistic scholarship. Finally, we must understand that while prosody is largely a matter of metrics, it is also the totality of structures controlling the significant movement of a poem's language.

III

Modern Poetry in the Metrical Tradition

Our inquiry begins with those poets who remained largely unaffected by the prosodical revolution of the 'teens and the twenties, and who composed the bulk of their work in syllable-stress metric. This does not mean that the poets of this chapter are unhappy holdovers from Victorianism, or representatives of an archaizing poetic spirit. They deal with the problems of our age; they write in an idiom derived from contemporary speech. But they catch and hold the rhythms of speech in metrical nets. Hardy is Victorian in origin and not a full-fledged "modern poet." He does not exhibit that neurotic sensitivity to the *Zeitgeist* characteristic of a poet like Auden. But Hardy's work reaches down into our time, surprising us again and again with its sudden aptness and vivid understanding. After reading Hardy's war poems, who can say he was not a man of the twentieth century?

Passages from these poets—they range from Hardy, Bridges, and Yeats to Edwin Muir and John Crowe Ransom—provide examples of traditional style in modern prosody. With no attempt to treat in depth the prosodic development of each poet or to make a detailed genetic study of origins and influences, the passages are offered as specimens for analysis so that we can see the richness, the variety, and the individuality possible within the traditional metrical system.

1 *Thomas Hardy*

Hardy's prosody often fails as an expressive form. In too many of his poems the versification is clumsy, neither subtle nor emphatic. Words are forced into the metrical patterns; the meters themselves are frequently inappropriate to the subject. After reading a large number of Hardy's poems, we feel bemused; there is a groping, clutching, sometimes aimless thrust to his rhythms. We come upon lines like these:

THE NEWCOMER'S WIFE

He paused on the sill of a door ajar
That screened a lively liquor-bar,
For the name had reached him through the door
Of her he had married the week before.

"We called her the Hack of the Parade;
But she was discreet in the games she played;
If slightly worn, she's pretty yet,
And gossips, after all, forget . . ."

The uncertain mixture of trisyllabic and iambic feet makes it difficult to hear the metrical direction; the fifth line above confirms us in the feeling that we are reading badly versified prose. It is difficult to read the line without placing an inappropriate stress on the second *the:*

"We cálled | her the Háck | of thé | Pa ráde . . .

Hardy's best poems move to a different music. In that little comic masterpiece, "The Ruined Maid," the anapestic base meter is exactly right to catch the querulous, jealous whine of the girl who stayed home, and the newly acquired insolence, and as yet tentative affectation of the girl who is "ruined." Here are the three last stanzas:

—"Your hands were like paws then, your face blue and bleak
But now I'm bewitched by your delicate cheek,
And your little gloves fit as on any la-dy!"—
"We never do work when we're ruined," said she.

—"You used to call home-life a hag-ridden dream,
And you'd sigh, and you'd sock; but at present you seem
To know not of megrims or melancho-ly!"—
"True. One's pretty lively when ruined," said she.

—"I wish I had feathers, a fine sweeping gown,
And a delicate face, and could strut about Town!"—
"My dear—a raw country girl, such as you be,
Cannot quite expect that. You ain't ruined," said she.

The appropriateness of the meter is no better illustrated than in the slight "wrenching" at the ends of the line:

And your lít | tle gloves fít | as on á | ny la-dý . . .
‸To knów | not of mé | grims or mél | an cho-lý . . .

Metrical stress forces a rise in pitch (la-*dy* . . . melancho-*ly*), mimicking the country girl's peevish complaint, and suggesting that her pronunciation of certain words is affected by the prevailing dialect. The meter also makes subtle what could never be fully expressed by the words alone: that the ruined girl's pride in her new clothes and recently acquired social status is qualified by certain misgivings. Her attitude is not quite jeering; she is really friendly—a little proud, but also a little ashamed. The meter supports a complexity of tone, providing, as in "Captain Carpenter," a prosodic irony to complement the ironies of character and circumstance.

The first stanza of "An August Midnight" mixes trisyllabic and disyllabic feet:

A shaded lamp and a waving blind,
And the beat of a clock from a distant floor:
On this scene enter—winged, horned, and spined—
A longlegs, a moth, and a dumbledore;
While 'mid my page there idly stands
A sleepy fly, that rubs its hands . . .

The measure is iambic tetrameter, though one line is mainly anapestic,

And the béat | of a clóck | from a dís | tant flóor

and one contains a monosyllabic foot,

On thís | scene én | ter—wínged, | hórned, | and spíned—

These rhythmic changes follow the poet's shifting perceptions. The clock beats trisyllabically; the "winged, horned, and spined" creatures enter in bumpy confusion. In the last line the recurrent labials (A slee(p)y (f)ly, that ru(b)s its hands) underscore the controlling tetrameter meter and the smooth, graceful movement of the fly.

Some stanzas from "In a Wood" show Hardy working in two-stress dactylic, a meter uncommon in English,[1] but suited to pathos and elegy:

Touches from ash, O wych,
    Sting you like scorn!
You, too, brave hollies, twitch
    Sidelong from thorn.
Even the rank poplars bear
Lothly a rival's air,
Cankering in black despair
    If overborne.

Since, then, no grace I find
    Taught me of trees,
Turn I back to my kind,
    Worthy as these.
There at least smiles abound,
There discourse trills around,
There, now and then, are found
    Life-loyalties.

Alternate lines are catalectic; the final foot lacks the two unstressed syllables:

Toúch es from | ásh, O wỳch,
    Stíng you like | scórn!
Yóu, too, bràve | hól lies twìtch
    Síde long from | thórn.

A feature of the odd lines is the heavy final stress, although in authentic dactyls falling rhythm would persist through the last foot. We have in effect, a cross rhythm; if we scan the lines as disyllabic, we get trochees and iambs:

Tóuch es | from ásh, | O wých,
Stíng you | like scórn!

Three against two. The final stressed syllable obviates the awkward and sometimes poetically embarrassing feminine rhyme. The fifth line of each stanza consists of two accentual amphimacs (or Cretics):

Éven the rànk | póp lars bèar . . .
Thére at lèast | smíles a bòund . . .

and from the first stanza (not quoted):

Whén the ràins | skím and skìp . . .

Whether or not we recognize the amphimac in syllable-stress prosody (it can always be rationalized into iambs and trochees), we recognize Hardy's awareness of metrical possibilities—an awareness sharpened by classical reading and musical training.

Hardy's music is not an accidental virtue, nor is it the mellifluous sound of vowels and consonants in regular sequences. Hardy's best poems show the advantages meter can afford the poet. In his poems which affect us like music, the music moves where feeling and order interact: at that level of metrical intensity and delicacy which allows language to shape itself into significant rhythmic forms. Hardy's theme in these stanzas is the oldest in the history of poetry—the pathos of mutability:

DURING WIND AND RAIN

They sing their dearest songs—
He, she, all of them—yea,
Treble and tenor and bass,
  And one to play;
With the candles mooning each face . . .
  Ah, no; the years O!
How the sick leaves reel down in throngs!

They clear the creeping moss—
Elders and juniors—aye,
Making the pathways neat
  And the garden gay;
And they build a shady seat . . .
  Ah, no; the years, the years;
See, the white storm-birds wing across!

They are blithely breakfasting all—
Men and maidens—yea,
Under the summer tree,
  With a glimpse of the bay,
While pet fowl come to the knee . . .
  Ah, no; the years O!
And the rotten rose is ript from the wall.

They change to a high new house,
He, she, all of them—aye,
Clocks and carpets and chairs
  On the lawn all day,
And brightest things that are theirs . . .
  Ah, no; the years, the years;
Down their carved names the rain-drop ploughs.

I scan only the last lines of each stanza; even in this brief analysis, we see the amazing rhythmical variety within a basic iambic pattern:

Hów the | sìck leáves | rèel dówn | in thróngs! . . .
Seé, the | whìte stórm- | bìrds wíng | acróss! . . .
And the rót | ten róse | is rípt | from the wáll . . .
Dówn their | càrved námes | the raín- | dròp ploúghs . . .

Hardy strains the meter with every possible variation: inverted, monosyllabic, and trisyllabic feet; heavy pauses and heavy rhetorical stresses. The family, depicted in all its activity, works and plays to the sometime hesitating, sometime headlong rhythms. Hardy gives a direct revelation of the curve of life, from birth and growth to decay and death. It is a revelation tormented by time; work, pleasure, and good fortune yield to the years. The prosody, with its nervous and passionate tension between meter and rhetorical stress, moves us along in time: the psychological time in which we experience the life of feeling.

2 *William Butler Yeats*

It is a critical commonplace that Yeats started out as a Victorian and ended up as a Modern. His earliest poems show Swinburnian fluency, especially in the use of triple meter:

> I would that we were, my beloved, white birds on the foam of the sea!
> We tire of the flame of the meteor, before it can fade and flee;
> And the flame of the blue star of twilight, hung low on the rim of the sky,
> Has awaked in our hearts, my beloved, a sadness that may not die.
>
> "The White Birds," 1893

But Yeats was dissatisfied with the current fashions of versification of the nineties: the long dactylic and anapestic lines; the elegant and overripe Alexandrine, popularized by Ernest Dowson and Lionel Johnson. Yeats remarks, in "The Symbolism of Poetry" (1900):

> . . . we would cast out of serious poetry those energetic rhythms, as of a man running, which are the invention of the will with its eyes always on something to be done or undone; and we would seek out those wavering, meditative, organic rhythms, which are the embodiment of the imagination.[2]

The casting out of the energetic and obvious rhythms is complete by the time Yeats published *Responsibilities* (1914). We find none of the inordinate prepositional stuffing of

> And the fláme | *of* the blúe | stàr *of* twí | light, hung lów | *on* the rím | *of* theský

to fill out the hexameter line. We do find sureness, subtlety, a controlled sensuousness, in the metric of "The Magi," perhaps the most remarkable of Yeats's pre–World War I poems. I scan the last four lines:

And áll | their hélms | of síl | ver hóv | er‿ing síde | by síde,
And áll | their éyes | still fíxed, | hóp ing | to fínd | once móre,
Bé ing | by Cál | va‿ry's túr | bu lénce | un sá | tis fíed,
The ún | con tról | la‿ble mýs | te‿ry ón | the bés | ti‿al flóor.

Yeats, like Milton, follows a principle of elision; syllables, ordinarily spoken in performance, do not count in scansion. *Hovering, Calvary, mystery,* and *bestial* are disyllabic. Whether Yeats himself said, in rich Irish brogue, *hov'ring* and *myst'ry,* does not matter; the metrical paradigm calls for six iambic feet in the line.

This is not, however, the hexameter of

> But when the storm is highest, and the thunders blare,
> And sea and sky are riven, O moon of all my night!
>
> Ernest Dowson, "Seraphita"

Yeats's rhetorical energy submerges all sense of metronomic metrical pulse; the astonishing last line has only four speech stresses:

> The uncontróllable mýstery on the béstial flóor . . .

The Magi seek another incarnation, not a repetition of Virgin and Dove, but as Yeats later conceived it in "Leda and the Swan," a bestial coupling of god and woman. The rhythmic change in this last line isolates it from the rest of the poem, holding it before our minds for special contemplation, frightening us into thought.

The opening lines of "The Second Coming" are strongly cross rhythmical. Overlaying blank verse metric is a falling rhythm of dactyls and paeons. Dotted lines mark the rhythmical periods; the solid lines mark metrical feet:

> Túrn ing | and ¦ túrn | ing in | the ¦ wí | den‿ing ¦ gýre
> Túrn ĭng ănd ¦ túrn ĭng ĭn thĕ ¦ wí dĕn ĭng ¦ gýre

The "interplay" of meter and rhythm produces a prosodic texture of opposing movement and feeling. The rhetorical "tune" of falling feet reappears in the last line:

‸Slóu | ches tówards | Béth le | hém to | be bórn . . . (meter)

Slóu ches̆ tŏwards ¦ Béth lĕ hĕm ¦ tó bĕ bŏrn . . . (rhythm)

Since the penultimate line is regular,

And whát | ròugh béast, | its hóur | come róund | at lást . . .

the last lines of the poem show symmetry and asymmetry in sharp rhythmical contrast. There can be no comfortable scansion of the last line; we might read its meter this way:

Slóu ches | towards Béth | le hém | to be bórn . . .

However conceived in scansion, the line is rhythmically unresolved. The poem ends taut with expectancy; prosodic energy does not diminish but reaches out into the surrounding darkness.

An earlier question returns: what is the relationship between meaning and prosody? Are the cross-rhythms of "The Second Coming" onomatopoeic; does Yeats's prosody *look like* the spiralling ascent of the falcon and *sound like* the shambling, mindless tread of the great stone beast? Do these rhythms represent the movements of falcon and beast? Not *represent* actions but *signify* feelings; rhythms are structures symbolic of feelings and not representations of things or actions. What we experience when we read "The Second Coming" is not kinaesthesia, "but how feelings go." Yeats's images, the observed falcon and imagined beast, are suffused with emotions of horror and awe. The function of the smoothly falling rhythm of the opening line, or the curiously broken rhythm of the last line is ". . . not communication but insight. . . ."[3] If we do not make this distinction, we could say the pattern,

/ ˘ ˘ ¦ / ˘ ˘ ˘ ¦ / ˘ ˘ ¦ /

sounds like the motion of a falcon in flight, and that prosody could *communicate* denotational sense. This is absurd when we realize that such a pattern can be found in poems ranging over a whole alphabet of feelings: from anger to xenophobia. Rather, the rhythmic pattern is contextually appropriate to the subject, and forms an emotional resemblance consonant with meaning. The rhythmic lurch of "Slouches towards Bethlehem to be born" gives a penetrating vision of indifferent, relentless, and uncontrollable movement; a sudden insight into the horrified and helpless feelings we might have when, at the next turn of history, the world erupts in apocalyptic violence.

Rhythmic structure is a contextually appropriate aural symbolism. I. A. Richards complains, with some justice, that prosodists neglect to show the important interaction of rhythmic form and propositional sense in the poem.[4] In "The Second Coming" we see how rhetorical stress, the rhythm of semantic emphasis, contradicts the expectations set up by the abstract meter. This new rhythm has a content of feeling generated by the meanings of words, but, at the same time, has formal movement of its own: structure not denotative of feelings, but articulating and re-enforcing them. The rhythmical irresolution of the last line can be explained in technical terms: the monosyllabic first foot, the trochaic second foot, etc. It is, however, the connotative power of *slouches,* together with the seesawing rhythm, that produces the powerful prosodic effect.

Among the triumphs of Yeats's versification are his poems in short lines. "Easter 1916" is written in three stress lines, built with exquisite rhythmical variety and balance. There is no regular foot, but each line modulates metrical periods; I quote and scan various sections from the poem:

> I have mét | them at clóse | of dáy
> Cóm ing | with ví | vid fá | ces
> From cóun | ter or désk | a mong gréy
> Éigh | teenth-cént | ury hóu | ses . . .
>
> Being cér | tain that théy | and Í
> But líved | where mót | ley is wórn:
> All chánged, | chànged út | ter lý:
> A tér | ri ble béau | ty is bórn . . .
>
> A hórse | hòof slídes | on the brím,
> And a hórse | plásh es | with ín | ít;
> The lóng- | leg ged móor | hèns díve,

And héns | to móor | còcks cáll;
Mín ute | by mín | ute they líve:
The stóne's | in the mídst | of áll.

We have great intricacy in apparent simplicity. Disyllabic and trisyllabic feet are interchanged freely; unaccented syllables provide either emphatic upbeats or delicate end assonance; lines are counterpointed by monosyllabic or inverted feet. Syntax tersely controls the argument, sometimes stopping at the end of the line, sometimes flowing over:

We know their dream; enough
To know they dreamed and are dead;
And what if excess of love
Bewildered them till they died?

Because Yeats arranges the poem into four alternating sections of sixteen and twenty-four lines and not into short stanzas, he must take special care to avoid the flaccid long sentence or the monotonous short one. The balance is nearly perfect; a short question is answered by the murmuring simile of mother and child, then followed by another question:

O when may it suffice?
That is Heaven's part, our part
To murmur name upon name,
As a mother names her child
When sleep at last has come
On limbs that had run wild.
What is it but nightfall?

In Yeats's poetry syntactical control deserves special notice. Although Yeats came under strong Symbolist influence, especially in the quality of his images, he rarely fails to supply the hard skeleton of logical thought which close syntactical form affords. The opening "Song" from *The Resurrection* is a good example of relating images, not by free grammatical apposition, but through a linking network of active verbs:

> I saw a staring virgin stand
> Where holy Dionysus died,
> And tear the heart out of his side,
> And lay the heart upon her hand
> And bear that beating heart away;
> And then did all the Muses sing
> Of Magnus Annus at the spring,
> As though God's death were but a play.

Yeats's images have, as they generally have in Symbolist poetry, meanings peculiar and private; and they must be understood in the context of Yeats's mythological philosophy of history. But no mystery attaches itself to the plot of the poem. *Stand, tear, lay, bear,* fully explain the activities of the savage virgin. The Muses *sing* as if they were the accompanying chorus in a festival tragedy performed at the great Athenian Dionysia.

A meter of absolute iambic regularity enforces the rigid syntax. The song is a hieratic chant and serves to introduce a play on the meaning of the Resurrection to the culture and stability of the Hellenic world. Christianity for Yeats was an irruption of the irrational in history, a force which would destroy the humane civilizations of Athens and Rome. The subject of the song is the violence of this new historical energy: a violence paradoxically rendered in regular metric and closely ordered syntax.

We find in Yeats's later verse a characteristic use of the monosyllabic and counterpointed foot which is a signature, a way of saying in rhythm, "This line is written by Yeats":

> I knów, | althóugh | when lóoks | méet
> I trém | ble tó | the bóne . . .

"Crazy Jane and Jack the Journeyman"

> Spéech af | ter lóng | sí | lence; ít | is ríght . . .

> Wráp | ping thát | fòul bó | dy úp . . .
> On Crúa | chan's pláin | slept hé
> That múst | síng in | a rhýme . . .

> Ó | but héart's | wíne shall | rún pure,
> Mínd's bread | grów swéet . . .

The last example sounds very much like Hopkins; the consecutive heavy stresses produce the typical movement of sprung rhythm. Much of the late verse pays little attention to syllabic count; Yeats clearly moves away from syllable-stress to strong-stress metric.

It is the strong-stress principle which dominates the lean textured verse of Yeats's penultimate play, *Purgatory* (1939). The crucial task of modern verse drama has been in discovering a poetic medium close to contemporary speech, unrelated to Shakespearean blank verse, yet capable of rhythmic emphasis at moments of dramatic necessity. The verse of *Purgatory* is Yeats's most successful fusion of colloquial naturalness and poetic intensity.

Boy. Half-door, hall door,
Hither and thither day and night,
Hill or hollow, shouldering this pack,
Hearing you talk.

Old Man. Study that house . . .
Great people lived and died in this house;
Magistrates, colonels, members of Parliament,
Captains and Governors, and long ago
Men that had fought at Aughrim and the Boyne . . .

Study that tree.
It stands there like a purified soul,
All cold, sweet, glistening light.
Dear mother, the window is dark again,
But you are in the light becausc
I finished all that consequence.

We have a norm of four stresses in the line. Yeats carefully spaces his stresses; at moments of poetic excitement, the stressed syllables crowd together in an effect of emotional acceleration:

Hálf-dóor, || háll dóor,

Híth er and thí ther || dáy and níght,

Híll or hóllow, || shóul der ing this páck . . .

All cóld, swéet, || glís ten ing líght . . .

When emotion slackens, the lines slow down; the freer use of unstressed syllables results in a more leisurely, conversational idiom:

> Great people lived and died in this house;
> Magistrates, colonels, members of Parliament,
> Captains and Governors, and long ago
> Men that had fought at Aughrim and the Boyne.

3 *Robert Bridges*

Bridges experimented ceaselessly to extend and widen the prosodic possibilities of English poetry. Devising, or adapting, rules and theories for quantitative, accentual, and syllabic verse, he then sought to apply them to his poetry. With what success, I assess below. First, we must note that Bridges is the only conscious and deliberate scholar-prosodist among the poets of the Late Victorian and Early Modern Period. He was aware of the free verse experimentation of the 'teens and twenties but rejected nonmetrical techniques. He theorized, with great point and cogency, that free verse encouraged monotony in poetic structure: it had little sustaining power; it required the poet to seek out an "absolute rhythm" for every thought and phrase; it identified line length with syntactical unit and consequently precluded the interplay between grammatical structure and prosodic stress.

Bridges attempted, by either reviving old or devising new meters, to escape the tyranny of syllable-stress metric.

> No art can flourish that is not alive and growing, and it can only grow by invention of new methods or by discovery of new material. In the art of English verse my own work has led me to think that there is a wide field for exploration in the metrical prosody, and that in carrying on Milton's inventions in the syllabic verse there is better hope of successful progress than in the technique of free verse as I understand it.[5]

A full account of Bridges' work in theoretical prosody and practical metrical invention goes beyond the scope of my study. Indeed, as Albert Guérard says, "A full account of Bridges' prosody would require a volume at least as large as the poet's own *Milton's Prosody*."[6] I refer the reader to Guérard's discriminating critique of Bridges' meters for more detailed technical information than

I offer here.[7] My effort is more pragmatically critical: is Bridges' poetry, in his new meters, vigorous and relevant; how much of this poetry is written for the metric, to test and illustrate a theory; how useful have Bridges' experiments been to the rhythmic life of twentieth-century verse?

Bridges wrote in the three meters possible, and in the one impossible, to the English language. His poems in syllable-stress meter reveal a musician's ear for quantity; as conscious a prosodist as Tennyson, Bridges pays close attention to vowel length and the placing of unstressed *long* syllables. An early sonnet in traditional meter shows consummate technical skill:

> Spring hath her own bright days of calm and peace;
> Her melting air, at every breath we draw,
> Floods heart with love to praise God's gracious law:
> But suddenly—so short is pleasure's lease—
> The cold returns, the buds from growing cease,
> And nature's conquer'd face is full of awe;
> As now the trait'rous north with icy flaw
> Freezes the dew upon the sick lamb's fleece,
>
> And 'neath the mock sun searching everywhere
> Rattles the crisped leaves with shivering din:
> So that the birds are silent with despair
> Within the thickets; nor their armour thin
> Will gaudy flies adventure in the air,
> Nor any lizard sun his spotted skin.

The Growth of Love, 24

Bridges has absorbed his influences well: Wordsworth, Keats, and Shakespeare are discernible but not obtrusive. One line moves with extraordinary rhythmic power and grace:

Flòods héart | with lóve | to práise | *Gòd's* grá | cious láw . . .

Floods and *God's* do not fall under the metrical ictus, but their position as rhetorically stressed long syllables singles them out for rhythmic emphasis. Since the metrical base is scarcely disturbed, we cannot consider the line sprung; however, Bridges occasionally "springs" a syllable-stress line with an extra-metrical syllable:

Gay Robin is seen no more:
He is gone with the snow,
For winter is o'er
And Robin will go . . .

Blithe Robin is heard no more:
He gave us his song
When summer was o'er . . .

The apparent influence of Gerard Manley Hopkins appears in a prosodically transitional poem, "The Downs" (1879). The poem is transitional because it hovers between traditional syllable-stress and strong-stress meter.

O bold majestic downs, smooth, fair and lonely;
O still solitude, only matched in the skies:
Perilous in steep places,
Soft in the level races,
Where sweeping in phantom silence the cloudland flies;
With lovely undulation of fall and rise;
Entrenched with thickets thorned,
By delicate miniature dainty flowers adorned!

———

The accumulated murmur of soft plashing,
Of waves on rocks dashing and searching the sands,
Takes my ear, in the veering
Baffled wind, as rearing
Upright at the cliff, to the gullies and rifts he stands;
And his conquering surges scour out over the lands . . .

We can scan it in traditional feet, but in some lines the strong stresses crowd together, in a characteristic Hopkins-like effect:

O bold majestic downs, smooth, fair and lonely . . .

Of waves on rocks dashing and searching the sands . . .

And his conquering surges scour out over the lands . . .

Compared to "The Wreck of the Deutschland" this is prosodically tame; Bridges was not the man to have closely followed his younger, more exuberant friend. Yet in developing the principles of his own strong-stress prosody (Bridges terms it *accentual verse*), he is close to Hopkins' strictures for the measurement of sprung rhythm. Indeed, Bridges and Hopkins make the same mistake about the nature of strong-stress meter; in their theoretic passion for reducing their metrical discoveries to *rules,* they apply a foot-scansion to what is essentially, and by nature, not a foot-measured meter.

Guérard tries manfully to scan Bridges' accentual verse according to the rules Bridges outlines in Part IV of *Milton's Prosody.*[8] His reading of the first stanza of "Nightingales" is

> Beautiful | must be | the mountains | whence | ye come,
> And bright | in the fruitful | valleys | the streams, | wherefrom
>   Ye learn | your song:
> Where are | those starry | woods? | O might | I wander | there,
>   Among | the flowers, | which in that | heavenly | air
>   Bloom the | year long![9]

Guérard concedes the poem may also be scanned on syllable-stress principles. All we need to recognize is the traditional substitution of trisyllabic for disyllabic feet, and we have a stanza of irregular line length in iambic meter:

> Beautiful | must be | the moun | tains whence | ye come,
> And bright | in the fruit | ful val | leys the streams, | wherefrom
>   Ye learn | your song . . . etc.

This scansion is not in accord with Bridges' metrical intention; but my ear cannot hear this as accentual or stress verse: I hear the limpid meters of romantic prosody, the facility of Shelley or the vowel-music of Tennyson.

Bridges' later poems in accentual meter have greater vigor: probably because he breaks his own rules and follows the native strong-stress line:

> Fool that I was: my heart was sore,
> Yea sick for the myriad wounded men,
> The maim'd in the war: I had grief for each one:

And I came in the gay September sun
To the open smile of Trafalgar Square;
Where many a lad with a limb fordone
Loll'd by the lion-guarded column
That holdeth Nelson statued thereon
Upright in the air.

"Trafalgar Square," 1917

Two defects weaken the metrical effect: the use of rhyme and the anapestic gallop:

The maím'd | in the wár: | I had gríef | for each óne:

And I cáme | in the gáy | Sep tém | ber sún . . .

Pound better exploits the rich possibilities of stress meter and uses it with greater power in his *The Seafarer:*

There come now no kings nor Caesars
Nor gold-giving lords like those gone.
Howe'er in mirth most magnified,
Whoe'er lived in life most lordliest,
Drear all this excellence, delights undurable!

This may be an odious comparison, but it shows what Bridges lacks in rhythmic distinction. One line of Bridges has strong movement,

Loll'd by the lion-guarded column . . .

but the next is doggerel,

That holdeth Nelson statued thereon . . .

Unlike Pound, Bridges cannot keep prosodical energy alive throughout the whole poem.

Bridges' other important metrical innovations were in syllabic meters. Unfortunately he confuses his terminology, calling syllable-stress meter "syllabic." In his "Letter to a Musician on English Prosody," he tells us that English blank verse, as practiced by Milton and Shakespeare, is "syllabic":

> I would not wish to seem to underestimate the extreme beauty to which verse has attained under the syllabic system. Shakespeare and Milton have passages of blank verse as fine as poetry can be. . . . On the simplest syllabic scheme it is impossible in English to write two verses exactly alike and equivalent, because of the infinite variety of the syllabic unit and its combinations. . . .[10]

We must, of course, sympathize; most prosodists come away torn and bleeding after an encounter with the Terminological Menace. Rather than recount the genesis and principles of Bridges' syllabic meter,[11] we offer some examples for analysis. The early syllabic poems were written in short "sixes"; extra-metrical syllables are elided ". . . the same as in Milton, and as with him optional; only it is less optional, since it is ruled by speech-practice and not by metrical demands. . . ."[12] Here are the first and fifth stanzas of "The West Front" (1920):

No country know I so well
  as this landscape of hell.
Why bring you to my pain
  these shadow'd effigys
Of barb'd wire, riven trees,
  the corpse-strewn blasted plain?

———

The tears of suffering
  and took aid of angels:
This was the temple of God:
  no mortuary of kings
Ever gathered the spoils
  of such chivalry and love:

Bridges abandons the foot; the metrical unit is a twelve-syllable line with a strong medial break. He emphasizes the caesura by splitting the line; actually the lines run

Of barb'd wire, riven trees, / the corpse-strewn blasted plain . . .

Ever gathered the spoils / of such chivalry and love . . .

We have no prescribed number of speech stresses; the first line above has eight, the second five or six, depending on how hard we hit *such.* The final *-y* of *chivalry* and the *a-* of *and* count in the meter as a single syllable.

Since the line is regulated neither by fixed numbers of feet nor by speech stresses, it can accommodate a great variety of rhythmic movement. "It was plainly the freest of free-verse, there being no speech rhythm which it would not admit. . . ."[13] Bridges developed his twelve-syllable line as a carry-all metric, using it in his most ambitious poetic undertaking, *The Testament of Beauty.* Unfortunately, I find Bridges' masterwork unreadable. His "loose alexandrines" (Book II, 841) lull rather than excite; his philosophic meanderings are priggish daydreams. Since I am not expert in Bridges' sources (Spinoza, Santayana *et al.*), I cannot comment on the poem's skillful philosophic eclecticism; however, what I can discover on my own—a mild naturalism, a still milder anti-intellectualism, the hope to reconcile pagan aesthetic with Christian ethic—has little power either as speculative philosophy or poetic vision. Perhaps the unhappiest feature of the poem is Bridges' Jovian detachment. He makes occasional reference to ordinary humanity and their all too human activities (the ways of the rich; crowds at football games, etc.); but *The Testament of Beauty* does not engage the world of common experience: it has no people in it, and consequently no human smell about it.

Finally we must mention Bridges' work in quantitative metric. My general remarks on adapting classical prosody to English need not be repeated here. I refer the reader back to Chapter II. However, the reader might like to play a little game to see if his ear can tell which of the following passages is composed in Bridges' "free" syllabic meter, which in his "English hexameters":

> Not knowing the high goal of our great endeavour
> Is spiritual attainment, individual worth,
> At all cost to be sought and at all cost pursued,
> To be won at all cost and at all cost assured;
> Not such material ease as might be attain'd for all
> By cheap production and distribution of common needs,
> Were all life level'd down to where the lowest can reach . . .[14]

> Turn our thought for awhile to the symphonies of Beethoven,
> Or the rever'd preludes of mighty Sebastian; is there
> One work of Nature's contrivance beautiful as these?
> Judg'd by beauty alone man wins, as sensuous artist . . .[15]

"Cadenced prose" would be the judgment of most readers. The second selection, from "Wintry Delights," was written to test the theories of Bridges' friend, William Johnson Stone.[16] "Wintry Delights" begins auspiciously; its rhythmic swing, however, derives more from *Piers Plowman* than from the *Aeneid:*

> Now in wintry delights, and long fireside meditation,
> 'Twixt studies and routine paying due court to the Muses,
> My solace in solitude, when broken roads barricade me
> Mudbound, unvisited for months with my merry children . . .

The distribution of heavy speech stresses and repetition of initial consonants suggest Middle English alliterative verse:

My sól ace in só li tude, || when bró ken róads bàr ri cáde me
Múd bound, un ví si ted || for mónths with my
mér ry chíl dren . . .

Again, this is not Bridges' prosodic intent. If we hum some hexameter music to ourselves (*Arma virumque cano,* or *This is the forest primeval*), we might be able to hear and scan

Nōw ĭn wĭn | trȳ dē | līghts, ānd | lōng fīre | sīde mĕ dĭ | tā tīon . . .

The two syllables *me-di-* are actually more than half as short as *side;* and we have, as C. S. Lewis points out, for the last two feet not the music of the slow movement of Beethoven's *Seventh Symphony* (♩ ♫ | ♩ ♩), but the "Ride of the Valkyries" (♩♬ ♩. ♩.).

One poem in the *Poems in Classical Prosody* stands out as a work of considerable rhythmic power, "Johannes Milton, Senex":

> Since I believe in God the Father Almighty,
> Man's Maker and Judge, Overruler of Fortune,
> 'Twere strange should I praise anything and refuse
> Him praise,
> Should love the creature forgetting the Crēator,
> Nor unto Himˇ in suff'ring and sorrow turn me:
> Nay how could I withdraw me fromˇ His embracing? . . .

Unlike the other quantitative poems these lines neither "limp nor twitch," but move with Miltonic sonority and smoothness. The classical meter imitated here is the Scazon or Choliambic: a six-footed iambic line with the final foot reversed:

> Sĭnce Ī | bĕ līeve | ĭn Gōd | thĕ Fā | thĕr Āl | mīgh tў̆ . . .

The poem's rhythmic success depends on a normative coincidence of vowel length with syllabic stress: we hear syllable-stress iambics underlying, and occasionally combating, the quantitative measure.

Our estimation of Bridges as prosodist and poet cannot be based on the effort and variety of his technical experimentation; his "new" meters have proved more interesting than useful. No great metric—like that of Eliot's "Gerontion"—evolved out of either his accentual or syllabic verse. His achievement as a poet rests on his lyrics in traditional meter. Even in these, exquisite as they are, I find none of the force or penetration of Hardy's metrically less sophisticated but rhythmically more impressive lyrics. If this seems a paradox, it is only saying that craftsmanship alone cannot produce great poetry—or great prosody. An impressive rhythm grows like a living thing out of the poem's feeling; the feeling is matured and shaped by the rhythm:

> O body swayed to music, O brightening glance,
> How can we know the dancer from the dance?

In Bridges' case feeling and rhythm move at low intensities. His poetry lacks vitality; even in his much admired "Low Barometer"—whose subject is the disorder of the human soul and the terrors of the night—the suave, almost gentle rhythms never rise to the pitch of feeling the subject requires.

4 Edwin Arlington Robinson and Robert Frost

In selected examples of Robinson's and Frost's loosened blank verse, metrical analysis shows how the lilt of New England speech gets into the versification. First, some passages from Robinson's *Isaac and Archibald:*

> Isaac and Archibald were two old men.
> I knew them, and I may have laughed at them
> A little; but I must have honored them
> For they were old, and they were good to me . . .
>
> But somewhere at the end of the first mile . . .

> I told him that I could not think of them . . .
>
> And that pleased me—for I was twelve years old . . .

Characteristic is Robinson's use of the inverted second foot:

> I knéw | thém, and | I máy | have láughed | at thém . . .
>
> But sóme | whére at | the énd | of the fírst míle . . .
>
> And thát | pléased me | —for Í | was twélve | yèars óld . . .

Inverting the second foot loosens metrical rigidity and brings the line close to ordinary speech. At times the metric—doubtless occasioned by the subject—turns Wordsworthian; we get monosyllabic rustic simplicity:

> It is not
> So much that he should come to his last hand,
> And leave the game, and go the old way down;
> But I have known him in and out so long,
> And I have seen so much of good in him
> That other men have shared and have not seen . . .

Those who do not like this kind of verse may mutter about low words creeping in dull lines; others will declare that the monosyllabic word has been a traditional source of power in English blank verse.

A longer passage shows other features of Robinson's blank verse:

> If you had asked me then to tell just why
> I made so much of Isaac and the things
> He said, I should have gone far for an answer;
> For I knew it was not sorrow that I felt,
> Whatever I may have wished it, or tried then
> To make myself believe. My mouth was full
> Of words, and they would have been comforting
> To Isaac, spite of my twelve years, I think;
> But there was not in me the willingness
> To speak them out. Therefore I watched the ground;
> And I was wondering what made the Lord
> Create a thing so nervous as an ant,
> When Isaac, with commendable unrest,
> Ordained that we should take the road again—

The syntax is close; smooth enjambments and grammatical precision urge along a steady narrative movement. We might also feel that the meter was as close as the syntax if we did not find lines like these:

> He saíd, | I shoúld | have góne | fár for | an án | swer
> What é | ver I máy | have wíshed | it, or tríed thén . . .

Lines of eleven syllables are common in the poem. These are often nonmetrical in structure, although we can rationalize them into scansion:

> At the énd | of an hoúr's wálk | ing áf | ter thát . . .

An anapest followed by a double foot dissolves the line into prose. Other eleven-syllable lines regularly employ trisyllabic feet in various positions; the effect is an overall softening of metrical pulse. In this line we find an anapest followed by contiguous Ionics—pure prose:

> And a frá | grance of óld súm | mers—the óld stýle . . .

Frost has followed Robinson in adapting the measure of blank verse to the rhythms of New England speech. Our example is from the dramatic dialogue, "West-running Brook":

> 'Fred, where is north?'
> 'North? North is there, my love.
> The brook runs west.'
> 'West-running Brook then call it.'

The speakers divide up a nearly strict blank verse line. Frost allows the metrical pulse to shade the feeling and meaning of three identical words:

> . . . is nórth?' |
> | 'Nòrth? Nórth | is thére . . .

Rhetorical stress falls nearly equally on the three *norths,* but since the second *north* falls between the metrically strong *norths,* its intensity is weakened. Meaning requires a lower level of stress: the second *north* has some emotive but no semantic value; it is

Fred's vocalized pause while remembering his directions. The meter ingeniously adjusts and modifies both concept and feeling. No wonder Frost so vigorously asserted that he would sooner play tennis without a net than write free verse!

Later in "West-running Brook" we find a line with six contiguous rhetorical stresses:

> And it is tíme, stréngth, tóne, líght, lífe and lóve—

Words of greater conceptual value fall beneath the ictus; *life* and *love* must be stressed slightly more than *strength* and *tone.* It may be possible to read the six nouns with absolutely level stress. But prevailing iambic movement and the slight variations in vowel length force greater emphasis on the fourth and fifth feet.

Frost may have had a Miltonic rhythm in his head ("Rocks, Caves, Lakes, Fens, Bogs, Dens and Shades of Death . . .") which suggested the context for the line above:

> And it is time, strength, tone, light, life and love—
> And even substance lapsing unsubstantial;
> The universal cataract of death
> That spends to nothingness—and unresisted,
> Save by some strange resistance in itself,
> Not just a swerving, but a throwing back,
> As if regret were in it and were sacred.

The learned Latinate punning and inverted syntax of

> And even substance lapsing unsubstantial . . .

echoes and parodies Milton: a fine example of rhythmic feeling preceding and stimulating an idea.

Like Robinson, Frost introduces many eleven syllable lines:

> It was to me—in an annunciation . . .
>
> Long, long before we were from any creature . . .
>
> Get back to the beginning of beginnings . . .

The hypermetrical syllable is generally unaccented; however, Saintsbury would have decried as deliberate metrical mischief the poem's last line:

To dáy | will bé | the dáy | of whát | we bo?th sáid . . .

and spluttered that *both* was a perversity. In context the line moves smoothly enough; the extra syllable allows the line to hang as a partial question in the air:

> 'Today will be the day
> You said so.'
> 'No, today will be the day
> You said the brook was called West-running Brook.'
>
> 'Today will be the day of what we both said.'

The slight bump in the rhythm slows the line down; we must speak the last words deliberately, hesitating, pondering, as if reaching carefully for every word.

Frost builds his prosody close to common speech as he builds his poetry close to man's recurrent experience. His rhythms issue from the meter in a way that seems without artifice; yet every line is a skillful modification of the metrical norm:

> And then—the watcher at his pulse took fright.
> No one believed. They listened at his heart.
> Little—less—nothing! —and that ended it.
> No more to build on there. And they, since they
> Were not the one dead, turned to their affairs.

from "Out, Out—"

The crushing and humiliating fact that life goes on despite human tragedy is the vital feeling in the rhythmical hesitations of the last lines:

> No móre | to búild | on thére. | And théy, | since théy
> Were nót | the óne | déad, || túrned | to théir | affáirs.

The caesura, a dead stop, coming in the middle of the foot, the spondaic foot itself with its two heavy stresses, are powerful evocations of feeling. The syntactical units are agonizingly short—each is a blow to head and body. We have rhythms symbolizing vital import; we feel the boy's death at basic levels. It is the prosody which images the nervous agony and the blank despair, the terrible concern and the even more terrible indifference.

5 *Edwin Muir*

Unjustly neglected, the poems of Edwin Muir are finally appearing in the standard anthologies. Muir shares certain qualities with Yeats; his poems in short lines have similar subtleties of rhythm, but their themes and images are less spectacular. Muir is haunted but not obsessed. The most powerful thematic influence on his work comes from modern German literature. Such allegorical pieces as "The Interrogation" or "The West" suggest Kafka's world where the ordinary and the fabulous mingle in mysterious relationships. "The Animals," "The Toy Horse," and "Orpheus' Dream" have affinities with Rilke; they are gnomic, abrupt in beginnings, concerned with the ineffable pathos of creatures and *things.*

His poems which derive from classical mythological sources possess singular power; however, unlike many modern poets who self-consciously adapt Greek myths, Muir tells of Ulysses and Penelope, Theseus and Orpheus with utter lack of literary affectation. "The Labyrinth" is about reality and illusion. Theseus, free of the labyrinth but dazed by memories, struggles on middle earth to shake himself free of his past:

Since I emerged that day from the labyrinth,
Dazed with the tall and echoing passages,
The swift recoils, so many I almost feared
I'd meet myself returning at some smooth corner,
Myself or my ghost, for all there was unreal
After the straw ceased rustling and the bull
Lay dead upon the straw and I remained,
Blood-splashed, if dead or alive I could not tell
In the twilight nothingness (I might have been
A spirit seeking his body through the roads
Of intricate Hades)—ever since I came out
To the world, the still fields swift with flowers, the trees
All bright with blossom, the little green hills, the sea,
The sky and all in movement under it,
Shepherds and flocks and birds and the young and old,
(I stared in wonder at the young and the old,
For in the maze time had not been with me;
I had strayed, it seemed, past sun and season and change,
Past rest and motion, for I could not tell
At last if I moved or stayed; the maze itself

Revolved around me on its hidden axis
And swept me smoothly to its enemy,
The lovely world)—since I came out that day . . .

The poem continues for twelve more lines before coming to its first full stop. Its remarkable, sustained syntax winds and turns upon itself, pausing in parenthesis, then moving on to complete its full statement only after thirty-five lines. The syntax *acts out* the journey of Theseus; when we emerge from the twisting, maze-like opening sentence, we issue on to the straight roads of the outer world. Once in the clear outside, the syntax is rapid and concise:

But taking thought
I'd tell myself, 'You need not hurry. This
Is the firm good earth. All roads lie free before you.'
But my bad spirit would sneer, 'No, do not hurry.'

The syntax offers us the sensation of wandering in the maze, then moves us along a straight road. The "silent rhythm of thought" powerfully directs our feelings to the experience behind words and meanings.

The strong syntax so dominates the prosody that the meter may seem to have little or no function. Indeed, Mr. J. C. Hall makes the astonishing claim that the poem is without meter: "In his poem 'The Labyrinth' Muir sustains the first sentence for 35 lines without metrical support and without forfeiting our attention—surely a remarkable achievement!"[17] We agree the poem's syntax undergirds its structure; but if we scan a few lines, it is clear that the poem has a blank verse base:

Since Í | e mérged | that dáy | from the lá | by rínth,

Dázed with | the táll | and éch | o‿ing pás | sa gés,

The swíft | re cóils, | so má | ny‿Í ál | most féared

I'd méet | my sélf | re túrn | ing at sóme | smòoth cór | ner . . .

Like much modern loosened blank verse, trisyllabic substitution allows Muir considerable rhythmic freedom. Many lines are phrased as prose:

Stairways and corridors and antechambers
That vacantly wait for some great audience . . .

and are absorbed into the metrical scheme without distortion or rhythmic upheaval. Muir carefully paces rhythmic movement; the lines proceed from regularity to freedom, and back to regularity. We can trace a gentle curve from steady iambic to prose statement:

> But they, the gods, as large and bright as clouds,
> Conversed across the sounds in tranquil voices
> High in the sky above the untroubled sea;
> And their eternal dialogue was peace
> Where all these things were woven; and this our life
> Was as a chord deep in that dialogue,
> An easy utterance of harmonious words,
> Spontaneous syllables bodying forth a world.

The first line above is normal iambic; the last two are nonmetrical. When the poem concludes, the prosody firmly returns to regular blank verse:

> Oh these deceits are strong almost as life.
> Last night I dreamt I was in the labyrinth,
> And woke far on. I did not know the place.

Among the many superb poems in short lines, I offer "The Fathers" and "The Animals" for prosodic scrutiny. They show how much variety is possible in the three-beat line; how the shifting of the strong stresses and an occasional trisyllabic foot control a realm of rhythmic possibility. The second stanza of "The Fathers" recalls, on first reading, Yeats:

> Archaic fevers shake
> Our healthy flesh and blood
> Plumped in the passing day
> And fed with pleasant food.
> The fathers' anger and ache
> Will not, will not away
> And leave the living alone,
> But on our careless brows
> Faintly their furrows engrave
> Like veinings in a stone,
> Breathe in the sunny house
> Nightmare of blackened bone,
> Cellar and choking cave.

A good poet may be measured by what he can, in matters of technique, get away with. Muir handles a line of three alliterated metrically stressed syllables

And *l*eave the *l*iving a*l*one . . .

*C*ellar and *ch*oking *c*ave . . .

by deftly modulating vowel length and quality. What might be an uncomfortable mouthful of consonants becomes song; the pattern of syllables, like a phrase of melody, carries a measured burden of feeling.

"The Animals" is Rilkesque. I give the first and last stanzas:

They do not live in the world,
Are not in time and space.
From birth to death hurled
No word do they have, not one
To plant a foot upon,
Were never in any place.

But these have never trod
Twice the familiar track,
Never never turned back
Into the memoried day.
All is new and near
In the unchanging Here
On the fifth great day of God,
That shall remain the same,
Never shall pass away.

On the sixth day we came.

Muir avoids every obvious poeticism; we have few adjectives, a simple diction, terse and correct syntax. The meter is compressed; a sense of powerful feeling, held in check, is conveyed by the use of the monosyllabic foot. Muir varies its position:

From bírth | to déath | húrled . . .

Áll | is néw | and néar . . .

On the síxth | dáy | we cáme . . .

A good example of "imitative meter" is the line

Né ver | né ver | turnèd báck

where the meter twice *turns back* in consecutive trochees and then comes to rights with a final heavy foot.

The last line is separated from the rest of the poem by a visual pause: a heavy silence indicated by the double line spacing. This device of fixing the poem's emotional climax in significant isolation is a frequent mannerism of Rilke's:

> Dann ist ein Hallen von dem vielen Hämmern,
> und durch die Berge geht es Stoss um Stoss.
> Erst wenn es dunkelt, lassen wir dich los:
> Und deine kommenden Konturen dämmern.
>
> Gott, du bist gross.

from *Das Stundenbuch*

Muir isolates his last line in a few other poems ("The Usurpers," "The Good Town," "Head and Heart"). These final lines are not portentous: not "clinching" afterthoughts or obvious précis. In "The Good Town" the last line makes a quiet observation, disturbed by a significant variation in the metrical pattern—an inverted third foot which belies the narrator's surface equanimity:

> We have seen
> Good men made evil wrangling with the evil,
> Straight minds grown crooked fighting crooked minds.
> Our peace betrayed us; we betrayed our peace.
> Look at it well. This was the good town once.'
>
> These thoughts we have, walking among our ruins.

6 *John Crowe Ransom*

Ransom and Winters, alone among the New Critics, have devoted meticulous attention to prosodical matters. I shall enlarge my previous, brief comments on Ransom's theories of metrical function, and make a distinction between Ransom's views expressed in the late thirties and forties and those he more recently holds. His most fully developed theory limits meter to providing aesthetic surface, or what he names "local texture" for the poem. In an article published in 1956, Ransom considers the matter of rhythm, apostrophizing it as "... the marriage of the meter and the language."[18] More of this blissful metaphor later. We must first note that Ransom's (from my point of view) cramped theorizing does not interfere with his sensitivity to metrical matters and with the soundness of his practical prosodical criticism. He can correctly scan a line of metered verse; he understands the foot structure of traditional meter; he can hear what the immediacies of metrical structure contribute to a line and to the whole poem.

"Ontology" and "ontological" are Ransom's favorite critical words; the mode of existence of the poem "is a *logical structure* having a *local texture.*" Ransom proceeds with an elaborate architectural conceit ("a negotiable trope"): the poem is a room whose beams, boards, and plaster are its structure; "... and perhaps it has been hung with tapestry, or with paintings, for 'decoration.' The paint, the paper, the tapestry are texture. It is logically unrelated to structure."[19] The structure-texture dichotomy is particularized for meter:

> The meter on the whole is out of relation to the meaning of the poem, or to anything else specifically; it is a musical material of low grade, but plastic and only slightly resistant material, and its presence in every poem is that of an abstractionist element that belongs to the art.[20]

Ransom rejects, of course, all "expressive" heresies. "It is not the business of the meters to be expressive of the meaning."[21] The meters enter into no logically accountable relationship with the propositional sense; nor do they, in their rhythmic varieties, suggest any qualities of feeling. Indeed, Ransom's poetics scarcely allow that poetry can have emotive meanings. Poets and readers *may* have gross and disorderly emotions at the moments of composition and reading; the poem, in its severe ontological purity, has only structure and texture. "Art is more cool than hot."[22] Reading Ransom, we are often seized with the infuriating notion that poems are neither written nor read; they exist, like the unborn and unconceived children of Kipling's "They," in their mysterious ontological heaven.

Ransom's views seem to me unnecessarily fastidious. They allow little of "the reek of the human" into the poem. I suspect Ransom's battle against "science" (his beckoning windmill) leads him to theoretical excess; he wants poetic discourse to be as tidy and rational as the universe of the scientists. We must also remember the historical situation. Ransom had been much impressed (as had every other New Critic) with the work of I. A. Richards in initiating a criticism ostensibly free of messy subjectivity. Neither Ransom's "ontology" nor Richards' neurology established a science of criticism; Ransom elegantly restates neoclassic poetics. The poem is a logical or prose discourse draped in poetic robes. What is Ransom's "texture" but neoclassic "ornament"? Meter enters into no intrinsic relationship with the meaning; its function is ornamental: paper and plaster for the poem. Ransom combats all Coleridgeian attempts to view the poem as an organism, preferring to consider "... the essential dualism of a poem ..." and poetry as "... an inorganic activity."[23]

Long ago Eliot observed that poets devise theories to defend the kind of poetry they write—or think they write. Ransom wrote, in an age of "free verse" and blank prose, richly textured and intricately metered poems. He strikes archaic attitudes, and he is fond of old words; we run to our dictionaries to discover the meaning of *transmogrifying, pernoctated, diuturnity, stuprate.* His theories, read together with his poetry, call us to his poetic devices and his craftsmanship. Everything that art can accomplish for poetry is lovingly bestowed on Ransom's verse. But like all theorizing poets, his poetry goes beyond anything his theory can account for; it is often a poetry which the theory would not recognize, or better, it is poetry superior to the theory.

We return to "Captain Carpenter" to see how it sanctions Ransom's views. The metrical peculiarities of the poem certainly furnish a texture distracting enough to the unwary reader. It draws, on first reading, sufficient attention to itself so that we might wonder what relationship exists between the meter and the meaning. We know Ransom roughens his lines to achieve an intended effect; if anyone thinks the versification of "Captain Carpenter" is inept or accidental, we have this self-conscious testimony:

> It is in no very late stage of a poet's advancement that his taste rejects a sustained phonetic regularity as something restricted and barren, perhaps ontologically defective. Accordingly he is capable of writing smooth meters and then roughening them on purpose.[24]

We have examined the metrical features of the poem in Chapter II. Ransom inverts the sensitive second and fourth feet; he also "wrenches" the accents:

The curse of hell upon the sleek up *start* . . .

The bitch bit off his arms at *the* el *bows* . . .

This handling of meter, far from proving distracting and irrelevant, supplies a prosodic tone which qualifies meaning. The wrenched accents allude to the metrical mannerisms of the popular ballads; the conflicts between meter and speech stress produce a rhythm which is itself "meaning."

If texture were ornamental, Ransom could have written

Captain Decatur rose up in his prime . . .

and would have achieved, if we can buy Ransom's theory, only another kind of irrelevancy. The meaning the meter complements, and interacts with, is the poem's complex irony: the calculated discrepancy between Ransom's fable and the way he feels about it. The meter tips us off about the feeling. By itself the meter could not carry Ransom's many ironies; the archaic diction and syntax and the macabre humor of Captain Carpenter's gradual dismemberment place the poem at its proper aesthetic distance. Captain Carpenter's quest is simple and commendable; singlehandedly, he sets out to rid the world of evil. Ransom judges the quest and finds it, all at once, Quixotic, horrible, comic, and deeply touching. The ironies do not blunt Ransom's total judgment: Captain Carpenter deserves our admiration and pity. Irony allows compassion without mawkishness. Ransom's sophisticated metrical manipulation—the "affective" contortions of the iambic line—infuses structure with texture and fits rhythm to feeling.

As deliberately metered as "Captain Carpenter," but without its textural eccentricities, is "The Equilibrists." Ransom counterpoints the meter in this poem, but adheres to the metrical code of traditional syllable-stress meter. He uses every "allowable" metrical variation: the substitution of trochee for iamb; the double or Ionic foot; the hypermetrical or "feminine" ending; the elision of two unstressed syllables to make up one metrical syllable.[25] Three selected stanzas exemplify all the possible departures:

1 Eyes talking: Never mind the cruel words,
2 Embrace my flowers, but not embrace the swords.
3 But what they said, the doves came straightway flying
4 And unsaid: Honor, Honor, they came crying.

5 But still I watched them spinning, orbited nice.
6 Their flames were not more radiant than their ice.
7 I dug in the quiet earth and wrought the tomb
8 And made these lines to memorize their doom:—

Epitaph

9 *Equilibrists lie here; stranger, tread light;*
10 *Close, but untouching in each other's sight;*
11 *Mouldered the lips and ashy the tall skull,*
12 *Let them lie perilous and beautiful.*

Lines three and four illustrate the feminine ending; the first foot of line four is a rising Ionic:

3 But whát | they saíd, | the dóves | came stráight | way flý | ing
4 And un saíd: Hó | nor, Hó | nor, théy | came crý | ing . . .

Lines six and seven show trisyllabic feet which are theoretically elided in scansion:

6 Their flámes | were nót | more rá | di‿ant than | their íce.
7 I dúg | in‿the quí | et eárth | and wróught | the tómb . . .

Lines nine and ten show inverted feet. The inversions, however, occur in the least sensitive positions—the first foot, and the foot after the caesura. The fourth foot of line ten is a rising Ionic:

9 E quí | li brísts | lie hére; | strán ger, | tread líght;
10 Clóse, but | un tóuch | ing in éach óth | er's síght . . .

The final couplet brings together initial inverted feet, the rising Ionic (fourth foot, line 11), and the rarer falling Ionic (second foot, line 12).

11 Móul dered | the líps | and á | shy the táll skúll,
12 Lét them | líe pé ri lous | and béau | ti fúl.

The last foot must be wrenched in scansion; in *reading* the line we would emphasize the prevailing falling rhythm.

Donne, "a great master of the meters,"[26] is Ransom's master in this poem. Metrical technique echoes the poem's metaphysical dissonances: honor against desire, Heaven against Hell, fire against ice, love against death. Metrical variation opens a world of feelings, balanced and opposed. There is no violent strain between meter and meaning; but rather, we have lines where the meter releases rhythms as unsettling as Ransom's alternation of feelings: anger and frustration, pity and admiration, and finally, wonder and religious awe. Ransom protests that meter cannot imply meaning, but what do the "procession of strong monosyllables"[27] and the curious falling Ionic do in this line:

Till cóld | wórds càme | dówn spí ral from | the héad . . .

but provide a rhythm contextually appropriate to sense and feeling? Do not the five contiguous speech stresses ". . . [open] up the possibilities of ambiguous meaning . . . and let [the reader] construe a meaning out of them, or a multiplicity of meanings"?[28]

My last three citations come from Ransom's statement in the *Kenyon Review's* symposium, "English Verse and What It Sounds Like" (Summer 1956). He considerably modifies his earlier views. He abandons the structure-texture dichotomy and clearly sees meter as a crucial means of semantic emphasis: "But it is surprising how often the stress at a new place puts a new light on a given situation; or rather, looks at the situation from a new but quite possible perspective."[29] He no longer seems concerned that the poem's existence be fixed in hygienic isolation. He talks about rhythm, feeling, and emotion; about the poem's "human materials," and its "deliverance of an emotional burden." Rhythm is the marriage of the meter and the language.

I give Ransom the last, significant words in this chapter. He is commenting on Arnold Stein's sensitive and brilliant readings of Milton's metric.[30] I am greatly mistaken if Ransom is not expounding, most eloquently and persuasively, the idea that prosody controls, modifies, and *signifies* emotive qualities in poetry:

> [Arnold Stein] . . . takes three short passages from Milton, and within them he goes from line to line to show what the meter is trying to do with the human materials, always against resistance but eventually with success, till we have to say that it has had its way with them and transformed them. The action focuses technically upon the conflict between the natural prose stresses and the ideal metrical ones, but in

every one of the picked passages a resolution or harmony is finally accomplished between the two orders. It is not a technical conflict only, as it might be if the game were being played just for the sport. The prose stresses define the deliverance of an emotional burden, but the passion would be undelivered if the meter prevailed too easily over them. It wins gradually, so that in the end the passion is spent, the troubled spirit is serene; and is there an inclination to say that the human spirit has attained to a heavenly peace?[31]

IV

Nineteenth-Century Precursors

The nineteenth century has been described as an age of many stylizations but no definite style: an age in which artists experimented, "and the experimenters all had one purpose in mind: to find a style instead of trying to get along with parodies of style."[1] Nineteenth-century prosodic style departs from the strict iambic discipline of the neoclassic closed couplet and end-stopped blank verse. We find, as early as Blake, free use of trisyllabic and inverted feet; we also find in Blake's Prophetic Books a long line of varying syllabic length which moves away from syllable-stress metric toward newer freedoms.

The general prosody of Romantic and Victorian poetry strains but does not abrogate the syllable-stress tradition. Eclecticism flourishes; Tennyson and Browning, the Victorian Establishment, are linked together in academic contexts, but their prosodies are miles apart. If a prevailing nineteenth-century prosodic style exists, Saintsbury confesses it has eluded him:

> . . . I have not attempted to sum up the general prosodic character of Mr. Swinburne and Mr. Morris, of Tennyson and Browning, even perhaps of Shelley and Keats.
>
> . . . I doubt whether the person is yet born—he is certainly not long out of his cradle—who can do this, or for many years will be able to do it. The perspective of the past is not yet firm enough for that.[2]

The nineteenth-century picture has become sharper, and for the viewer fifty years after Saintsbury, the perspective shows different relationships. The prosodies of Shelley, Tennyson, and Swinburne move toward a distant horizon; Blake, Whitman, Hopkins, and Browning are now in the foreground, recognized as crucial influences and important points of prosodic departure. The nineteenth century swung gradually away from the dominance of syllable-stress metric toward open rhythms. In our own prosodic age—post-Saintsbury—a spate of experimental prosodies has obscured the main streams of prosodical practice, but this seems clear: the nineteenth-century movement toward greater prosodical flexibility culminated in the "free verse" movements of the 'teens and twenties; with Auden in the early thirties, prosody once more stabilized itself in traditional metric.

Before we assay the prosodies of our contemporaries, we turn to Browning, Whitman, and Hopkins: three poets who struggled against the English prosodic norm and who foreshadowed the revolt of the early twentieth century—the temporary dislodgement of the syllable-stress foot. Each of these poets arrived at a new prosody in ways important to later poets; each, though vaguely aware of the others' activities, found his own solutions. Browning, Whitman, and Hopkins are the ancestors whose progeny have increased and multiplied; the prosodical innovations of our age have their origins in their practice or influence.

1 Robert Browning

The "irregularities" in Browning's prosody dismayed his Victorian contemporaries who were nurtured on Shellyean and Tennysonian suavities. Yet Browning's verse scans according to the letter of metrical law. More objectionable than the supposed roughness of his metrical practice are the irritating rhythms which establish themselves in lines like these:

> At the midnight in the silence of the sleep-time,
>   When you set your fancies free . . .
>
> No, at noonday in the bustle of man's work-time
>   Greet the unseen with a cheer! . . .

Epilogue to *Asolando*

Such rhythmical tunes persist in the memory long after critical discrimination rejects Browning's noisy and automatic optimism. These lines—as many of Browning's do, when he is seized with the affirmative mood—*march* to a procession of strong equal stresses. That they march with equal boisterousness *in the silence of the sleep-time* and at noonday is a mark of Browning's prosodical insensitivity.

It is not, however, Browning's prosodical mannerisms but his handling of traditional blank verse which becomes important for modern prosody. In the famous dramatic monologues he took blank-verse measure and trimmed and stretched it to fit the rhythms of colloquial speech. The garrulous apology of "Mr. Sludge, The Medium" illustrates Browning's mature practice and the general tone of the later monologues. Mr. Sludge, a fraudulent spiritualist, has been nearly strangled by one of his victims:

> Well, if the marks seem gone,
> 'T is because stiffish cock-tail, taken in time,
> Is better for a bruise than arnica.
> There, sir! I bear no malice: 't is n't in me.
> I know I acted wrongly: still, I've tried
> What I could say in my excuse,—to show
> The devil's not all devil . . . I don't pretend,
> He's angel, much less such a gentleman
> As you, sir! And I've lost you, lost myself,
> Lost all-l-l-l- . . .

Browning intends American speech: the original "Sludge" was D. D. Home, a notorious American medium who had duped the credulous Mrs. Browning. After her death Browning published "Sludge." It is a savage attack—doubtlessly a release of Browning's suppressed rage and chagrin.

The lines show a wealth of strong rhetorical stresses and some anomalous feet:

> 'T ís be | cause stíf | fish cóck- | tàil, tá | ken in tíme . . .
> Thére, sír! | I béar | no má | lice: 't ís | n't in mé . . .
> As yóu, | sír! And | I've lóst | you, lóst | my sélf . . .

The main departures from normal metrical procedure are the spondee (line two, first foot) and the inverted second foot (line three). But the rhythmical freedom of these lines does not issue from gross violation of metrical law; their suppleness is a matter of syntactical phrasing. Syntax tumbles and rushes along, combating the meter at caesuras and the ends of lines:

Well,
if the marks seem gone,
'T is because stiffish cock-tail,
taken in time,
Is better for a bruise
than arnica.
There, sir!
I bear no malice:
't is n't in me.
I know I acted wrongly:
still, I've tried
What I could say in my excuse . . .

Browning breaks up the line into short speech periods; the effect, in working against the persistent meter, is taut and hesitant.

The practice of multiplying the number of caesuras in the blank verse line—actually, a process of rhetorical fragmentation—increases in Browning's later work. In *The Ring and the Book* (1868–69) we find lines broken by as many as four heavy pauses:

To stop song, loosen flower, and leave path.
  Law . . .
You were wrong, you see: that's well to see,
  though late . . .
There, I was born, have lived, shall die, a fool!

Caponsacchi, 94, 141, 179.

A complete passage from *The Ring and the Book* reveals a metric that is prophetic; we find here the early Pound and Eliot:

Oh, though first comer, though as strange at the work
As fribble must be, coxcomb, fool that's near
To knave as, say, a priest who fears the world—
Was he bound brave the peril, save the doomed,
Or go on, sing his snatch and pluck his flower,
Keep the straight path and let the victim die?
I held so; you decided otherwise,
Saw no such peril, therefore no such need
To stop song, loosen flower, and leave path. Law,
Law was aware and watching, would suffice,
Wanted no priest's intrusion, palpably
Pretence, too manifest a subterfuge!

Caponsacchi, 86–97.

The meter is frequently counterpointed; some heavily stressed lines bear a superficial resemblance to Hopkins:

> Wás he | boúnd bráve | the pér | il, sáve | the dóomed . . .
> Tó stóp | sóng, lóos | en flówer, | and léave | páth. Láw . . .

We have Hopkins-like distortion of grammar ("bound brave the peril"), and much spondaic springing. The lines are metrically precarious, but Browning always recovers the meter at the point when it seems ready to dissolve in the uncontrolled excitement of passionate speech.

Eliot protests—too loudly I think—that Pound's verse and his own owe nothing to Whitman.[3] Possum-like, he is less explicit about Browning's influence on their prosodies. On superficial examination these lines appear as "free" as the *Song of Myself:*

> "My nerves are bad to-night. Yes, bad. Stay with me.
> "Speak to me. Why do you never speak. Speak.
> "What are you thinking of? What thinking? What?
> "I never know what you are thinking. Think."
>
> *The Waste Land,* II.

But scansion shows their metrical structure: a jazzing of the normal blank-verse line:

> "Spéak to | me. Whý | do you né | ver spéak. | Spéak.
> "Whát are | you thínk | ing óf? | What thínk | ing? Whát?

Rhythmic character here is determined by the same nervous hesitancies, the expressive pauses within the line, which we found in Browning.

2 *Walt Whitman*

Whitman's prosody shows no development from traditional syllable-stress metric. It is our first great *nonmetrical* prosody in English, relying on the various techniques of enumeration, syntactical parallelism, and (Hopkins' term) "figures of grammar" to shape words to rhythm. Eliot tells us that Whitman is a great prose writer. Eliot is mistaken; the formal bases of Whitman's prosody are as open to analysis as those of the traditional meters. We must remember, however, that the scansion of stressed and unstressed syllables has no relevance to Whitman's prosody (as traditional scansion has no relevance to the later poems in sprung rhythm by Hopkins). Occasionally Whitman's lines fall into scannable hexameters, but their rhythmic base is not provided by a pattern of metrical feet. The proof of this is the total absence of counterpointing, or syncopation, in Whitman's verse. Nowhere in Whitman do we find the *jazzing* that we have shown in the lines from Eliot. *Jazzing* is possible only against a distinctly felt pattern of metrical expectancy—as in the syncopations of jazz which contradict with predictable irregularity a steady pulse in double or common time.

It may seem that we belabor the obvious in insisting that Pound and Eliot are not heirs to Whitman's prosody. Or to be more accurate: they did not find, as young poets, Whitman's rhythms appropriate to their tone and subject. The monotony of Prufrock's life could not be imaged in the long, open cadences of *Out of the Cradle;* his boredom and triviality are neatly rendered in a tetrameter couplet:

> In the room the women come and go
> Talking of Michelangelo.

Whitman's prosody is formal and ceremonious. Despite Whitman's occasional and misguided attempts to use what he thought was common speech, his diction is part of a self-conscious literary dialect. His proper mode is not speech but invocation; not conversation, but chant and ceremony. Significantly enough, we catch echoes of the Whitmanian hexameter in Eliot's later liturgical music:

> I do not know much about gods; but I think that
> the river
> Is a strong brown god—sullen, untamed and
> intractable . . .

Robert Graves gleefully believes that Eliot is here "true to a boyhood's admiration for Longfellow's *Evangeline*. . . ."[4] Our impulse is more charitable: the music of *Fóur Quartets* is closer to Whitman than Longfellow.

Whitman's revolution in prosody was so simple and complete that it has never been properly assessed. Whitman did not fuss about his innovations in technique, as did Hopkins who agonized over every stress and syllable; consequently the theorists have left Whitman's prosody untouched.[5] Whitman's basic contribution was the substitution of syntax for meter as the controlling prosodic element in his poetry. The syllable-stress foot has no primary function in Whitman's verse, although these feet occur frequently enough as decorative but never as integral parts of rhythmic structure. The primary rhythms of Whitman's verse are all the various functions of syntax.

This leaves us with Donald Davie's contention that Whitman may belong with those poets who exploit "syntax like music."[6] Davie points out that certain modern poets, especially those who came under the influence of Symbolism, abandoned the logical forms of grammar and attempted to articulate the *feelings of an experience* without clearly defining the experience. A celebrated example of "syntax like music" occurs in Eliot's "Gerontion":

In the juvescence of the year
Came Christ the tiger

In depraved May, dogwood and chestnut, flowering judas,
To be eaten, to be divided, to be drunk
Among whispers; by Mr. Silvero . . .

By Hakagawa, bowing among the Titians;
By Madame de Tornquist, in the dark room
Shifting the candles; Fräulein von Kulp
Who turned in the hall, one hand on the door.

If we scrutinize the grammar of these lines with any care, we see there are numerous ambiguities of reference, modification, and sentence structure. Do the eating and drinking of Christ (or is it the flowering judas which is consumed?) refer to actual communion or to mere symbolic participation in a meaningless act? Who are the characters in this drama? Where did they come from; why are they doing the things they are doing? Did Fräulein von Kulp invite Mr. Silvero into her room; or is it only a passing thought that made her hesitate before she closed her door? Only feeling, given its form by the movement of the syntax, is clearly articulated in these lines; the experience which generated the feeling is left vague and undefined. We sense mystery, fraud, a general unwholesome quality—without ever knowing exactly what Madame de Tornquist was doing in the darkened room, or why Hakagawa was bowing among the Titians rather than among the El Grecos.

Like music these lines affect the reader by movement of sound; they offer the structure of feeling without denoting the human problems that gave rise to the feelings. Music is the art which deals with emotion in the abstract; the joy or agony we feel when we listen to music is never an explicit joy or agony. By suppressing the logical forms of grammar and blurring the edges of experience, Eliot achieves a quasi-musical effect. Syntax, the very form of thought, becomes a means for conveying feeling; we respond to Eliot's lines without fully comprehending them. Rhythm tends to become autonomous and separate itself from the rational structure of the poem.

Musical syntax is an important element in the newer prosodies. Whitman first discovered its resources and showed how much could be done to communicate feeling by manipulating the order of words. Violence must be committed on grammar to produce syntactic rhythm and its attendant music, but like the "organized violence" of meter, it is often salutary mayhem. The most important single device in Whitman's prosody is syntactical parallelism; each line comprises a rhythmical unit whose grammar is precisely echoed in subsequent lines (the following examples are all taken from *When Lilacs Last in the Dooryard Bloom'd*):

> As I stood on the rising ground in the breeze in the cool transparent night,
> As I watch'd where you pass'd and was lost in the netherward black of the night,
> As my soul in its trouble dissatisfied sank, as where you sad orb,
> Concluded, dropt in the night, and was gone.

The order of words is stiff and formal; rhythm rises to the last line and then quietly falls with the western star. Whitman uses various and intricate forms of parallel techniques. We find numerous passages in *anaphora:*

> Coffin that passes through lanes and streets,
> Through day and night with the great cloud darkening the land,
> With the pomp of the inloop'd flags with the cities draped in black,

> With the show of the States themselves as of crape-veil'd
> women standing,
> With processions long and winding and the flambeaus of the
> night,
> With the countless torches lit, with the silent sea of faces and
> the unbared heads . . .

The passage in which these lines are set is grammatically elliptical: a sentence is begun, continued with great rhetorical sonority, but never completed. Each line is a solemn rhythm, and the syntax controls the prosody without relating one line to the next. The structure which holds the lines together is a logic of feeling, not the "authentic syntax"[7] which can follow the silent rhythm of man thinking. Whitman's syntax exerts no intellectual control; it functions nearly exclusively *as prosody,* creating and organizing rhythmic structure. Whitman has no narrative talent: to tell a story requires the traditional close syntax and its conscious ordering of human experience into intelligible relationships.

We shall note two other features of Whitman's prosodical method. First, the technique of enumeration. Again the passage shows *ellipsis;* Whitman makes music with the order of words:

> Lo, the most excellent sun so calm and haughty,
> The violet and purple morn with just-felt breezes,
> The gentle soft-born measureless light,
> The miracle spreading bathing all, the fulfill'd noon,
> The coming eve delicious, the welcome night and the stars,
> Over my cities shining all, enveloping man and land.

We have no proper syntax at all, nor is any necessary to render Whitman's impression of the growing and then fading day. Feeling is all. Our last example of syntactical rhythm shows Whitman gradually expanding, then contracting the line:

> And I saw askant the armies,
> I saw as in noiseless dreams hundreds of battle-flags,
> Borne through the smoke of the battles and pierc'd with
> missiles I saw them,
> And carried hither and yon through the smoke, and torn
> and bloody,
> And at last but a few shreds left on the staffs, (and all in
> silence,)
> And the staffs all splinter'd and broken.

The danger of Whitman's method is that it persuades many who command rhetoric into believing that they command a prosody. Rhetoric and the music of syntax can simulate prosody, giving us the illusion that the poet is feeling when he is pretending emotion. Sandburg and Jeffers fill out their Whitmanized lines with only clumsy equivalents for rhythmic movement:

> While this America settles in the mold of its vulgarity,
> heavily thickening to empire,
> And protest, only a bubble in the molten mass, pops and
> sighs out, and the mass hardens,
> I sadly smiling remember that the flower fades to make fruit,
> the fruit rots to make earth.
> Out of the mother; and through the spring exultances,
> ripeness and decadence; and home to the mother.

Jeffers is telling us about the cycle of decay, the inevitable processes of life, and the sad grandeur of historical destiny. Meaning fights through the morass of the rhythms; syllable, stress, and syntax do not move but writhe, heave, grunt, and lie down again, gasping with the effort. The heavy stresses, impaled by alliteration, die on the page:

> I sadly smiling remember that the flower fades to make
> fruit . . .

A platitude is thought without style; rhythmic platitude is movement without grace and direction. Platitude of thought and rhythm produce doggerel, and it is nonetheless doggerel in free or open verses. Our objection to Poe's "The Raven" centers on its meaningless metric with its appalling double meters and insistent repetitions. The result is a simulacrum of feeling, aimless gesture, *howl.* Whitman's nonmetrical prosody is as capable of doggerel as Poe's metronome. Neither the restraint of a rigidly imposed metrical form nor the freedom of syntactical cadence can guarantee a prosody which quickens language with rhythmic purpose.

3 Gerard Manley Hopkins

Hopkins, like Whitman, violated "prosodic nature" and originated a rhythmic form which cannot be scanned by syllable and foot. Long after Hopkins had died, but a decade before his influence was even vaguely felt, Saintsbury was aware of his troubled and troubling spirit:

> Speaking prosodically, not of general poetry or literature, I do not know that Mr. Stevenson's verse requires special notice. Much more might be given to that of Father Gerard Hopkins, if it were not that, as his friend Mr. Bridges (who knew him long after I had lost sight of him, and with whose ideas on prosody he was much more in agreement than with mine) admits, he never got his notions into thorough writing-order. They belonged to the anti-foot and pro-stress division. But, even if it were not for old things and days, it would be unfair to criticise lines like
>
> I want the one rapture of an inspiration
>
> [from the sonnet "To R. B."]
>
> —which you can, of course, scan, but where 'one' seems to be thrust in out of pure mischief—or many others. He never published any; and it is quite clear that all were experiments.[8]

Since Hopkins' experiments in prosody have been so generally acknowledged as clear triumphs, and these triumphs loudly and with great confusion trumpeted to a prosodically naive world, it is refreshing to hear a slightly skeptical voice. Saintsbury touches, albeit briefly, on three major points: that Hopkins was engaged in experimentation; that his prosody "... belonged to the anti-foot and pro-stress division"; that Hopkins was not above deliberate metrical distortion.

The experimental nature of Hopkins' prosody has given rise to much confused and contradictory theorizing. Consider the chewed-over matter of sprung rhythm. Paull F. Baum comes to the exasperated conclusion that "... Sprung Rhythm is not a form of verse, to be scanned by feet, but a form of Prose Rhythm not amenable to scansion and therefore not to be explained as verse."[9] We partially agree. Hopkins' most sophisticated sprung rhythm cannot be scanned as syllable-stress meter; its prosodic character is nonmetrical. Hopkins drew a red herring of theory across the track of his achievements; he insisted that the nonmetrical form of sprung rhythm might be scanned from the strong syllable. Indeed, it can be, but so can any passage of rhythmical prose. In the poems in developed sprung rhythm, Hopkins discards the metrical foot and works with rhetorical rather than metrical units. We would not, however, say that Hopkins' poetry cannot be explained as verse. The bases of his prosody rest on complex matters of descent and development.

"Springing," as a metrical effect in English verse, probably owes its origin to early confusions between the older strong-stress meters and the post-Chaucerian syllable-stress meters. Measuring the line of verse, simply by counting the strong stresses and letting the unstressed syllables shift for themselves, was the native metrical tradition. The later syllable-stress meters eventually replaced the falling rhythms of accentual prosodies with the characteristic iambic—a rising rhythm. We find early verses which ambiguously teeter between strong-stress and syllable-stress metric:

Old Mother Hubbard
Went to her cupboard
To fetch her poor dog a bone
But when she came there
The cupboard was bare
And so the poor dog had none.

These lines do not scan comfortably. The rhyming couplets fall into strong-stress meter:

Óld Mother Húbbard || Wént to her cúpboard . . .

But whén she came thére || The cúpboard was báre . . .

Yet clearly there are metrical feet in the third and sixth lines:

To fétch her póor dóg a bóne . . .

And só the póor dóg had nóne.

How do these feet arrange themselves: do we have an iamb, an anapest, and an iamb, in this distribution:

To fétch | her poor dóg | a bóne . . .

or do we have a monosyllabic foot in the third position of the line:

To fétch | her póor | dóg | a bóne . . .

And só | the póor | dóg | had nóne . . . ?

Mother Hubbard had not made up her metrical mind. Two principles cross each other; the falling rhythm of *Old Mother Hubbard/Went to her cupboard* is contradicted by *To fetch her poor dog a bone.*

One kind of sprung rhythm results when the older stress metric intrudes upon the "prosodic norm" or conventional syllable-stress meter. This happens frequently in our poetry; a fine example is the line quoted earlier from Yeats:

> Spéech af | ter lóng | síl | ence; ít | is ríght.

Yvor Winters gives a similar example from Wyatt:

> With ná | ked fóot, | stálk | ing ín | my chám | ber.[10]

In both cases we have a monosyllabic foot in the third position.

In his poems in sprung rhythm, Hopkins makes this intrusion of stress metric a deliberate principle of composition. Wyatt and Yeats were composing in syllable-stress meter, and the crowding of accents disturbs but does not shatter the metrical norm. Hopkins allows so many heavy stresses to enter the normal syllable-stress line that eventually he writes a new metric. Sprung rhythm is not a sudden or consistent development in Hopkins, nor is it sufficient to say that Hopkins revives Old English meter and measures his verses by strong stresses and dipodies. Like Old Mother Hubbard, individual poems scan equally well as stress verse or syllable-stress verse:

INVERSNAID

> This darksome burn, horseback brown,
> His rollrock highroad roaring down,
> In coop and in comb the fleece of his foam
> Flutes and low to the lake falls home.

The rhythm is "sprung" because the lines contain stresses which cannot be comfortably counted in normal scansion; we must rationalize them as monosyllabic "feet":

> This dárk | some búrn, || hórse back | brówn . . .
> Flútes | and lów || to the láke | fàlls hóme.

Of course we may read these lines as stress verse pure and simple. We find the pronounced medial caesura, the four strong beats, and the alliteration which characterize the Old English meter.

Whether we measure these lines as syllable-stress or strong-stress meter, they are clearly metrical. Hopkins' poems in his characteristic, fully developed sprung rhythm move away from measured verse and into nonmetrical prosody. He arrived at his "new rhythm" through the native tradition of stress metric, through musical analogies, and by extending the practice of "springing" the line until all traces of syllable-stress meter vanish. "The Windhover," "Spelt from Sibyl's Leaves," or these fragments ("Ash-boughs"),

> Not of áll my eyes see, wandering on the world,
>
> Is anything a milk to the mind so, so sighs deep
>
> Poetry tó it, as a tree whose boughs break in the sky

represent the most sophisticated form of sprung rhythm; they defy scansion as syllable-stress meter unless we are willing to admit into traditional metrical paradigms wholesale and indiscriminate use of the monosyllabic foot, paeons, and other anomalous structures.

To understand Hopkins' practice of sprung rhythm, we must make distinctions beyond those he makes in his Author's Preface. Sprung rhythm is obviously a matter of degree and a name given to a number of different prosodical techniques. Hopkins is himself not clear about his practice. He distorts the metrical base of "Spring and Fall" by placing inappropriate speech stresses on metrically unstressed syllables:

> Márgarét, are you gríeving
>
> Over Goldengrove unleaving?
>
> Léaves, líke the things of man, you
>
> With your fresh thoughts care for, can you?
>
> Áh! ás the heart grows older
>
> It will come to such sights colder . . .

Do we understand that Hopkins means us to say, "*Mar* ge *ret,* are you grieving . . . / *Ah! as* the heart grows older . . ."? If so, Hopkins could not distinguish between metrical pattern and highly idiosyncratic reading. Despite Hopkins' markings, the lines are not sprung but trochees and dactyls in alternate trimeter and tetrameter:

> Mar ga ret, | are you | griev ing
> Ov er | Gol den | grove un | leav ing?
> Leaves, like the | things of | man, you
> With your | fresh thoughts | care for, | can you?

There is considerable evidence that Hopkins gave assent to the performative heresy. He was eager that poetry be reinstated as a spoken art: ". . . abovc all remember what applies to all my verse, that it is, as living art should be, made for performance and that its performance is not reading with the eye . . ."[11] Hopkins confuses the speaking of verse with meter, rhetorical stressing with basic structure. In his search for "instress" and "inscape," for rhythmic forms to express his excitements and exultations, he violates a simple meter. The result is not greater expressiveness but a puzzling dramatic distortion.

Hopkins' Preface does not distinguish between metrical and nonmetrical sprung rhythm; we must deduce from his practice that poems as prosodically dissimilar as "The Wreck of the Deutschland" and "The Leaden Echo and the Golden Echo" embody different principles of versification. "The Wreck of the Deutschland" is composed in intricate strong-stress meter. Analogous lines in an expanding stanza contain identical numbers of stresses; composition is consistent throughout the poem, and the verse, though sprung, is metered:

Stresses per line	4
2	I am soft sift
3	In an hourglass—at the wall
4	Fast, but mined with a motion, a drift,
3	And it crowds and it combs to the fall;
5	I steady as a water in a well, to a poise, to a pane,
5	But roped with, always, all the way down from the tall
4	Fells or flanks of the voel, a vein
6	Of the gospel proffer, a pressure, a principle, Christ's gift.

6

2 Not out of his bliss
3 Springs the stress felt
4 Nor first from heaven (and few know this)
3 Swings the stroke dealt—
5 Stroke and a stress that stars and storms deliver,
5 That guilt is hushed by, hearts are flushed by and melt—
4 But it rides time like riding a river
6 (And here the faithful waver, the faithless fable and miss).

We cannot, of course, scan these lines by feet; Hopkins is not thinking in syllable-stress meter, but in numbers of stresses per line. There is no interplay between the precise expectations of foot prosody and rhetorical stress; in sprung rhythm we find that close coincidence of rhetorical and prosodical pattern which obtains in Old English verse.

Hopkins meters "The Wreck of the Deutschland" on stress principles. "The Leaden Echo and the Golden Echo" has no metrical base. Its prosody is close to Whitman's practice; rhythmic periods are defined by syntactical arrangement, repetitions, and musical imitation. Here is the coda of the "Golden Echo":

O then, weary then whý should we tread? O why are we so
 haggard at the heart, so care-coiled, care-killed, so
 fagged, so fashed, so cogged, so cumbered,
When the thing we freely fórfeit is kept with fonder a care,
Fonder a care kept than we could have kept it, kept
Far with fonder a care (and we, we should have lost it) finer,
 fonder
A care kept.—Where kept? Do but tell us where kept,
 where.—
Yonder,—What high as that! We follow, now we follow.—
 Yonder, yes yonder, yonder,
Yonder.

Sound overrides sense as words serve as abstract musical structures; the movement of words is obviously meant to suggest the slowly fading echo. Gertrude Stein comes to mind; but more insistently, the end of *Anna Livia Plurabelle,* composed by another poet who brought musical method to bear on English prosody:

> . . . Night! Night! My ho head halls. I feel as heavy as yonder stone. Tell me of John or Shaun? Who were Shem and Shaun the living sons or daughters of? Night now! Tell me, tell me, tell me, elm! Night night! Telmetale of stem or stone. Beside the rivering waters of, hitherandthithering waters of. Night![12]

Joyce's "prose" can be scanned according to strong-stress principles:

> Níght! Níght! || My hó head hálls.
> I féel as héavy || as yón der stóne.
> Whó were Shém and Sháun
> the líving sóns || or dáughters óf?

Which brings us full circle. Hopkins has told us, in so many words, that sprung rhythm can be rhythmic prose: "Sprung Rhythm is the most natural of things . . . it is the rhythm of common speech and written prose, when rhythm is perceived in them." To dichotomize prose and verse, however, compounds confusion; I call sprung rhythm one of the many kinds of modern nonmetrical prosodies. Thus we can see that Hopkins' experiments parallel Whitman's assault on syllable-stress metric. Unlike Whitman, Hopkins broke down traditional metric by counterpointing and intruding upon it lines built on strong-stress principles. We can see the gradual disintegration of syllable-stress metric in these examples, selected from the twenty-year period of Hopkins' development:

> Elected Silence, sing to me
>
> And beat upon my whorlèd ear . . .

"The Habit of Perfection," 1866.

> Lovely the woods, waters, meadows, combes, vales,
> All the air things wear that build this world of Wales . . .

"In the Valley of the Elwy," 1877.

Not, I'll not, carrion comfort, Despair, not feast on thee;
Not untwist—slack they may be—these last strands of man
In me ór, most weary, cry *I can no more.* I can . . .

"Carrion Comfort," 1885.

Earnest, earthless, equal, attuneable, vaulty, voluminous, . . stupendous
Evening strains to be tíme's vást, womb-of-all, home-of-all, hearse-of-all night.

"Spelt from Sibyl's Leaves," 1885.

Yes I cán tell such a key, I dó know such a place,
Where whatever's prized and passes of us, everything that's fresh and fast flying of us, seems to us sweet of us and swiftly away with, done away with, undone . . .

"The Golden Echo," 1882

"The Habit of Perfection" scans as regular iambic tetrameter. The lines from "In the Valley of the Elwy" are strongly counterpointed; the second line should be noted for its spondee and monosyllabic foot:

Áll | the áir | thíngs wéar | that buíld | this wórld | of Wáles . . .

The next three examples are not amenable to foot-scansion. "Carrion Comfort" is perhaps closest to traditional metric with its strongly varied hexameter lines. The last two examples are prosodically nonmetrical: sprung rhythm in its characteristic form.

4 *Toward the Twentieth Century*

Browning, Whitman, and Hopkins forecast the three major prosodic developments of the modern period. I hesitate to call them influences; they established no schools, attracted no immediate disciples. Whitman's effect has been so various and far-reaching that it is nearly impossible to assess; Hopkins had no impact on modern poetry until the late twenties and early thirties. It is true that Pound caught Browning's rhythms and owes much to Browning's adaptation of blank verse to modern speech. But our three Victorians were prophets rather than practical reformers; their prosodies point a way rather than specify a program. Poets who start from the common iambic, who, in expanding or tightening traditional meter, work toward looser rhythms, descend from Browning. Poets who compose to the music of syntactical arrangement, who pursue "the figure of grammar," follow Whitman. And those poets whose rhythm is marked by the energy of strong stressing are the spiritiual, if not the actual, heirs of Hopkins.

Our convenient categories do not account for all modern prosodies; the webs of practice are a tangle of individual development and often untraceable influence. Eliot knew Pound and had read Browning; his prosody changed after he came to Europe, but some of its essentials were worked out while he was still an undergraduate at Harvard. Pound himself was wildly eclectic, blown about in the winds of his shifting enthusiasms. Yet the main streams of modern prosody flow in the directions indicated by our Victorian ancestors. Despite all the smoke screens of propaganda thrown up by Pound, he and Eliot start from traditional meter. Pound began as a disciple of Provence and assimilated the colloquial iambics of Browning to the complex Provençal patterns. Whitman is the source of most contemporary "free verse," and has fathered the nonmetrical prosodies of Sandburg, Jeffers, Fearing, and many others. Even the Imagists, who maintained a strict policy of nonrecognition toward Whitman, often based their rhythms on the principles of syntactical parallelism.

Free verse is the prosodist's most troublesome term. It frequently designates prosodic fads or gaucheries: certain kinds of imagistic *vers libre,* Whitmanized prose, bad iambic pentameter. Many readers link *free verse* with particular subject matter and associate unscannable poetry with atheism and anarchism. Those who cannot distinguish dipodies from tripods are also apt to confuse *free love* and *free verse.* Since our aim is to provide categories of technical distinction and historical descent, we might better avoid *free verse* as a generic term and speak rather of *nonmetrical prosody. Nonmetrical prosody* has social and political neutrality; we can say a poet writes nonmetrically without implying anything about his politics or sex life. *Nonmetrical* also possesses technical neutrality; we need not think of a nonmetrical poet as an anarchist of poetic form. And in the sixties of our benighted century, *free verse* and *free-verse poet* are irrevocably dated. To the unsentimental young, *free verse* was written in the dark 'teens and dim twenties by proper Bostonians who were kicking over the traces. Not that it is easy to make distinctions; we have quasi-metrical prosody, such as Delmore Schwartz's:

IN THE NAKED BED, IN PLATO'S CAVE

In the naked bed, in Plato's cave,
Reflected headlights slowly slid the wall,
Carpenters hammered under the shaded window,
Wind troubled the window curtains all night long,
A fleet of trucks strained uphill, grinding,
Their freights covered, as usual.
The ceiling lightened again, the slanting diagram
Slid slowly forth.

These lines are set to a highly varied but unmistakable blank-verse rhythm; they recall the energetic forward motion and sudden compressions of "Gerontion." Although Schwartz's lines "are as well written as good prose," they no more resemble prose than these:

We hear the earth and the all-day rasp of the grasshoppers:
It was we laid the steel on this land from ocean to ocean:
It was we (if you know) put the U.P. through the passes . . .

It was we did it: hunkies of our kind:
It was we dug the caved-in holes for cold-water:
It was we built the gully spurs and the freight sidings . . .

MacLeish, from "Frescoes for Mr. Rockefeller's City"

Behind Schwartz's lines stand the practice of Eliot and ultimately Browning and the Jacobean dramatists; MacLeish's prosody here is 100 percent American with its end-stopped lines, repeated syntax, and primitive-sounding enumerations—Whitman *redivivus*.

Nonmetrical prosody appears in many forms: modified traditional metric, Whitmanesque syntactical cadence, and Hopkinesque sprung rhythm. Modern poets will mix their prosodic modes; Auden combines strong-stress and iambic in these lines:

Doom is dark and deeper than any sea-dingle:
Upon what man it fall
In spring, day-wishing flowers appearing,
Avalanche sliding, white snow from rock-face,
That he should leave his house . . .

Pound experimented with a number of nonmetrical prosodies, but his free verse approaches a quantitative norm. His line always carefully measured and weighed syllabic durations—before he gave up prosody for economics. In the lines below, the rhythms are controlled by a musician's sense of syllabic length:

DANCE FIGURE

Dark eyed,
O woman of my dreams,
Ivory sandalled,
There is none like thee among the dancers,
None with swift feet.

I have not found thee in the tents,
In the broken darkness.
I have not found thee at the well-head
Among the women with pitchers . . .

Pound's ear for quantity has been justly celebrated; but we must also recognize the parallelisms or "rhythmic constants" of the Authorized Version:

I have not found . . .
In the . . .
I have not found . . .
Among the . . .

We examined in Chapter III some of the great modern poetry written in traditional metric. We turn now to the aggressively and subtly "modern" prosodies. Much twentieth-century verse (though not necessarily the best) does not turn on the armature of syllable-stress meter. Some of it seems without immediate prosodical ancestry; the visual rhythms of the Imagists and others strike the analyst as an unprecedented technical innovation—until he takes a historical bearing and remembers the pattern poems of the Metaphysicals. But a prosody need not be nonmetrical to be modern. Traditional metric, to be sure, is foot measured; however, modern prosodies may be measured by strong-stress and syllabic count. Since 1912 we have witnessed myriad attempts to energize language with new rhythms; we have heard and seen a spate of new prosodies: some strict, some "free," some berserk. Time allows us to see that if experimentation with nonmetrical prosodies has led into blind alleys, it has also opened out into wildly beautiful landscapes and pleasant meadows.

V

Imagism and Visual Prosody

1 T. E. Hulme and Others

What we ordinarily think of as "modernist poetry" begins with the Imagist movement. Details of the movement's history and politics need not concern us here; we discover a zeal for poetic reform and experimentation tangled in a mesh of self-advertisement, mutual influence, and energetic feuding. Critical opinion has been cautious about the leading personalities of Imagism and who contributed what to theory and practice. Fifty years later, three figures emerge from the ruins of forgotten controversy: T. E. Hulme the idea man; Ezra Pound the public-relations man; Amy Lowell the business manager. Around this trinity is clustered a host of names, angels of greater and lesser brightness. H. D., D. H. Lawrence, F. S. Flint, John Gould Fletcher; even Yeats and T. S. Eliot were known, willingly and unwillingly, and at one time or another, as "imagists."

Wide divergence exists between Imagist theory and practice. The poetry published in the four Imagist anthologies (1914–1917), and the critical principles, issued like military commands in the various forewords and manifestos, scarcely make up a body of coherent doctrine and practice. Imagism was not a "school" of poetry but a visitation of the *Zeitgeist;* like all spectral phenomena, it soon faded after its first exciting appearances. But during the brief period of Imagism's active life, modern poetry developed two of its leading conventions: the use of precise, sometimes startling images, and the programmatic use of the nonmetrical prosodies.

The Imagists were loud propagandists for *vers libre,* though there was considerable disagreement about exactly what made *vers libre.* In one of his earliest pronouncements, Pound offers a famous musical analogy: "As regarding rhythm: to compose in sequence of the musical phrase, not in sequence of the metronome."[1] Pound later urges upon the would-be poet the intensive study of music to develop his sense of *duration:* the relative time values of syllabic length. Hulme also recommends free verse but for reasons contradictory to those Pound advances.

Hulme believes the essence of the new poetry lies in the visual: "This new verse resembles sculpture rather than music; it appeals to the eye rather than to the ear."[2] Free verse, Hulme argues, is less musical than metered verse; for this reason it should carry the new poetry. The crudity of Hulme's thought is revealed in his speculations on meter and verse:

> I quite admit that poetry intended to be recited must be written in regular metre, but I contend that this method of recording impressions by visual images in distinct lines does not require the old metric system.
>
> The older art was originally a religious incantation: it was made to express oracles and maxims in an impressive manner, and rhyme and metre were used as aids to the memory. But why, for this new poetry, should we keep a mechanism which is only suited to the old?
>
> The effect of rhythm, like that of music, is to produce a kind of hypnotic state, during which suggestions of grief or ecstasy are easily and powerfully effective, just as when we are drunk all jokes seem funny. This is for the art of chanting, but the procedure of the new visual art is just the contrary. It depends for its effect not on a kind of half sleep produced, but on arresting the attention, so much so that the succession of visual images should exhaust one.
>
> Regular metre to this impressionist poetry is cramping, jangling, meaningless, and out of place. Into the delicate pattern of images and colour it introduces the heavy, crude pattern of rhetorical verse. . . .[3]

Hulme's major heresy, which has been of considerable consequence to subsequent poetry and poetics, inheres in his belief that poetry must be primarily "this method of recording visual images in distinct lines." Hulme goes so far as to deny that sound is the basic material of verse: "This material, the ὕλη of Aristotle, is image and not sound. It builds up a plastic image which it hands over to the reader, whereas the old art endeavoured to influence him physically by the hypnotic effect of rhythm."[4] Hulme's insensitivity to music—Michael Roberts reports: "It seemed to him time spent in listening to music would have been better spent in conversation"[5]—and his overwhelming interest in painting and sculpture must be partly responsible for Hulme's indifference to sound values in poetry. Hulme talks of poetry as if it were a spatial and not a temporal art. This confusion about the basic material of poetry—language, which is organized sound moving in time—dismisses prosody as of no central importance in poetic structure.

No poet quite took Hulme at his word and abandoned prosody for a poetry of purely visual surface: unless it was E. E. Cummings or Pound of the later *Cantos.* Nor did it require a Hulme to call attention to *vers libre; vers libre* and modern French poetry had thoroughly permeated the pre-World War I atmosphere. The impact of Symbolist and later French poetry had been everywhere felt: by Eliot at Harvard, by Hulme and Pound in Europe. Hulme observed that it was *vers libre* itself which released and stimulated the extraordinary French poetic activity during the decades preceding World War I: "With the definite arrival of this new form of verse in 1880 came the appearance of a band of poets perhaps unequalled at any time in the history of French poetry."[6]

Two articulate proselytes of the new French prosody, the poets Georges Duhamel and Charles Vildrac, published in 1910 a brief treatise on *vers libre, Notes sur la technique poétique.* Amy Lowell, a close student of the modern French poets, mentions Duhamel and Vildrac's work; Pound refers to it repeatedly.[7] Others in the Imagist group were undoubtedly familiar with this seminal little book. The *Notes* are an excited defense and analysis of *vers libre* method, written in a series of aphorisms—much like Pound's treatises and ABC's. How much Pound derived from Duhamel and Vildrac, in form, content, and pungency, may be seen if we compare the "Don'ts for Imagists" with some passages from the *Notes:*

> Aujourd'hui, les gens qui défendent la versification régulière avec le dogmatisme et l'intransigence glapissante d'un Dorchain sont aveugles ou imbéciles.
>
> Les vieilles cadences soulignaient trop ces rapports; nous pouvons danser maintenant sans grosse caisse, nous pouvons chanter sans métronome.[8]

In the light of the *Notes,* we might do well to go back to origins, and examine a characteristic example of *vers libre:*

> Tourne à jamais la flamboyante gloire du Christ
> C'est le beau lys que tous nous cultivons
> C'est la torche aux cheveux roux que n'éteint pas le vent
> C'est le fils pâle et vermeil de la douloureuse mère
> C'est l'arbre toujours touffu de toutes les prières
> C'est la double potence de l'honneur et de l'éternité
> C'est l'étoile à six branches
> C'est Dieu qui meurt le vendredi et ressuscite le dimanche
> C'est le Christ qui monte au ciel mieux que les aviateurs
> Il détient le record du monde pour la hauteur

These lines are from Apollinaire's "Zone." This poem might have been written by a slightly surrealistic, disillusioned Whitman. The versification is "free" in that it exceeds, and recedes from, the twelve-syllable norm of the alexandrine; we have a half-line of six syllables,

> C'est l'étoile à six branches . . .

and long lines of fourteen or fifteen syllables,

> C'est Dieu qui meurt le vendredi et ressuscite le dimanche
> C'est le Christ qui monte au ciel mieux que les aviateurs . . .

Rhyming is not systematic but used for clinching effects:

> C'est le Christ qui monte au ciel mieux que les aviateurs
> Il détient le record du monde pour la hauteur

Most importantly, we have a "figure of grammar": the music of deliberate syntactical parallelism in the phrases, *C'est le beau . . . C'est la torche . . . C'est la fils,* etc.; like Whitman, Apollinaire bases his rhythmic structure on the effects of parallel and repeated syntax rather than strict syllable-count.

Duhamel and Vildrac explain how syntactical manipulation rhythmically energizes free verse. They name the various "figures of grammar" the *constante rythmique,* the *équilibre rythmique,* and the *symétrie rythmique.* In French the rhythmic constant may be merely a sequence of phrases containing equal numbers of syllables; this example is from the *Notes:*

La voix retentit comme un hymne paré d'étoiles
parmi les drapeaux et les miroirs de fête;
des cadences *de marteaux géants* dans des forges
hantées *de chanteurs athlètes* . . .

Gustave Kahn

More frequently, the structure of *vers libre* shows the familiar syntactical parallelisms—as in the lines from Apollinaire. *Vers libre* does not rest on a controlling metric of syllabic count—"Les équilibres rythmiques ne se produisent pas seulement selon des rapports numeriques des syllabes"—but is formed on syntax, on the forms of grammar, and on *les repos de la voix:*

> La syntaxe et les repos de la voix aident le plus souvent à ces rapports. La nature même des mots, leur qualité syntaxique peuvent déterminer le balancement de la phrase, donnant, à certain hemistiches correspondants, la valeur colorée des adjectifs, à d'autres le poids des substantifs, à d'autres encore l'énergie motrice du verbe.[9]

Who among the later nineteenth-century French poets first wrote *vers libre* is something of a historical mystery. Gustave Kahn was among the earliest practitioners of the new form; by the nineties a group including Verhaeren and Vielé-Griffin were publishing as *vers librists.* But both Rimbaud and Laforgue had earlier written verse which breaks the old prosodic forms. Rimbaud's *Marine* has every quality the Imagists admired: sharply defined visual effects; a laconic brevity which "presents an intellectual and emotional complex in an instant of time";[10] a free prosody organically developing out of the material of the poem:

MARINE

Les chars d'argent et de cuivre—
Les proues d'acier et d'argent—
Battent l'écume—
Soulèvent les souches des ronces.
Les courants de la lande,
Et les ornières immenses du reflux,
Filent circulairement vers l'est,
Vers les piliers de la forêt,
Vers les fûts de la jetée,
Dont l'angle est heurté par des tourbillons de lumière.

[1886]

The poem satisfies other canons of Imagist poetic practice; it makes no moral comment on the experience it renders and offers an emotion seemingly uninvolved with the poet's personality.

The political leaders of Imagism, Pound, Flint, and Amy Lowell (Hulme dropped out in 1914 to pursue another enthusiasm, war) were generally at odds with each other about fundamental principles. Flint objected to the restrictions on subject matter proposed by Amy Lowell; Pound believed in the image and in the principle of verbal precision, but felt that Imagism was more a corrective to the deliquescence and sentimentality of post-Victorian poetry than a complete formula for the new verse. Only Amy Lowell, in her theories, and H. D. in her poetry, kept close to the letter of original Imagist law. And by 1915, three years after the movement's founding, Imagism finally became a matter of prosody:

> The 1915 preface [to Amy Lowell's *Some Imagist Poets*] not only accepted *vers libre* as Imagistic but elevated it to a position of central importance in its doctrine. That Imagist attention was now fixed primarily upon the rhythms of poetry is further indicated by the explanation given this principle in the 1916 anthology: 'Poetry is a spoken and not a written art.'[11]

2 *Des Imagistes*

"Poetry is a spoken and not a written art." Yet when we examine Imagist poetry we are struck by how often the poem's appearance on the page constitutes its chief prosodic feature. Typography, not sound, controls the rhythms in these lines:

> The trees are like a sea;
> Tossing,
> Trembling,
> Roaring,
> Wallowing,
> Darting their long green flickering fronds up at
> the sky,
> Spotted with white blossom-spray.

from "Green Symphony," by John Gould Fletcher

A similar example, from Amy Lowell's "An Aquarium":

> Streaks of green and yellow iridescence,
> Silver shiftings,
> Rings veering out of rings,
> Silver—gold—
> Grey-green opaqueness sliding down,
> With sharp white bubbles
> Shooting and dancing,
> Flinging quickly outward.
> Nosing the bubbles,
> Swallowing them,
> Fish.

The length of line contracts with the syntax, until we get the subject-noun, *Fish,* in clean visual isolation. Amy Lowell does not neglect sound-values; we have harshly stressed lines,

> With sharp white bubbles . . .

as well as the smoothly modulating vowels in

> Grey-green opaqueness sliding down . . .

The line also serves to isolate each separate image and hold it up to the eye for contemplation. Syntax is fragmentary; we have participles and nouns but no authentic verbs.

The dislocation of syntax generates a prosody of sorts in Amy Lowell's "Violin Sonata by Vincent D'Indy":

> A little brown room in a sea of fields,
> Fields pink as rose-mallows
> Under a fading rose-mallow sky.
>
> Four candles on a tall iron candlestick,
> Clustered like altar lights.
> Above, the models of four brown Chinese junks
> Sailing round the brown walls,
> Silent and motionless.

Again we have free-floating images without grammatical orientation. By carefully suppressing all verbs, Amy Lowell presents rather than comments on an experience. Such method denies the importance of human action in poetry and limits it to perceptual reporting. As part of the reform movement in modern poetry, Imagist techniques were historically useful in clearing out excessive sentiment and cleaning up the rhetoric; keeping an eye, unclouded by the steam of one's own emotions, on the object was the salutary aim of Imagism. But reform movements often go too far: the Imagists, in throwing out the rascals of excessive interest in feeling and subject matter, came dangerously close to writing poetry cleansed not only of rhetoric but also of human concerns.

None of the above, however, is true of H. D., the best poet in the Imagist group. (I am, of course, excepting Pound.) H. D. follows the Imagist practice of writing in short lines; she concentrates on visual detail and keeps careful control of the emotion that delicately moves between her imagery. Her prosody articulates rather than fragments the elements of her poetry. While she is aware of the effect of visual rhythms, she orders her prosody primarily by means of sound and active verbs. Our example is a complete poem, "Along the Yellow Sand":

Along the yellow sand
above the rocks,
the laurel-bushes stand.

Against the shimmering heat,
each separate leaf
is bright and cold,
and through the bronze
of shining bark and wood,
run the fine threads of gold.

Here in our wicker-trays,
we bring the first faint blossoming
of fragrant bays:

Lady, their blushes shine
as faint in hue,
as when through petals
of a laurel-rose,
the sun shines through,
and throws a purple shadow
on a marble vase.

(Ah, love,
so her fair breasts will shine
with the faint shadow above.)

H. D. does not follow the Imagist practice of writing in sentence fragments; her syntax is complete and active. Note the verbs: *stand, run, bring, shine, throws.* Metrically, the lines are dominated by iambic movement and punctuated by occasional rhymes. Individual lines are mainly trimeter or dimeter:

> . . . and thróugh | the brónze
> of shín | ing bárk | and wóod,
> rún the | fìne thréads | of góld.

A train of Greek votive maidens brings offerings of laurel to Aphrodite,

> . . . so her fair breasts will shine
> with the faint shadow above.

The subtle rhythmic shift in the last line emphasizes the suppressed excitement, the breath suddenly withdrawn, as the girls become aware of Lady Aphrodite's physical beauty. Unlike many Imagist poems "Along the Yellow Sand" has recognizable plot; H. D. is not fixing an image in a moment of time but recording significant human action.

H. D.'s Hellenism shapes both the spirit and form of her work. Her long poem, *Helen in Egypt,* is written in a stanza of three short lines, evidently suggested by the cryptic *Palinode* of Stesichorus:

> *Οὐκ᾽ ἔστ᾽ ἔτυμος λόγος οὗτος·*
>
> *οὐδ᾽ ἔβας ἐν ναυσὶν εὐσέλμοις,*
>
> *οὐδ᾽ ἵκεο πέργαμα Τροίας.*

> That story is not true.
> You never sailed in the benched ships.
> You never went to the city of Troy.
>
> translation by Richmond Lattimore

"According to the Palinode, Helen was never in Troy. She had been transposed or translated from Greece into Egypt. Helen of Troy was a phantom, substituted for the real Helen, by jealous deities. The Greeks and Trojans alike fought for an illusion."[12]

H. D.'s technique transcends the narrative limitations of Imagist theory. Pound's doctrine of the image does not provide for connections between images; poetry is to proceed by a series of instantaneous, intense perceptions, a "sense of sudden growth."[13] Narrative is impossible within this poetic canon. But H. D. follows a different procedure in *Helen in Egypt.* She is, like Pound, essentially a lyric poet whose gifts do not include the epic grasp. *Helen in Egypt* has its own form: a series of visions or scenes, held together by brief connecting links in prose. Each vision is a lyric meditation; and the voices (Helen, Achilles, Paris, Theseus) shift as they dream in remembrance or prophesy the future. The prose links preserve the narrative line, yet allow Helen to ". . . encompass infinity by intense concentration on the moment. . . . She will bring the moment and infinity together 'in time, in the crystal, in my thought here.'" Admittedly, such a method is a compromise; it allows H. D. to keep her cake of poetry and at the same time take sustenance from the prose. She can sustain poetic intensity and maintain narrative coherence.

The three-line stanza gives firmness to the prosody and solves the problem of a "carrying metric." The lines are short, but within the limitations of two to four stresses, H. D. gets considerable expressive variety:

> . . . few were the words we said,
> but the words are graven on stone,
> minted on gold, stamped upon lead;
>
> . . . he, Achilles, piling brushwood,
> finding an old flint in his pouch,
> 'I thought I had lost that';
>
> few were the words we said,
> 'I am shipwrecked, I am lost,'
> turning to view the stars,
>
> swaying as before the mast,
> 'the season is different,
> we are far from—from—'
>
> *let him forget,*
> *Amen, All-father,*
> *let him forget.*

The easy prose movement tightens into a strong-stress pattern when the language thickens into metaphor:

míntėd on góld, || stámped upon léad . . .

Another kind of movement images the actions of Achilles,

turning to view the stars,
swaying before the mast . . .

The section concludes with Helen's prayer in two-stress lines. At one point Helen remembers the scenes and noises of the Trojan War; the lines lengthen into English heroic measure, blank verse:

whether they floundered on the Pontic seas
or ran aground before the Hellespont,
whether they shouted Victory at the gate,

whether the bowmen shot them from the Walls,
whether they crowded surging through the breach,
or died of fever on the smitten plain . . .

H. D. wisely avoids attempting the English hexameter to render a sense of Greek meter.

Richard Aldington, a member of the original Imagist group and H. D.'s husband, also wrote verse to visual rhythms. Length of line gives prosodic shape to his verse, emphasizing important words and syntactic groups:

THE FAUN SEES SNOW FOR THE FIRST TIME

Zeus,
Brazen-thunder-hurler,
Cloud-whirler, son-of-Kronos,
Send vengeance on these Oreads
Who strew
White frozen flecks of mist and cloud

Over the brown trees and the tufted grass
Of the meadows, where the stream
Runs black through shining banks
Of bluish white. . .

The expanding rhythm of the first stanza makes an especially strong impression on the ear; the heavy stressing in lines two and three is resolved by the smooth iambics of

> Whìte fró | zen flécks | of míst | and clóud . . .

We also hear rhythmic echoes: the iambics in line six are heard, with lessened dynamic intensity, in line four:

> Send vén | geance ón | these Ó | re áds . . .

Within a basic iambic pattern such echoing would be inaudible; where the verse moves freely, a line in regular meter becomes suddenly arresting—as when we glimpse the shadowy form of a tree or a man in the paintings of the abstract expressionists.

Most free verse shows these appearances of regular metric. In good free verse a metrical line will intensify an image or an idea, or mark the climactic point of the rhythm. Such marking must be subtle; if the poet strains too hard for an "absolute rhythm," or attempts a literal matching of rhythm to the emotion or situation, the effect can be highly artificial. The final lines of Amy Lowell's "Patterns" move to obviously contrived rhythms; one line (the sixth below) has a completely inappropriate swing:

> I shall go
> Up and down,
> In my gown.
> Gorgeously arrayed,
> Boned and stayed.
> And the softness of my body will be guarded
> from embrace
> By each button, hook, and lace.

The swaying of the amphimacers (Í sh̆all gó / Úp ănd dówn, / Ín mў gówn. / . . . Bóned ănd stáyed) rather naively suggests the lady walking in her heavy gown; the sixth line, in the unmistakeable trochaic meter of "Locksley Hall," unfortunately suggests:

> As the husband is, the wife is; thou art mated with a clown,
> And the grossness of his nature will have weight to drag thee
> down.

In the open territory of free prosody, occasional metrical lines are often crudely and dangerously intrusive; the especially strong trochaic line coupled to the silly sentiments about the lady's chastity destroys the poem's emotional unity. If Amy Lowell had been working in a conventional meter, such a solecism as, "And the softness of my body . . . ," would have been glaringly apparent. As these lines stand, they have neither the rhythmic neutrality of genuine prose nor the meaningful intensities of well-handled meter.

3 *Marianne Moore*

Marianne Moore saw the need for greater prosodical discipline than that offered by Imagist *vers libre.* Early and loosely associated with the Imagist group (Richard Aldington was her "discoverer"), she developed a metrical idiom which had no immediate source and has had no successful imitators. The distinction of her verse scarcely lies in its "freedom" but in its studied complexity. Her meter combines Imagist concern for the visual shape of line and stanza with careful syllabic count and the systematic use of rhyme. The result is a prosody of high technical contrivance which beautifully works. We can see and hear its workings in some stanzas from a recent poem, "In the Public Garden":

> Boston has a festival—
> compositely for all—
> and nearby, cupolas of learning
> (crimson, blue, and gold) that
> have made education individual.
>
> My first—an exceptional,
> an almost scriptural—
> taxi-driver to Cambridge from Back Bay said
> as we went along, "They
> make some fine young men at Harvard." I recall
>
> the summer when Faneuil Hall
> had its weathervane with gold ball
> and grasshopper, gilded again by
> a -leafer and -jack
> till it glittered. Spring can be a miracle
>
> there—a more than usual
> bouquet of what is vernal—
> "pear blossoms whiter than clouds," pin-
> oak leaves barely showing
> when other trees are making shade, besides small

fairy iris suitable
for Dulcinea del
Toboso; O yes, and snowdrops
in the snow, that smell like
violets. Despite secular bustle . . .

An almost breathless anecdotal rhythm—the talk of an intelligent and observant woman rapidly leaping from description to idea and back again—is held in check by the formal metrical elements. Miss Moore counts syllables, more or less strictly; the pattern in analogous lines is 7, 6, 9, 6, 11. A rhyme scheme binds the entire poem together: the first and second and final lines of each stanza end with either a light or heavy stress on the syllable *l*. Miss Moore also measures as well as counts her syllables, adding a consort of vowels to the orchestration of her lines:

Toboso; O yes, and snowdrops
in the snow . . .

The end of "In the Public Garden" grows more intense in its music; the strict syllabism and severe stanzaic shape break down, and in their place we hear the more immediate effects of assonance and consecutive rhyming:

There are those who will talk for an hour
without telling you why they have
come. And I? This is no madrigal—

no medieval gradual—
but it is a grateful tale.
Without that radiance which poets
are supposed to have—
unofficial, unprofessional, still one need not fail

to wish poetry well
where intellect is habitual—
glad that the Muses have a home and swans—
that legend can be factual;
happy that Art, admired in general,
is always actually personal.

Madrigals are part songs with intricate contrapuntal textures; graduals are liturgical hymns sung from the steps of the altar. Miss Moore modestly tells us her poem has neither richness nor authority; it is a simple tale told with Muses and swans and gratitude.

An earlier poem, "The Monkeys," deals in aesthetics and the nature of poetry. The poetry Miss Moore talks about in these lines is like her own: fastidious in craft and "malignant / in its power over us. . . ." I quote the whole poem; its prosody begins with the title and carries the poem to its last word:

THE MONKEYS

winked too much and were afraid of snakes. The zebras,
supreme in
their abnormality; the elephants with their fog-coloured skin
and strictly practical appendages
were there, the small cats; and the parakeet—
trivial and humdrum on examination, destroying
bark and portions of the food it could not eat.

I recall their magnificence, now not more magnificent
than it is dim. It is difficult to recall the ornament,
speech, and precise manner of what one might
call the minor acquaintances twenty
years back; but I shall not forget him—that
Gilgamesh among
the hairy carnivora—that cat with the

wedge-shaped, slate-gray marks on its forlegs and the resolute
tail,
astringently remarking, 'They have imposed on us with their
pale
half-fledged protestations, trembling about
in inarticulate frenzy, saying
it is not for us to understand art; finding it
all so difficult, examining the thing

as if it were inconceivably arcanic, as symmet-
rically frigid as if it had been carved out of chrysoprase
or marble—strict with tension, malignant
in its power over us and deeper
than the sea when it proffers flattery in exchange for
hemp,
rye, flax, horses, platinum, timber and fur.'

The scene of the poem is the zoo; the monkeys are offered as a synechdoche for the other animals. Children always remember the vividness of the monkeys; adults tend to be oppressed by their human resemblances. (The poem was originally titled "My Apish Cousins.") The monkeys, like their human cousins, find art and poetry disturbing, even—to use Miss Moore's neologism—*arcanic:* possessed of strange, perhaps curative, powers. Poetry frightens them because the understanding of poetry requires some submission to its influence. Monkeys, like men, prefer things as they are. Poetry offers, in exchange for real goods (vegetable, animal, mineral), only a dubious flattery.

We must read the whole poem before we understand why the monkeys feared the snakes. Snakes are like poems: frigid, tense, and symmetrical. Miss Moore's characteristic syllabic prosody enforces *symmetry*—even in the ironic splitting of this word (first line, last stanza) to maintain her syllabic equivalence. The first two lines of the last stanza abandon the prevalent rhyme: as if to assert the freedom of poetry immediately after submitting to its formal exactions. Miss Moore regards the limitations of her prosodic method as means rather than ends; the strictness of the form must be broken if subject and feeling demand ampler latitude for expression. Basic to Miss Moore's aesthetic is "the principle of accommodation": that even meticulous good taste and craftsmanship can be carried to excess,

> that excessive conduct augurs disappointment,
> that one must not borrow a long white beard and tie it on
> and threaten with the scythe of time the casually curious:
> to teach the bard with too elastic a selectiveness
> that one detects creative power by its capacity to conquer
> one's detachment;
> that while it may have more elasticity than logic,
> it knows where it is going . . .
>
> "The Labours of Hercules"

Poetry and its form must balance the opposing requirements of logic and elasticity; ". . . it knows where it is going . . ." yet it must, in its own special and precise way

> . . . convince snake-charming controversialists
> that it is one thing to change one's mind,
> another to eradicate it—that one keeps on knowing
> 'that the Negro is not brutal,

that the Jew is not greedy,
that the Oriental is not immoral,
that the German is not a Hun'.

"The Labours of Hercules"

In "The Labours of Hercules" Miss Moore makes many accommodations. The verse adjusts to the seemingly casual movements of Miss Moore's mind and interests, but displays no prosodical uncertainty. Her prosody closely follows "the figure of grammar," mapping its course along a series of repeated verbal and modifier word groups. If we skeletonize the grammatical structure, in a manner analogous to the two-voice framework of musical analysis, the prosodical scheme becomes apparent. As in all of Miss Moore's poems, we begin with the title:

THE LABOURS OF HERCULES [are]

To popularize the mule . . .

to persuade one of austere taste . . .

that the piano is . . . that his 'charming tadpole notes' . . .

to persuade those self-wrought Midases . . .

that excessive conduct . . .
that one must not . . .

to prove to the high priests of caste
that snobbishness is a stupidity . . .

. . . —that we are sick of the earth,

sick of the pig-sty, wild geese and wild men . . .

etc.

Syntax like music, we say. The poem is built on two motifs, the verbal group beginning with *to* (infinitive), and the modifier group beginning with *that* (dependent clause). Modern structural linguistics calls both infinitives and dependent clauses *head-tail* groups and describes the similarity of their rhythmic structure.[14] The overall grammatical structure consists of the title as subject, the copula *are,* and the poem itself as a complex complement.

The poem is a single sentence, and since here Miss Moore does not count syllables or construct stanzas, the syntax carries the chief prosodical burden. The method is a refinement on Whitman's more obvious syntactical parallelisms. Miss Moore acknowledges no debt to Whitman, but rather to their common source, Hebrew poetry:

> 'Hebrew poetry is
> prose with a sort of heightened consciousness.' Ecstasy affords
> the occasion and expediency determines the form.
>
> "The Past Is the Present"

We may be puzzled by Miss Moore's statement about expediency and ask what can be expedient about a method so carefully contrived and formally exact. But remembering that *expedients* are simply means and resources, we understand that syllable, stanza, and grammatical arrangement enable the poet to gain political advantages in the kingdom of language. Miss Moore is cunningly adept in the game of getting the most out of every word she uses. Hers is a limited ecstasy—her reference to Hebrew poetry strikes the mind as calculated irony. The unemphatic movements of her prosody suit the demands of her feeling and subject. A syllabic-syntactic prosody gives no "beat"; it resembles certain songs by Campion and Dowland where rhythm has nothing to do with bar lines and accents. Miss Moore's rhythms proceed without strong accentuation; they convince our minds and ears that rhythms are not crass patterns of phonetic recurrence but definitions of time. The spatial elements, the heritage of Imagism in her prosody, help arrange the illusion of time; they are expedients to a calculated end. A heavily accented foot or stress prosody would impede the quick and delicate movements of her feeling; it would clot the fineness of her observations, slow down the darting and sensible eye of her intelligence.

4 William Carlos Williams

Our first contact with William Carlos Williams' verse makes us jump; nothing, and certainly nothing in the way of a deliberate metric, seems to intervene between us and the sensibility of this extraordinary man. Our first example, a fragment Williams reprints from *Paterson,*[15] delights both ear and eye with its carefully spaced lines and young girl voice:

> I bought a new
> bathing suit
>
> Just pants
> and a brassiere—

I haven't shown
it

to my mother
yet.

As in Imagist poetry, the lines are arranged for rhetorical emphasis; the half-rhymes (*suit / it / yet*) mark slight hesitations in the young lady's brief and pithy discourse. (We must sternly suppress, as being critically undemonstrable, our inclination to see in the shape of the poem an emblem of its subject: both poem and bathing suit share a tantalizing brevity.) Williams was early associated with the Imagists; his first literary friends were Pound and H. D., and Pound included a poem by Williams in *Des Imagistes* (1914). But Williams never officially joined the Imagists nor signed their manifestos. He went to Europe on trips, preferring to remain an American sightseer rather than take up the uncertain life of an expatriate. His aggressive and positive Americanism resembles Pound's aggressive, *negative* Americanism.

Both Williams and Pound take an antihistorical stand. Williams shows his contempt for history simply by ignoring it; he tells us again and again he prefers direct experience to the ash-heaps of the past. Pound's antihistoricism makes more devious but nevertheless followable tracks. He became a scholar, digested what he needed, and rejected the rest. The "philosophy of history" informing the *Cantos* retells history as Pound, from his odd angle of vision, sees it. We find no "history," of course: only mythology animated by demonology. Pound brought his American brashness to Europe and started a poetic revolution; Williams stayed home, practiced medicine in Rutherford, and cultivated his sensibility.

We see a clue to Williams' position, both technical and spiritual, in his tirade against Eliot. I quote from *The Autobiography of William Carlos Williams:*

> . . . To me especially [*The Waste Land*] struck like a sardonic bullet. I felt at once that it had set me back twenty years, and I'm sure it did. Critically Eliot returned us to the classroom just at the moment when I felt that we were on the point of escape to matters much closer to the essence of a new art form itself—rooted in the locality which should give it fruit. . . .
>
> If with his skill he could have been kept here to be employed by our slowly shaping drive, what strides might

> we not have taken! We needed him in the scheme I was half-consciously forming. I needed him: he might have become our adviser, even our hero. By his walking out on us we were stopped, for the moment, cold. It was a bad moment. Only now, as I predicted, have we begun to catch hold again and restarted to make the line over. This is not to say that Eliot has not, indirectly, contributed much to the emergence of the next step in metrical construction, but if he had not turned away from the direct attack here, in the western dialect, we might have gone ahead much faster. . . .[16]

After discounting Williams' considerable personal antipathy for Eliot,[17] we understand his cry against the calculated craftsmanship, the dazzling metrical virtuosity of *The Waste Land.* To Williams, *The Waste Land* seemed a step backward into the prosodical past; it returned the poet "to the classroom." Williams found no use for Eliot's meters: which scarcely demolishes Eliot but helps to explain Williams. We need not quarrel with Williams about Eliot's repudiation of America; Eliot *had* to go to Europe just as Williams *had* to remain in New Jersey. Matters of temperament determined their location as well as their style. Style is the man; and the man is the air he breathes, the food he eats, the ground on which his house is built.

Williams built his poetic line on "the western dialect" and on the idea that the poem assumes a rhythmic shape congruent to its shape as a presented *object.* The Objectivist theory

> . . . argued the poem, like every other form of art, is an object, an object that in itself formally presents its case and its meaning by the very form it assumes. Therefore, being an object, it should be so treated and controlled—but not as in the past.[18]

Williams did not make clear whether the poem-object existed in space or time; he implies the poem exists in time *and* space ("like a symphony or cubist painting"). Objectivist theory emphasized the concreteness of the poem, the "thingness" of its words; Williams discovered in the writings of Gertrude Stein ". . . [a] feeling of words themselves, a curious immediate quality quite apart from their meaning, much as in music different notes are dropped, so to speak, into a repeated chord one at a time, one after another—for itself alone."[19] A word in a poem must function as a discrete perceptual entity; it must be given, with all its physical immediacy, to hearing, vision, or touch. The poet and his reader must revive their childhood belief that words are indeed the things and qualities they symbolize; words like *rough, smooth, round* possess for the mind perceptual roughness, smoothness, roundness.

Objectivist theory represents another variety of the spatial heresy and the attempts of modern poets to fight the medium. Language is stubbornly conceptual; poets must resist abstraction and struggle to make their words vivid to eye, ear, and touch. The objectivist poem achieves its vividness by stopping time; the poem sits on the page in its unmoving "thingness":

BETWEEN WALLS

the back wings
of the

hospital where
nothing

will grow lie
cinders

in which shine
the broken

pieces of a green
bottle

Nothing happens; the verbs (*lie, shine*) present little action and function nearly as copulas. The poem's significance is implied, not stated. We understand that the back of the hospital, the infertile cinders, and the shattered bottle, add up to a feeling of sudden desolation. The sun, catching the green glass, points up the bleak surroundings.

Such a poem requires a bare minimum of prosodic means. The lines are alternately long and short and hold two and one stress respectively. Important words stand by themselves or at the ends of lines: *nothing, cinders, broken, green.* The poem is composed in space, and the eye comes to rest on *green.* Perhaps *green* suggests fertility, in contrast to the barren back of the hospital. But Williams would probably snort at this "interpretation," and maintain ". . . The feeling is of words themselves, a curious immediate quality, quite apart from their meaning. . . ." As words detach themselves from their meanings, prosody becomes static.

Rhythmic structure moves in time, but the Objectivist poem does not move; like the Gumbie Cat it "sits and sits and sits and sits," maintaining its inscrutability.

Not all of Williams' poems, however, sit motionless, pinned down by typography and visual form. "The Dance" has a boisterous, even catchy, swing:

> In Breughel's great picture, The Kermess,
> the dancers go round, they go round and
> around, the squeal and the blare and the
> tweedle of bagpipes, a bugle and fiddles
> tipping their bellies (round as the thick-
> sided glasses whose wash they impound)
> their hips and their bellies off balance
> to turn them. Kicking and rolling about
> the Fair Grounds, swinging their butts, those
> shanks must be sound to bear up under such
> rollicking measures, prance as they dance
> in Breughel's great picture, The Kermess.

The lines stomp along in heavily accented triple time: the German *Ländler* with its ONE-two-three, OOM-pah-pah. Interior rhyme and a firm anapestic meter hold the poem together:

> their híps | and their bél | lies off bál | ance
>
> to túrn | them.∧ Kíck | ing and ról | ling a bóut |
>
> the Fair Gróunds, |∧ swíng | ing their bútts, | those
>
> shánks | must be sóund . . .

We cannot miss the obvious music of "The Dance." Williams' eye is sharp but his ear is equally sharp. We hear finer, more intricate music in other poems. Hoagy Carmichael reads "Tract" (*I will teach you my townspeople / how to perform a funeral*) over a pulsing jazz accompaniment; his soft Southern voice gracefully picks out the rhythms and we know that Williams writes for the ear as well as the eye.

Most of Williams' poems are composed in characteristic short lines. However, he has written a number of poems using a longer and more conventional line. These are the concluding tercets from "The Yachts":

> Arms with hands grasping seek to clutch at the prows.
> Bodies thrown recklessly in the way are cut aside.
> It is a sea of faces about them in agony, in despair
>
> until the horror of the race dawns staggering the mind,
> the whole sea becomes an entanglement of watery bodies
> lost to the world bearing what they cannot hold. Broken,
>
> beaten, desolate, reaching from the dead to be taken up
> they cry out, failing, failing! their cries rising
> in waves still as the skillful yachts pass over.

The lines approximate blank verse—the modern, loosened kind with free use of substitution and hypermetrical effects. Rhythmic beauty is achieved by a long *rallentando,* a gradual slowing down of prosodic movement. The first tercet has the normal rising rhythm of blank verse, but beginning with the last line of the second tercet, the rhythm begins to shift. A pattern of trochaic words, *Broken, beaten, reaching, failing, rising,* crosses the rising iambic base; like the waves themselves, we have a rocking movement generated by the falling metrical units of trochee and dactyl:

beát en, | dé so late, | reách ing from | the deád | to be tá | ken úp

they crý | oút, faíl | ing, faíl | ing! their críes | rí sing . . .

The final lines evoke a nearly unbearable pathos—nearly, but not quite; the passionately well-ordered metric keeps the feeling within bounds. "The Yachts" is among Williams' best poems; it ranks with the best poems of our age.

5 E. E. Cummings

Imagist techniques pushed first the image, then the individual word toward prosodic isolation. The typographical prosody of E. E. Cummings is a by-product of Imagism; however, Cummings goes a step further. Not only does he break down the line into visual shapes and give the separate word rhythmic autonomy, but he fragments words themselves. Each letter of the alphabet assumes importance in the rhythmic scheme. In the following poem Cummings distorts typography, but does not paint a picture of the poem's ostensible subject. The typographical derangements, the capital *O*'s evidently enhance the *moon*-ness of the poem; it is a matter of quality, not photography:

mOOn Over tOwns mOOn
whisper
less creature huge grO
pingness

whO perfectly whO
flOat
newly alOne is
dreamest

oNLY THE MooN o
VER ToWNS
SLoWLY SPRoUTING SPIR
IT

1 from *no thanks*

Even when the typographic fit is upon him, Cummings is a more versatile technician than he is usually given credit for. He is the master of several visual styles. The well-known grasshopper poem works like a cubist painting; we must piece together the shattered words and disarranged punctuation to discover what the poem *says*. (It reads, as near as I can make out, "The grasshopper, who as we look up now, gathering into PPEGORHRASS, leaps! arriving to become, rearrangingly, a grasshopper!") I am unable to discover what rationale lies behind the poem's punctuation. What the poem is *doing* is leaping, flying apart in midair, and rearranging itself on the page:

r-p-o-p-h-e-s-s-a-g-r
who
a)s w(e loo)k
upnowgath
PPEGORHRASS
eringint(o-
aThe):l
eA
!p:
S a
(r
rIvInG .gRrEaPsPhOs)
to
rea(be)rran(com)gi(e)ngly
,grasshopper;

13 from *no thanks*

The poem apparently resembles its subject: the disintegrating and reintegrating grasshopper. Actually, the poem does not so much *look like* the grasshopper's action as give the feel of action. Cummings uses an elaborate technique of synaesthesia, a complex visual and aural derangement, to signify emotional meaning. We must, in order to read this poem, "see" sounds and "hear" shapes.

Synaesthesia is, of course, nothing new to poetry. Blake can see sound,

> And the hapless Soldier's sigh
> Runs in blood down Palace walls . . .

or Dame Edith Sitwell hear light,

> Jane, Jane, tall as a crane,
> The morning light creaks down again . . .

and we grant them necessary poetic license. Baudelaire mixes the senses of smell, sight, and sound in a three-way *correspondance:*

> Il est des parfums frais comme des chairs d'enfants,
> Doux comme les hautbois, verts comme les prairies . . .

The equation for successful synaesthesia takes this general form: a stimulus, perceived by one sense, is metaphorically apprehended by another. The method of synaesthesia holds considerable potential for emotional violence; the sigh that runs in blood and the fragrances soft as oboes affect us with great and peculiar power—peculiar, because the sensuous derangement of a Blake or a Baudelaire conducts a shock of sudden insight.

Such is the intention of the grasshopper poem. But we have shock without the suddenness; it takes time to construe the anagrammatized words and the disjunct punctuation and syntax. What should be grasped in an instant must be slowly deciphered. Our reaction is not passionate surprise but that Cummings is a very clever fellow. The poem lacks one term of the equation for workable synaesthesia. We have the visual stimulus, the poem's eccentric shape, but the metaphorical gap between eye and ear remains unfilled. The poem exists without significant aesthetic surface: apprehensible phonetic qualities.

Which is not to say that Cummings' work with typography has no merit. Poetry has been, for a long time, a printed art;

unless we read on a very primitive level, we do not "mouth" words when our eye moves over the page. But with visual symbols only, which cannot be transformed and perceived by the ear, the poet severely limits his range of feeling. Ultimately our admiration for Cummings' shape poetry is intellectual; the pattern or hieroglyphic poem belongs to the genre of wit poetry. George Herbert before Cummings "possessed the fantastic idea that a poem should resemble its subject in typographical appearance. . . ."[20] The poem's printed appearance forms a metaphorical structure, a conceit; we question whether to interpret the shape of the pattern poem rhetorically or rhythmically. Is the shape a matter of figurative language or prosody?

In Metaphysical shape poetry we have no doubt what is intended. The visual element in Herbert's *Easter-wings* is metaphorical; the length of line is both metaphorical and prosodical:

My tender age in sorrow did beginne:
And still with sicknesses and shame
Thou didst so punish sinne,
That I became
Most thinne.
With thee
Let me combine
And feel this day thy victorie:
For, if I imp my wing on thine,
Affliction shall advance the flight in me.

The line thins down from pentameter to monometer, then expands back to full pentameter again. Meter controls rhythmic structure; the phonetic pattern is prosodically dominant. Shape functions rhythmically but does not by itself carry the prosody.

Cummings also writes the kind of shape poem where meter as well as visual pattern make a prosody. The poet is explaining to a somewhat obtuse woman that war is not glorious. He counts out his feelings in lines of one to nine syllables—as he might show a child a problem in simple arithmetic on his fingers. The expanding and contracting shape of the poem conducts the reader through the dynamics of feeling; the longest line lengthens to an irritated ". . . O / what the hell . . ."; the last, short lines drop down to a hopeless "i am / dead." The poem's triangular shape indicates, like the crescendo fork of musical notation, where the reader must raise and lower the intensity of his voice:

i'm
asking
you dear to
what else could a
no but it doesn't
of course but you don't seem
to realize i can't make
it clearer war just isn't what
we imagine but please for god's O
what the hell yes it's true that was
me but that me isn't me
can't you see now no not
any christ but you
must understand
why because
i am
dead

40 from *XAIPE*

Cummings has a technical advantage over the Metaphysical pattern poets: he composes on the typewriter and can see how the printed poem will appear. It is perhaps worth mentioning that the typewriter has had perceptible influences on modern writing. The rhythms of modern prose have been affected by it. Certainly the particular iconographic effects Cummings achieves with the distribution of individual letters and punctuation would be impossible without it. With the typewriter the poet can fully exploit the spatial possibilities of a blank sheet of white paper; the page itself enters into the composition of his poem. Other poets who compose on the typewriter, Eliot for one, have used the blank space, the isolated line or word, and the pregnant indentation to poetic and rhythmic advantage.

6 *"The Visual in the Verbal"*

By itself, the notion of "the visual in the verbal" was a lively, needed, fructifying heresy.[21] Imagism stimulated interest once again in the problems of poetic form and technique; the new visualism brought a discipline of seeing with precision and recording with accuracy. A new technique, as Hulme pointed out, became a source of creative excitement and urged poets to new themes and subjects. The concern with sharp images strengthened certain textural features of the new verse; although these lines are iambically based, we feel a rhythmic hardness not found in Georgian poetry:

> Wipe your hand across your mouth, and laugh;
> The worlds revolve like ancient women
> Gathering fuel in vacant lots.
>
> T. S. Eliot, "Preludes"

Eliot was never a card-carrying Imagist; in his poetry seeing, feeling, and thinking fuse in ways that transcend mere poetic doctrine.

The limitations of Imagism prevented prolixity and rhythmic flabbiness. A successful Imagist poem was, by definition and decree, a short poem usually composed in short lines. Such brevities discouraged dealings in abstractions and unrealized emotion. If the Imagist poet were going to treat ideas as well as sense impressions, his eyes had to see what his brain formulated. As a result, Imagist poets had few transactions with the world of ideas; orthodox Imagism began and ended with recording acts of simple perception. A man could hardly be sentimental in a poem such as this:

> Black swallows swooping or gliding
> In a flurry of entangled loops and curves;
> The skaters skim over the frozen river.
> And the grinding click of their skates as they impinge
> upon the surface,
> Is like the brushing together of thin wing-tips of
> silver.
>
> John Gould Fletcher, "The Skaters"

But the impact of Imagism on prosody proved, in the historical long run, more of a force for confusion and weakness than a stimulus toward new and useful rhythmic forms. A poetic so committed to what the eye saw rather than what the ear heard was doomed, from the very beginning, to run ". . . upstream, against / The grain of language and the course of change."[22] Imagist rhythms relaxed, almost inevitably, into the slackness of prose; the line rather than the sentence or paragraph became the verse unit. Most of Whitman's lines end with a full rhythmic cadence; so do the *vers libre* poems of Pound:

> Go, my songs, to the lonely and the unsatisfied,
> Go also to the nerve-wracked, go to the en-
>   slaved-by-convention,
> Bear to them my contempt for their oppressors.
> Go as a great wave of cool water,
> Bear my contempt of oppressors.
>
> "Commission"

The methods of syntactical manipulation, practiced by Whitman and the French *vers librists* and recommended by Duhamel and Vildrac, have only limited rhythmical interest. The most sympathetic reader of *Song of Myself* wearies of Whitman's "gab and loitering": a weariness occasioned by the monotonous end-stopped lines and syntactical meanderings.

Imagist poetry favored a dislocated syntax, a network of images unrelated by strict grammatical connections. While it is possible that a metrical prosody can support syntactical looseness —Hart Crane and Dylan Thomas are both poets who, though careless of their syntax, maintain a regular metric—the combination of free verse and free syntax shatters the continuity of poetic structure. The long poem becomes impossible; the prosodical forms of Imagism prevent both discursive and narrative movement. Imagism, at least in theory, dedicated itself to new freedoms of ear and eye; *vers libre* and immediate visual perception were the new orders in poetry.

But these orders were in fact destructive elements. Without the support of close syntax and with only the very weak support of *vers libre,* Imagist poetry relied more and more on visual effects. Imagist theory, in the speculations of Hulme, and, for a brief period, Imagist practice, tried to make poetry a spatial art: to turn words into pictures and rhythms into palpable surfaces. Many poems by Cummings, Williams, and Pound elevated orthography and the minor eccentricities of print to leading features of poetic structure: such poems are the logical and absurd reductions of Hulme's belief that the newest poetry must resemble painting and sculpture. Poetry becomes a species of picture writing scarcely requiring a prosody of phonetic surface. The next step would be poetry without language, the abandoning of the larger aural symbolism of which prosody is a significant part. Even Hulme and Pound would hardly consciously countenance such a violation. But Hulme's theories and Pound's poetry contain the seeds of higher irrationality; how much versified and syntactical language do we find on any single page of Pound's *Thrones,* the latest fourteen *Cantos?* Or have the ideogram and "the ideogrammatic method," the apotheosis of "the visual in the verbal," replaced syntax and prosody, the rational structures of poetry?

VI

"The Celebrated Metric" of Ezra Pound

"It is ill dealing with the prophets. They themselves may be approachable, serene, and simple, but about them their disciples soon cast such a mirage of words that the seeker is blinded and baffled, if he is not utterly repelled."[1] These words begin Paul Elmer More's brilliant essay on Walt Whitman; they also express my own misgivings and trepidations in dealing with Pound's eminence as a master of English verbal music. No poet has been more lavishly admired for prosodical skill than Pound; no poet has elicited such praise for his ear. To the Poundlings it is a simple truism that Pound is always and everywhere an infallible craftsman; to many who believe Pound holds distorted views on matters of human importance, it assuages guilt to qualify criticism with *But he has the finest ear of the twentieth century.* During the unfortunate Bollingen Award controversy, John Berryman offered the ultimate in extravagant judgments: "Fifteen years of listening have not taught me [Pound's ear] is inferior to the ear of the author of *Twelfth Night.*"[2]

Well, so be it. Mr. Berryman is certainly entitled to the opinions of *his* ears. But such eulogy inhibits genuine criticism: Pound needs no belying with false compare; his virtues as a prosodist are evident enough without placing him alongside the author of *Twelfth Night.* (Is Mr. Berryman coyly sidestepping the question of whether Pound's ear is as good as the author of *The Tempest*'s?) Prosodical excellence is not discerned by geewhiz wonder but by quotation and analysis. In a less ecstatic mood Mr. Berryman does indeed quote and analyze; he scans one line from the *Pisan Cantos,* reading it as "a spondee–two dactyls–and trochee":[3]

So old Elkin had only one glory . . .

The beauty of this line emerges from the interplay of quantity with a brief procession of syllable-stress anapests. We hear the meter (⏑ ⏑ ´) and Pound's careful positioning and *timing* of the *o* and *l* sounds. Mr. Berryman scans the quantities: a matter to which we later return.

Eliot first heard the subtleties of Pound's music. In 1917 he published anonymously ("I was so completely unknown that it seemed more decent that the pamphlet should appear anonymously . . ."[4]) *Ezra Pound / His Metric and Poetry.* This, Eliot's first critical book, might serve as a model for prosodical criticism; its twenty-five pages define Pound's method in precise aphorisms:

> The freedom of Pound's verse is rather a state of tension due to constant opposition between free and strict. There are not, as a matter of fact, two kinds of verse, the strict and the free; there is only a mastery which comes of being so well trained that form is an instinct and can be adapted to the particular purpose in hand.[5]

Metric precedes *poetry* in the title; Eliot comments little on Pound's subjects but centers his observations on the technical accomplishment of the verse. Eleven years later Eliot takes the same tack in his introduction to the Faber edition of Pound's *Selected Poems.* He praises the *Selected Poems* as a "textbook of modern versification," and brilliantly generalizes on *vers libre,* technique and inspiration, and "the relation of a poet's technical development and his personal development. . . ."[6] Similarly, Eliot professes admiration for the versification of the *Cantos,* though he expresses distaste for their "philosophy."

Most of the pieties heard about Pound's metric echo what Eliot said forty-five years ago. The reluctance to deal directly and critically with Pound's verse can be traced to Eliot's sensitive and authoritative remarks; few trust their own ears sufficiently to quarrel with Eliot's judgments. But we know Eliot's criticism was hardly disinterested. During the years 1917–22 Pound and Eliot took in each other's washing; what they then said must be understood in a context of mutual admiration and the defiance of the Philistines. Pound's disciples are still fighting the battles of the 'teens and twenties; most of the talk about Pound's metric is charged with outdated polemic and unnecessary apology. Few have taken the trouble to submit Pound's lines to careful prosodic scrutiny.

We shall examine Pound's verse as if we had heard none of the fervent propaganda of his disciples. We shall take with sufficient salt what Pound himself has said about prosody: statements often made in jest, in irritation, or in the querulous voice of the "village explainer."[7] In his *Treatise on Metric* Pound tells us that the supposed rules of prosody cannot teach us to become poets: "Prosody and melody are attained by the listening ear, not by an index of nomenclatures, or by learning that such and such a foot is called spondee."[8] No poet has ever been seriously injured by learning the craft of versification and discovering which foot is called a spondee. Pound himself bothered to learn a great deal about prosody—including the nonexistent rules. He studied, with professorial thoroughness, the forms of Provençal verse; he learned how to write English quantity and strong-stress meter.

And no poet has been so damaged by the dogmatic adulation of his friends and disciples. Many of Pound's remarks on metric are illuminating and of great practical value; others are obvious, defensive, or obscurely paradoxical. He has written poetry of unequaled rhythmic splendor and delicacy; he has written broken and incoherent passages which abandon prosodic control. Consequently, I do not read his utterances, either in prose or verse, as chapter and verse of a sacred book: I regard him neither as a legislator (acknowledged or unacknowledged) of the world, nor as the poet who never made a metrical mistake. The task here is to examine poetry, not to propitiate a god.

I

A persistent melomania dominates Pound's statements on prosody. In one of his early exhortations, he urged the poet to "behave as a musician, a good musician, when dealing with that phase of your art that has exact parallels in music."[9] At the same time, and perhaps unaware of the contradiction, Pound proclaimed first the Image, and later the Ideogram the essence of the poetic. Curiously, as he increasingly made musical knowledge a *sine qua non* for the aspiring poet, his own prosody forsook musical virtues and became steadily more visual. The early lyrics aspire happily toward the condition of music ("Pound quotes approvingly the dictum of Pater"[10]); the later *Cantos* are marked by the famous Chinese characters and other appeals to the eye.

Pound's own musical gifts and his relationship to musical art are perplexing matters. There exist numerous stories about his musical talents; Yves Tinayre reports that Pound had no ear (!), could not carry a tune, but "sang rhythmically."[11] William Carlos Williams corroborates Tinayre's report and observes that Pound's interest in music lay in the rhythm, "the time variants," and that "Tones, I am certain, meant nothing to him, can mean nothing."[12] Whatever handicaps of tone deafness Pound suffered, they did not deter him from writing an opera or "composing" a violin sonata.[13] He even tried his versatile hand at music theory and wrote *Antheil and the Treatise on Harmony* (1927). It is in this book that Pound expatiates most fully on music, rhythm, and their relationships to prosody.

The title is misleading: Pound obviously does not know a dominant ninth from a tromba marina. We find nothing about harmony—except one mysterious statement that chords in a musical composition must be separated by proper intervals of time. We find the intellectual's usual snobberies about music: the nineteenth century was a ruinous period; polyphony is better than harmony; down with the piano, up with ancient instruments, etc. But picking carefully among Pound's enthusiasms and prejudices, we can piece together his idea of a musically inspired poetic doctrine:

> I believe in an absolute rhythm.
> E. P. 1910 with explanations.
>
> In 1910 I was working with monolinear verbal rhythm but one had already an adumbration that the bits of rhythm used in verse were capable of being used in musical structure, even with other dimensions. (pp. 13–14)

I am inclined to think that the horizontal merits faded from music, and from the rhythm of poetry, with the gradual separation of the two arts. A man thinking with mathematical fractions is not impelled toward such variety of *raga* as a man working with the necessary inequalities of words. But the verbal rhythm is monolinear. It can form contrapunto only

> against its own echo, or against a developed expectancy. (p. 47)

> Again I emphasize the value of these different rhythm roots as above that of a tired and mechanical accent-metric. (p. 125)

> A rhythm is a shape; it exists like the keel-line of a yacht, or the lines of an automobile engine, for a definite purpose, and should exist with an efficiency as definite as that which we find in yachts and automobiles. (p. 126)[14]

Pound reacts, at least in theory, against traditional syllable-stress metric. An earlier injunction warned the aspiring poet, "Don't chop your stuff into separate *iambs.* Don't make each line stop dead at the end, and then begin every next line with a heave."[15] Pound has composed, of course, in iambic verse—which does not invalidate his remarks about suppleness and variety. He has never favored a heavily stressed line; his translation of "The Seafarer" keeps to the strong-stress quadruple meter, but offers melody rather than emphatic beat:

> Storms, on the stone-cliffs beaten, fell on the stern
> In icy feathers; full oft the eagle screamed
> With spray on his pinion.

The rhythm overrides the metrical divisions as a good tune will move across the bar lines.

The statements about "absolute rhythm," "monolinear rhythm," and "contrapunto" (if I properly understand them) refer to the problem of finding a rhythmical form for a long poem. Pound had already begun composition of the *Cantos;* the early poems were behind him. An "absolute rhythm" worked for the shorter poems—especially the ones in Pound's Imagistic manner. But absolute rhythm can sustain itself only for a limited number of lines; Pound was considering a musical method for the *Cantos.* ". . . bits of rhythm used in verse were capable of being used in musical structure, even with other dimensions. . . ." Pound is evidently proposing the use of "bits of rhythm" thematically, as short *motifs* are repeated in a musical work. ". . . even with other dimensions" puzzles me: unless Pound had a sudden insight that the structure of the *Cantos* was going to collapse into a jigsaw puzzle of visual forms.

Perhaps unwittingly, Pound admits the impossibility of the method he proposes. Verbal rhythm can form "contrapunto only against its own echo"; this means that similar rhythmic structures must be quite close together if we are going to experience any "contrapuntal" effect. Verbal rhythm also forms counterpoint ". . . against a developed expectancy," that is, against a regular meter. "The necessary inequalities of words" must be welded into rhythmic form either by strong, close syntax or by regular meter; neither obtains in the *Cantos.* Close syntax—using repeated, parallel, or incremental grammatical forms—makes rhythmic echoes possible; a regular meter allows the greatest possible variety of echoes "against a developed expectancy."

The Treatise on Harmony explains, not clearly, that *music* inheres in the verbal surface of poetry, and also affords larger, architechtonic possibilities. Pound recognizes that rhythmic forms of music and poetry move in time and vary in intensity and duration. The later *Treatise on Metric* hammers home the importance of rhythm as a *shape in time:*

> Rhythm is a form cut into TIME, as a design is determined SPACE. . . .
>
> In making a line of verse (and thence building the lines into passages) you have certain primal elements:
>
> That is to say, you have the various 'articulate sounds' of the language, of its alphabet, that is, and the various groups of letters in syllables.
>
> These syllables have differing weights and durations
>
> A. original weights and durations
>
> B. weights and durations that seem naturally imposed on them by the other syllable groups around them.
>
> Those are the medium wherewith the poet cuts his design in TIME.[16]

We recall Mr. Berryman's scansion of the line from the *Pisan Cantos:* spondee–two dactyls–and trochee. He does not scan syllable-stress feet, but hears the relative syllabic lengths, the rhythm of English quantity:

So old | El kin had | on ly one | glo ry

He hears the musical shape the line makes in time. Pound's ear has (if we may be permitted some salutary synaesthesia) an extraordinary feel for duration. Three unaccented long syllables slow down the prevailing movement of anapests (or dactyls: the line is too brief to decide):

So old Él | kin had ón | ly *one* gló | ry

The quantitative-hexameter paradigm represents one of Pound's favorite "bits of rhythm"; we have quoted earlier a fragmentary line-and-a-half of Virgilian verse:

so | light is the | ur ging, so | or dered the | dark pe tals of | ir on

we who have | passed ov er | Leth e.

Canto LXXIV

Our "quantitative" scansion shows a dactylic-anapestic base. We have *something* resembling the *Evangeline* measure, but infinitely more subtle in its management of duration and weight. (That Pound is Longfellow's *metrical* grandnephew remains unproved![17])

Pound's *Treatises* admonish the poet to use his ears, to pay the closest possible attention to the aural surface of his art. The tenor of all Pound's statements on rhythm and meter indicates a preference for a quantitative prosody; he does not, however, advocate Greek and Latin meters in English. The poet must exercise care in the handling of his syllables, not make the impossible attempt, as Bridges did, of devising grammatical rules for English quantity. An early statement (1917) *Re Vers Libre* warns the poet against trying to imitate the Greek and Latin meters:

> I think the desire for vers libre is due to the sense of quantity reasserting itself after years of starvation. But I doubt if we can take over, for English, the rules of quantity laid down for Greek and Latin, mostly by Latin grammarians.
>
> . . . I think progress lies rather in an attempt to approximate classical quantitative meters (NOT to copy them) than in carelessness regarding such things.[18]

A still earlier statement (1913)—it is remarkable that the further back we dig in Pound's critical work, the more lucid and detailed are his perceptions—sums up everything of value in Pound's doctrine of *ut musica poesis:*

> . . . The movement of poetry is limited only by the nature of syllables and of articulate sound, and by the laws of music, or melodic rhythm. Space forbids a complete treatise on melody at this point, and forbids equally a complete treatise on all the sorts of verse, alliterative, syllabic, accentual, and quantitative. And such treatises as the latter are for the most part useless, as no man can learn much of these things save by first-hand untrammeled, unprejudiced examination of the finest examples of all these sorts of verse, of the finest strophes and of the finest rhyme-schemes, and by a profound study of the art and history of music.[19]

2

Our first example, from the 1909 *Personae,* descends from Yeats and the Pre-Raphaelite line; we have the sound of Yeats's *fin de siècle* mood music. Pound's world-weariness, however, has more exuberance than languor:

> O smoke and shadow of a darkling world,
> These, and the rest, and all the rest we knew.
> 'Tis not a game that plays at mates and mating,
> 'Tis not a game of barter, lands and houses,
> 'Tis not 'of days and nights' and troubling years,
> Of cheeks grown sunken and glad hair gone grey;
> There *is* the subtler music, the clear light
> Where time burns back about th'eternal embers.
> We are not shut from all the thousand heavens:
> Lo, there are many gods whom we have seen,
> Folk of unearthly fashion, places splendid,
> Bulwark of beryl and of chyrsophrase.
>
> ———
>
> Thou hooded opal, thou eternal pearl,
> O thou dark secret with a shimmering floor . . .
>
> "The Flame"

Most readers will notice that Pound's technique is showing, that he is trying hard for the rich, full effect:

> Of cheeks grown sunken and glad hair gone grey . . .
>
> Folk of unearthly fashion, places splendid,
> Bulwark of beryl and of chrysophrase.

Rhythmically, the lines are static; one line stops dead "at the end," the next begins "with a heave." But some lines "go" with a strikingly individual movement:

> These, and the rest, and all the rest we knew . . .
>
> There *is* the subtler music, the clear light
> Where time burns back about th'eternal embers . . .

In the first line above, Pound splits the inverted first foot with a caesura; in the next two lines, we find the rising Ionic flowing over the end of the line and into the next:

> There *ís* | the súb | tler mú | sic, the cléar líght
> Where tíme | *burns* báck | a bóut | th'‿é ter | nal ém | bers.

We note the holding effect of the unstressed long syllable in the second foot of the line above; the length of *burns* is approximately twice that of *back*, on which the metrical ictus falls. We have blank verse in *tempo rubato;* the right hand, freely moving and pausing among the quantities, plays over the steady syllable-stress base line.

A new rhythm distinguishes a somewhat later example of Pound's blank verse; here is the opening of the second part of "Near Perigord" (*Lustra,* 1915):

> End fact. Try fiction. Let us say we see
> En Bertrans, a tower-room at Hautefort,
> Sunset, the ribbon-like road lies, in red cross-light,
> Southward toward Montaignac, and he bends at a table
> Scribbling, swearing between his teeth; by his left hand
> Lie little strips of parchment covered over,
> Scratched and erased with *al* and *ochaisos.*
> Testing his list of rhymes, a lean man? Bilious?
> With a red straggling beard?
> And the green cat's-eye lifts toward Montaignac.

The rhythmical tune sounds familiar; we heard it before in *The Ring and the Book:*

> To stop song, loosen flower, and leave path . . .

Pound stretches the line both tighter and looser than Browning does. We have blank verse compressed to four beats—a strong-stress line:

> The dull round towers encroaching on the field,
> The tents tight drawn, horses at tether
> Farther and out of reach, the purple night,
> The crackling of small fires, the bannerets,
> The lazy leopards on the largest banner . . .

We have the verse flowing out in hexameters:

> Stray gleams on hanging mail, an armourer's torch-flame . . .
>
> 'Say that he saw the castles, say that he loved Maent!'

The brilliant metrical surface of "Portrait d'une Femme" strikes the ear differently; many individual lines scan as blank verse, but the movement is highly varied and frequently a matter of vocal cadence:

> Great minds have sought you—lacking someone else.
> You have been second always. Tragical?
> No. You preferred it to the usual thing:
> One dull man, dulling and uxorious,
> One average mind—with one thought less, each year . . .

This kind of "irregularity" does not clash with other rhythms. Pound leads up to a metrical half-close by gradually bringing each line nearer to the iambic norm. The verse period begins with a half-line,

> And takes strange gain away:

works into three lines where trisyllabic and trochaic feet unsettle the verse,

Trophies fished up; some curious suggestion;
Fact that leads nowhere; and a tale or two,
Pregnant with mandrakes, or with something else . . .

and then slips back into regular iambic,

That might prove useful and yet never proves,
That never fits a corner or shows use,
Or finds its hour upon the loom of days . . .

Pound demonstrates his prosodical brilliance in other than syllable-stress meters; *Ripostes* (1912) contains the strong-stress "The Seafarer" and the quantitative "Apparuit." There is little point in arguing whether "The Seafarer" is translation or "re-creation"; such lines as

Cuckoo calleth with gloomy crying
He singeth summerward, bodeth sorrow,
The bitter heart's blood. Burgher knows not—

combine Ye Olde Englishe with Pound's favorite pidgin Eskimo. The use of the definite article—"*The* burgher knows not"—would hardly disturb the rhythm. It is not Pound's occasional mistranslations that set the reader's teeth on edge, but his lapses occasioned by straining after "flavor." His translation of

. . . þaer mec oft bigeat
nearo nihtwaco aet nacan stefnan
þonne he be clifum cnossað . . .

is close enough to satisfy even the dustiest Old Englishman:

. . . and there I oft spent
Narrow nightwatch nigh the ship's head
While she tossed close to cliffs.

But why the archaic and cute *oft* and *nigh? Near* would be the subtler orchestration, with its modulated vowel and its delicate alliteration with *narrow.*

All criticism, however, seems mean and carping given the poem's rhythmic magnificence. The strong-stress meter describes the slow arc of feeling; the continuous falling movement is the perfect vehicle for Pound's favorite theme, "Time is the evil. Evil." (*Canto XXX*). Pound handles the meter more strictly than not, maintains a norm of three alliterated and four stressed syllables in each line, and varies the position of the medial pauses:

> Waneth the watch, but the world holdeth.
> Tomb hideth trouble. The blade is layed low.
> Earthly glory ageth and seareth.

Waneth the watch, but the world holdeth reproduces the meter of the original quite faithfully but mistakes the meaning of

> wuniað þa wacran   and þas woruld healdaþ . . .

"Weak men endure and inherit the earth." Perhaps Pound was too lazy to consult his dictionary and relied on his ear. The ear triumphs and only pedants regret the loss of the original meaning.

We offered a stanza from "Apparuit" in Chapter II as an example of pseudo-quantitative meter. Pound uses the Sapphic stanza whose paradigm is

— ⏑ | — ⏓ | — ⏑ ⏑ | — ⏑ | — ⏓

repeated for three lines, followed by a short line (the Adonic):

— ⏑ ⏑ | — ⏓

We see how closely Pound adheres to the pattern; I give the last two stanzas:

> Half the graven shoulder, the throat aflash with
> strands of light inwoven about it, loveli-
> est of all things, frail alabaster, ah me!
> swift in departing.
>
> Clothed in goldish weft, delicately perfect,
> gone as wind! The cloth of the magical hands!
> Thou a slight thing, thou in access of cunning
> dar'dst to assume this?

Stress underlines quantity; the normal word accent coincides with (but in only one place, *access,* combats) the length of vowel. The suppleness and ease of Pound's handling may be contrasted to Swinburne's—one of Pound's acknowledged masters. Swinburne's "Sapphics" are stiff and uncomfortable, the lines nearly awkward:

All the night sleep came not upon my eyelids,
Shed not dew, nor shook nor unclosed a feather,
Yet with lips shut close and with eyes of iron
Stood and beheld me.

Then to me so lying awake a vision
Came without sleep over the seas and touched me,
Softly touched mine eyelids and lips; and I too,
Full of the vision . . .

Pound's Sapphics are unquestionably superior in syntax and in the rightness of the quantities; they catch the rhythm—and hence the spirit—of their great original:

κὰδ δέ μ'ἴδρως κακχέεται, τρόμος δὲ
παῖσαν ἄγρει, χλωροτέρα δὲ ποίας
ἔμμι, τεθνάκην δ' ὀλίγω'πιδεύης
φαίνομ' ἀλαία.

Sappho, "To a Bride"

And the sweat breaks running upon me, fever
shakes my body, paler I turn than grass is;
I can feel that I have been changed, I feel that
death has come near me.

translation by Richmond Lattimore

I am less impressed by Pound's original poems in the Provençal stanzas. They seem exercises or virtuoso pieces, although the early *Canzon: of Incense* contains such fine lines as these:

Thy gracious ways,
O Lady of my heart, have
O'er all my thought their golden glamour cast;
As amber torch-flames, where strange men-at-arms
Tread softly 'neath the damask shield of night,
Rise from the flowing steel in part reflected,
So on my mailed thought that with thee goeth,
Though dark the way, a golden glamour falleth.

No such lines distinguish the *Sestina: Altaforte,* cautiously praised by Eliot as "perhaps the best sestina that has been written in English. . . ."[20] (Pound seems not to concur with Eliot's nearly half-century old judgment; he has recently withdrawn permission to quote or reprint the *Sestina.* Readers may consult the *Sestina* in the American (New Directions) edition, *Personae, The Collected Poems of Ezra Pound,* pages 28–29; or in the Faber edition, *Ezra Pound, Selected Poems,* pages 52–53.) The poem is excessively noisy, largely bluster and fee-fi-fo-fum. Pound's intention was a celebration of masculine vigor, a paean to the gods of war; the result is a set of variations that never progress from their theme.

The structure of the sestina, with its six recurring end-words, presents a formidable trap for the unwary. If the poet carelessly selects his end-words—words that are too loud or too obtrusive—he finds that his poem cannot move but remains stubbornly chained to the end of each line. Four of Pound's end-words (*crimson, clash, rejoicing, opposing*) stop every line dead, forcing the *Sestina* into unmetrical and even ungrammatical sequences. The envoy contains three of the worst lines Pound has written: a crescendo of successive shrieks. It remained for Auden, perhaps taking his cue from the *Sestina: Altaforte,* to reestablish the sestina and properly domesticate it for modern English poetry.

3

Pound's nonmetrical prosody comes in several varieties. "The Alchemist," from *Ripostes,* plays variations on a number of rhythmic constants. The poem is subtitled "Chant for the Transmutation of Metals" and is a catalogue of exotic proper names collected from Pound's reading on medieval alchemy. The rhythms are established through enumerations, anaphora, and repeated syntax:

> Sail of Claustra, Aelis, Azalais,
> As you move among the bright trees;
> As your voices, under the larches of Paradise
> Make a clear sound . . .
>
> Bring the saffron-coloured shell,
> Bring the red gold of the maple,
> Bring the light of the birch tree in autumn
> Mirals, Cembelins, Audiarda,
> Remember this fire . . .

Midonz, with the gold of the sun, the leaf of the
    poplar, by the light of the amber,
Midonz, daughter of the sun, shaft of the tree,
    silver of the leaf, light of the yellow of the
    amber,
Midonz, gift of the God, gift of the light, gift of
    the amber of the sun,
                                Give light to the metal . . .

Pound uses a great variety of enumerative and parallel techniques in the *Lustra* volume. "Salutation," "Salutation the Second," and "Commission" all descend prosodically from Whitman; Pound, with some surliness, acknowledges his debt in "A Pact":

I make a pact with you, Walt Whitman—
I have detested you long enough.
I come to you as a grown child
Who has had a pig-headed father . . .

We have one sap and one root—
Let there be commerce between us.

Evocative handling of quantity sustains the syntactic rhythms; the first two lines of "Surgit Fama" suggest Virgilian hexameters:

There is a | truce a mong | the gods, / Kore is |
    seen in the | North . . .

The last lines echo the rhythm of the first with Pound's favorite mixture of spondees and dactyls:

'Once more in Delos, once more is the altar a-quiver.
Once more is the chant heard . . .

Other poems in *Lustra* which move to free quantitative measures include "Dance Figure" and "Gentildonna." The latter poem is made up of two distichs, one hexameter, the other pentameter:

She passed and left no quiver in the veins, who now
Moving among the trees, and clinging
in the air she severed,
Fanning the grass she walked on then, endures:

Grey olive leaves beneath a rain-cold sky.

This poem figures among Pound's imagistic pieces, though the "purity" of his method might be questioned. He names as well as presents his emotion ("left no quiver"); the prosody approaches the syllable-stress norm.

A number of the Imagist poems in *Lustra* approximate the syllabic haiku. The following examples contain nineteen instead of the prescribed seventeen syllables:

FAN PIECE . . .

O fan of white silk,
clear as frost on the grass-blade,
You also are laid aside.

LI PO

And Li Po also died drunk.
He tried to embrace a moon
In the Yellow River.

The prosody of Pound's Imagist period relies little on visual effects, line arrangement, stanzaic shaping, and other vagaries. The permanent, and probably damaging—we shall speak of this below—contribution of Pound's 1912–15 years was the fashioning of "prose song." Pound reviewed Ford Madox Ford's *Collected Poems* and praised lines like these for their "leisurely, low toned" qualities:

'Though you're in Rome you will not go, my You,
Up to that Hill . . . but I forget the name.
Aventine? Pincio? No, I never knew . . .
I was there yesterday. You never came.

I have that Rome; and you, you have a Me,
You have a Rome, and I, I have my You . . .[21]

Pound's affection for Ford must have deafened his ears; if this is "the prose tradition in verse," then flatness and ineptness must be virtues.

At the time (1915) Pound's own practice hardly follows Ford's; music, not ineptness, created "The River Song." This is an adaptation (through Fenollosa) from the Chinese poet Li Po:

> This boat is of shato-wood, and its gunwales
>   are cut magnolia,
> Musicians with jewelled flutes and with pipes of gold
> Fill full the sides in rows, and our wine
> Is rich for a thousand cups.
> We carry singing girls, drift with the drifting water,
> Yet Sennin needs
> A yellow stork for a charger, and all our seamen
> Would follow the white gulls or ride them.
> Kutsu's prose song
> Hangs with the sun and moon . . .

This may be poetry "as well written as prose," but its rhythm depends on the delicate balancing of the metrical with the non-metrical. Only a poet who wrote well in regular meter could have written the superb hexameter:

> We carry singing girls, drift with the drifting water . . .

The iambic movement is softly muted by the inverted fourth foot and the feminine ending. To call this "prose song" was misleading to all the Poundlings who never learned to sing. Just as many poets thought they wrote like Whitman because they began each line with the same sequence of words, so some thought they wrote like Pound because they stitched together lines of varying length and stultifying flatness.

It is a misnomer to call "The River Song" free verse; the lines, in scansion, fall easily into metrical feet. No line in our example has more than two consecutive unstressed syllables—which reduces the authentic prose effect. We hear a more obvious prose movement in "Villanelle: The Psychological Hour." This poem relies on line arrangement for deliberate rhetorical emphasis; Pound also uses an italicized refrain:

> I had over-prepared the event,
>   that much was ominous.
>   With middle-ageing care
>   I had laid out just the right books.
> I had almost turned down the pages.

Beauty is so rare a thing.
So few drink of my fountain.

So much barren regret,
So many hours wasted!
And now I watch, from the window,
the rain, the wandering busses . . .

The refrain is metered in trochees and fits smoothly with the freer, nonmetrical lines. A falling rhythm predominates, lightening the lugubrious self-pity:

Beauty would drink of my mind.
Youth would awhile forget
my youth is gone from me. . . .

The dying fall of the last line

my yóuth | is góne | fróm me.

gives the necessary ironic tone to the voice. A man barely thirty cannot be discovered, in all seriousness, lamenting his fled youth.

4

When Pound and Eliot were new friends, benefiting from each other's stimulation, they resolved to do something about the general state of English prosody circa 1918–20. Pound recommended a return to traditional meters:

> . . . at a particular date in a particular room, two authors, neither engaged in picking the others' pockets, decided that the dilutation of *vers libre,* Amygism, Lee Masterism, general floppiness had gone too far and that some counter current must be set going . . . Remedy prescribed 'Émaux et Camées' (or the Bay State Hymn Book). Rhyme and regular strophes.
>
> Results: Poems in Mr. Eliot's second volume . . . also 'H. S. Mauberley.'[22]

Mauberley displays an overall rhythmical hardness combined with an accomplished freedom. Its metrical *cantus firmus* derives, as Pound explains, from the octosyllabic couplet used in Gautier's *vers de société, Émaux et Camées.* Gautier counts syllables, of course, and rhymes his stanza *abab:*

CONTRALTO

On voit dans le musée antique,
Sur un lit de marbre sculpté
Une statue énigmatique
D'une inquiétante beauté.

Est-ce un jeune homme? est-ce une femme,
Une déesse, ou bien un dieu?
L'amour, ayant peur d'être infâme,
Hésite et suspend son aveu.

Pound does not copy Gautier's stanza but adapts it to English meter. He measures accents rather than syllables; the opening section of *Mauberley* moves in four- and five-stress lines:

For three years, out of key with his time,
He strove to resuscitate the dead art
Of poetry; to maintain 'the sublime'
In the old sense. Wrong from the start—

No, hardly, but seeing he had been born
In a half-savage country, out of date;
Bent resolutely on wringing lilies from the acorn;
Capaneus; trout for factitious bait . . .

The rhyming is *abab* in sections I and II; in section III Pound changes to a more relaxed scheme of rhyming only the second and fourth lines:

Faun's flesh is not to us,
Nor the saint's vision.
We have the Press for wafer;
Franchise for circumcision.

All men, in law, are equals.
Free of Pisistratus,
We choose a knave or an eunuch
To rule over us.

O bright Apollo,
τίν ἀνδρα, τίν'ἥρωα τίνα θεὸν,
What god, man, or hero
Shall I place a tin wreath upon!

The use of macaronic rhymes (*theon, upon*) can also be traced to Gautier; we find in the *Émaux et Camées* such grotesqueries as

> Tom, qu'un abandon scandalise,
> Récite "Love's labours lost",
> Et Fritz explique à Cidalise
> Le "Walpurgisnachtstraum" de Faust.
>
> from "Le Chauteau du souvenir"

Mauberley's rhyming deserves detailed scrutiny. Some of the double-rhymed feminine endings strike the note of comic doggerel:

> Knowing my coat has never been
> Of precisely the fashion
> To stimulate, in her,
> A durable passion;
>
> Doubtful, somewhat, of the value
> Of well-gowned approbation
> Of literary effort,
> But never of The Lady Valentine's vocation . . .

Pound rhymes with Byronic slap and dash; *Mauberley* has yet to be fully recognized as essentially comic: not only in theme but in details of technique. John Espey minimizes the comic and Byronic impulses in *Mauberley,*[23] but lines like these are out of *Don Juan:*

> Nothing, in brief, but maudlin confession,
> Irresponse to human aggression,
> Amid the precipitation, down-float
> Of insubstantial manna,
> Lifting the faint susurrus
> Of his subjective hosannah.

A romantic ironist, Pound turns the weapons of satire and ridicule upon himself. The rhythms trickle into sand in the above passage; the rhymes, *confession / agression, manna / hosannah,* are tired inspirations. These are intended effects; Pound makes fun of himself—up to a point. Self-pity replaces self-ridicule in the next quatrain:

Non-esteem of self-styled 'his betters'
Leading, as he well knew,
To his final
Exclusion from the world of letters.

How much of Pound is Mauberley, or whether Mauberley bears *any* resemblance to Pound, has been a critical asses' bridge. Mauberley's complaint of "Exclusion from the world of letters" has no biographical relevance. After his arrival in Europe, Pound quickly entered literary circles, experienced little difficulty in getting published, was friend and equal to Yeats, Joyce, and Eliot. Who excluded Pound—or could have? The character Mauberley is a fiction, compounded out of Pound's fragile ego, some shrewd self-criticism, and much projective rhetoric. The versification testifies to this compounding. Gautier's quatrain supplies the basic metrical melody, but we hear this melody only briefly. The opening quatrains are heavily counterpointed; indeed, scansion shows no regular foot:

For three | years, out | of key | with his time . . .

In the old sense. | Wrong from | the start—

In a half-sav | age coun | try, out | of date . . .

Nonmetrical lines fit easily into this scheme:

Bent resolutely on wringing lilies from the acorn . . .

The chopped seas held him, therefore, that year . . .

The stanza shrinks down to two beats; the rhythm diminishes:

Turned from the 'eau forte
Par Jacquemart'
To the strait head
Of Messalina:

'His true Penelope
Was Flaubert',
And his tool
The engraver's.

In the recapitulation ("THE AGE DEMANDED") rhythm is augmented; the movement leisurely, Whitmanian:

> Incapable of the least utterance or composition,
> Emendation, conservation of the 'better tradition',
> Refinement of medium, elimination of superfluities,
> August attraction or concentration.

Here Pound builds his rhythm by the enumeration of Latin polysyllables. Mauberley enters tropical waters and slowly drifts into nonexistence. The metric meanders and murmurs, finally peters out in slow dimeter and monometer:

> 'I was
> And I no more exist;
> Here drifted
> An hedonist.'

All that remains of Gautier's stanza is the rhyme, *exist / hedonist.*

The *persona* Mauberley, beauty struck and fashionably alienated, has been described by Pound himself as ". . . mere surface. Again a study in form, an attempt to condense the James novel."[24] The metrical surface is similarly condensed. The rhythm moves toward extreme compression; the tempo is quick, nervous with "Syncopation from the Greek . . ."[25] The base rhythm, provided by the Gautier stanza, holds together the loose texture of images, impressions, and *vignettes de société.* Without this carrying rhythm, the poem would break apart into unshored and ruinous fragments. With it, the poem achieves a special vitality and coherence and a place in the canon of twentieth-century poetry.

Although the *Homage to Sextus Propertius* (1917) precedes *Mauberley* in composition, its overall poetic method and specific prosodical character bring it close to the *Cantos.* I regard the *Homage,* as Eliot does, as "the necessary prolegomena to the *Cantos*": their immediate technical and spiritual precursor. Its sudden transitions, oblique references, and entanglement of mythological and personal allusion are the familiar devices of Pound's epic. The *Homage* also resembles the *Cantos* in versification. Pound adapts from Propertius' elegiac meter a loosely dactylic line with its falling rhythm. The *Cantos* are an extreme prosodic mixture and in many sections forsake formal versification, but what traces I discern of a carrying metric sound like Pound's favorite dactylic-spondaic—the basic feet in the elegiac paradigm. In both the *Homage* and the *Cantos* the rhythm is wide open, of course; it can accommodate the freest cadence of slang or the most elegantly polished hexameter.

Pound found in Propertius a kindred spirit. Propertius is enigmatic, gloomy, "difficult," and given to contradictory and violent moods. Like Pound he is a historical pessimist, believing in the imminent collapse of civilization, and complaining, like any contemporary *poète maudit,* of a culture hostile to poets and poetry. He also displays Pound's odd emotional polarity: a sense of absolute personal defeat alternating with wild and extravagant hopes. He argues, as Pound argued in the 'teens and twenties, that the poetry of the latest age is distended and overblown, that it has sacrificed craft to "Caesar's affairs":

> Annalists will continue to record Roman reputa-
> tions,
> Celebrities from the Trans-Caucasus will belaud
> Roman celebrities
> And expound the distentions of Empire,
> But for something to read in normal circumstances?
> For a few pages brought down from the forked hill
> unsullied?

And like Pound, Propertius believes fate has destined him to purify the Muse:

> Now if ever it is time to cleanse Helicon;
> to lead Emathian horses afield . . .

Propertius shows amusing ambivalence toward the epic. However much he mocks the Virgilian organ tones and imperial stance, he yearns to sing the larger strain and change from reeds to trumpets. He projects a poem celebrating the excitements of Caesar Augustus' expanding empire:

> The primitive ages sang Venus,
> the last sings of a tumult,
> And I also will sing war when this matter of a girl
> is exhausted.

I with my beak hauled ashore would proceed in a
 more stately manner,
My Muse is eager to instruct me in a new gamut, or
 gambetto,
Up, up my soul, from your lowly cantilation,
 put on a timely vigour.

O august Pierides! Now for a large-mouthed product . . .

This is *Propertius through Pound.* The *Homage* paraphrases and fills out Propertius' text with the emotional contents of Pound's temperament. Pound enlarges and applies to himself the self-mockery and heavy irony he discovers. The originality of the *Homage* rests in this technique of expanding the feeling, of making something intensely personal out of the Latin. Pound also wanted to move from personal involvement and lyric form—*Mauberley* is essentially a suite of lyrics—to larger themes. Pound's and Propertius' comic trepidations have sudden relevance; did Pound suspect that his epic notions were tinged with megalomania, that the projected *Cantos* might come off merely as "a large-mouthed product"?

Propertius writes in the meter common to Latin, and earlier Greek, elegiac poets. This meter, rather than any particular subject or emotion, names as elegiac the poetry of Horace, Tibullus, and Propertius. An elegiac poem consists of a series of couplets; each couplet is made up of a line of hexameter followed by a line of pentameter:

Sunt aliquid Manes: letum non omnia finit,
 Luridaque evictos effugit umbra rogos.
Cynthia namque meo visast incumbere fulcro,
 Murmur ad extremae nuper humata viae,
Cum mihi somnus ab exequiis penderet amoris,
 Et quererer lecti frigida regna mei.

Propertius, 4.7.

Like its English cousin, the heroic couplet, the elegiac holds in two lines a complete thought in a finished syntactical unit.

Propertius handles the couplet with great expressiveness and colloquial vigor. In the first line below, the spondaic third foot, divided at the caesura, is a metrical doubletake, a gasp of comic fright when Propertius sees Cynthia's "pale shade":

Sūnt ălĭ | quīd Mā | nēs : || lē | tūm nōn | ōmnĭă | fīnĭt,

Lūrĭdă | (quē) e vīc | tōs || ēffŭgĭt | ūmbră rŏ | gōs . . .

The pentameter parodies the more dignified hexameter; it actually is a truncated hexameter with a catalectic foot before the caesura and in the last position.

Pound freely renders Propertius' meter and catches the abrupt syntactical patterning, the quick turns of speech, and the overall descending movement. Pound makes no attempt to reproduce the quantitative structure but rather demonstrates his usual genius in handling syllabic weights and durations. Comparison gives valuable information:

> Nox media, et dominae mihi venit epistula nostrae:
> Tibure me missa iussit adesse mora,
> Candida qua geminas ostendunt culmina turres,
> Et cadit in patulos lympha Aniena lacus.
> Quid faciam? obductis committam mene tenebris,
> Ut timeam audaces in mea membra manus?

Propertius, 3.16.

This is Pound's version:

> Midnight, and a letter comes to me from
> our mistress:
> Telling me to come to Tibur:
> *At* once!!
> "Bright tips reach up from twin towers,
> "Anienan spring water falls into flat-spread pools."
>
> What *is* to be done about it?
> Shall I entrust myself to entangled shadows,
> Where bold hands may do violence to my person?

Pound maintains Propertius' dialectic: the sudden pause and question, the balance of one line against the other. Pound gets the sense of extreme compression which the Latin conveys and the sense of exact rhythmic balancing. In the Latin we have metrical echos:

Nōx mĕ dĭ | ā; Quīd fă cĭ | ām; Ūt tĭ mĕ | ām.

Pound also balances "bits of rhythm": *Midnight; At once; Bright tips.* The spondee becomes a structural element. Sound values also carry over into the English; the sharp *s's* of

Tibure me missa iussit adesse mora

become equally sharp *t's:*

Telling me to come to Tibur:
At once!!

What prosodic inspiration Pound takes from Propertius can be seen in comparing other passages. The exquisite balance of the Latin, the give and take of hexameter and pentameter stand behind these lines:

The moon will carry his candle,
the stars will point out the stumbles,
Cupid will carry lighted torches before him
and keep mad dogs off his ankles.

Behind these, the magnificent sonority of the Latin vowels:

For long night comes upon you
and a day when no day returns.
Let the gods lay chains upon us
so that no day shall unbind them.

Nox tibi longa venit nec reditura dies.
Atque utinam haerentes sic nos vincire catena
Velles, ut numquam solveret ulla dies!

Occasionally Pound falls into the actual swing of the Latin, and we have the best English equivalents of the quantitative hexameter:

Death has his tooth in the lot,
Avernus lusts for the lot of them,
Beauty is not eternal, no man has perennial fortune,
Slow foot, or swift foot, death delays but for a
season.

5

The *Cantos* enlarge upon the material and method of the *Homage*. Pound's scope widens from Augustan Rome to nearly all history; anachronism, which has merely local and comic functions in the *Homage*,

> My cellar does not date from Numa Pompilius,
> Nor bristle with wine jars,
> Nor is it equipped with a frigidaire patent...

develops into a major principle of composition in the *Cantos*. The mingling of myth and personal history, of gossip and chronicle, of indisputable fact with the wildest prejudice has qualitative affinities with the adaptations from Propertius. But in length and intention the *Cantos* loom as a monstrous expansion; their sheer bulk dwarfs the earlier poem. I stress the importance of length; the *Cantos* raise special questions of syntax and prosody, and more crucially than the *Homage*, questions of structural coherence. I also stress Pound's "history" and his anachronistic mode of presenting it.

Pound's intended purpose in the *Cantos* is to tell the truth about History; the jacket of *Section: Rock Drill, Cantos 85–95* announces that the *Cantos* are

> —the tale of the tribe... it is their purpose to give the true meaning of history as one man has found it: in the annals of ancient China, in the Italian Renaissance, in the letters and diaries of Jefferson, the Adamses and Van Buren, in the personalities of his own time. The lies of history must be exposed; the truth must be hammered home by reiteration, with the insistence of a rock-drill.

The *Cantos are* history: completely, aggressively, staggeringly so. They bulge with facts and supposed facts, teem with men and events. Much of the substance of the *Cantos* we recognize as direct chronicle, the matrix out of which rational histories have been written. Pound gives the documents, letters, papers, and anecdotes. It would be hard to deny that the *Cantos* are "the tale of the tribe."

Pound's peculiar telling of the tale, however, creates vexing formal difficulties and becomes an instrument for destroying the *Cantos* as poetry. Pound sets out to annihilate sequential time in his epic by fixing events in deliberate temporal disorder. His compositional method depends on the wholesale use of anachronism; in the prophetic mind of the poet, "All ages are contemporaneous."[26] Queen Elizabeth I, von Moltke, Andrew Jackson, and St. Ambrose, the fourth-century Bishop of Milan, simultaneously live in a timeless world:

"JESUS!!"

quoth the Queen, 1584 anno Domini, "sterling,
pund sterling how much? 13,000. It is not to be looked for."
From ploughing of fields is justice,
and if words be not solid
Von Moltke, Fontainebleau, 1867, "a stag hunt"
"In locis desertis

"laetamur, silvis in mediis.
"tondentur, occiditis, mulgentur
"quibus agrum colitis.
"Cruorem funditis,
"carnes intrinsecus vos onerant
"Corporum sepulcra mortuorum viventia."
Ambrose "De Brachmanorum".
"That Virginia be sovreign," said Andy Jackson
"never parted with . . ."
Oh GAWD ! ! ! that tenth section . . .
"any portion of . . ."
DAMN IT.

Canto 100

This passage, from one of the latest *Cantos,* is an extreme example of temporal distortion and historical compression. But an earlier instance, from *Canto III,* illustrates Pound's odd historiography: that the past need not be considered in its conventional chronological order and its putative pattern of cause and effect.

My Cid rode up to Burgos,
Up to the studded gate between two towers,
Beat with his lance butt, and the child came out,
Una niña de nueve años,
To the little gallery over the gate, between the towers,
Reading the writ, voce tinnula:

That no man speak to, feed, help Ruy Diaz,
On pain to have his heart out, set on a pike spike
And both his eyes torn out, and all his goods sequestered,
"And here, Myo Cid, are the seals,
The big seal and the writing."
And he came down from Bivar, Myo Cid,
With no hawks left there on their perches,
And no clothes there in the presses,
And left his trunk with Raquel and Vidas,
That big box of sand, with the pawn-brokers,
To get pay for his menie;
Breaking his way to Valencia.
Ignez da Castro murdered, and a wall
Here stripped, here made to stand.
Drear waste, the pigment flakes from the stone,
Or plaster flakes, Mantegna painted the wall.
Silk tatters, "Nec Spe Nec Metu."

The passage deals with three eras: eleventh-century Spain, fourteenth-century Portugal, and fifteenth-century Italy. There is a probably accidental progression from the eleventh to the fifteenth century; but it is not chronology which affords this passage unity. The historical instances exemplify pathetic change; we witness the Cid's frustrated heroism, the cruel and senseless murder of Ignez de Castro, and the slow decay of a fresco by Mantegna. Emotion and rhythm hold these lines together. As long as Pound maintains rhythmic force, a prosody which the ear can hear, the *Cantos* possess at least the unity of tone and sound.

The opening of *Canto I* augurs well for the prosodic health of the whole poem. The measure is that of *The Seafarer,* strong-stress meter with four heavy beats to the line. (These lines are scanned in Chapter II.) Pound's first choice of metric was a good one; the strong-stress line sustains narrative, modulates with easy fluency from formal to gamey speech, and escapes the iambic domination which has crippled the long poem ever since Milton. While it is hard to say what exactly the carrying prosody of the *Cantos* is, it is easy to discover what it is not. Blank verse or any variation on the iambic norm figure minimally in the *Cantos.* We have occasional passages of Browningesque "stretched blank verse,"

> We also made ghostly visits, and the stair
> That knew us, found us again on the turn of it,
> Knocking at empty rooms, seeking for buried beauty . . .

but the iambic movement is weakened by tri-syllabic substitution.

Pound combines the strong-stress meter with other, freer rhythms. *Canto III* opens in Pound's most luminous and limpid "quantities":

> I sat on the Dogana's steps . . .
>
> Gods float in the azure air,
> Bright gods and Tuscan, back before dew was shed.
> Light: and the first light, before ever dew was fallen.
> Panisks, and from the oak, dryas,
> And from the apple, mælid,
> Through all the wood, and the leaves are full of voices . . .

The same rhythms move through *Canto IV:*

> The silver mirrors catch the bright stones and flare,
> Dawn, to our waking, drifts in the green cool light;
> Dew-haze blurs, in the grass, pale ankles moving.
> Beat, beat, whirr, thud in the soft turf
> under the apple trees . . .

We recognize Pound's prosodical signature, the dactylic-anapestic and spondaic paradigms:

Líght: and the | fírst líght, | before év | er déw | was fáll | en . . .

Dáwn, to our | wák ing, | drífts in the | gréen cóol | líght . . .

Béat, béat, | whírr, thúd, | in the sóft túrf . . .

This signature is written on almost any page of the *Cantos;* for random verification I cite and scan lines from all sections of the poem:

Évil and | fúrther | évil, and a | cúrse cúrsed |
on our chíl | dren . . .

Canto II

And the síl | ver béaks | rí sing and | cróss ing.
Stóne trées, | whíte and | róse-whíte | in the dárk | ness . . .

Canto XVII

And in Áu | gust that yéar | díed Pópe | Al es sán | dro
Bór | gia . . .

Canto XXX

The shá dow | of the tént's péak | tréads on its | cór ner peg
márk ing the | hóur. ∧ The | móon splít, | no clóud | néarer
than | Lúcca . . .

Canto LXXVIII

Till the blúe gráss | turn yél | low
and the yél | low léaves | flóat in | áir . . .

Canto 99

Chárity | Í have had | sóme tímes |
Í cannot | máke it | flów thrú . . .

Canto 116

Our "scansions" lay the lines down in Procrustean beds; we are not reading structural meter but showing an approximate rhythmical direction. A predominant dactylic-spondaic foot generates a falling rhythm—which prevails in the *Cantos* when rhythm is present.

Throughout the *Cantos* the sustaining movement is intermittent. No unifying mode of versification establishes itself. Beginning with *Canto XXX,* the initial rhythmic impetus begins to falter and is broken by large blocks of prose. Beginning with *Canto LII,* Chinese ideograms and other visual devices gradually supplement audible prosodic means. Without an overall *sounding* rhythm, syntax (never Pound's strong point) staggers. An audible rhythm can cover the lack of syntactical closeness: truncated word groups, omitted articles, and shorthand grammar may have charm when rhythmically supported:

Sun up; work
sundown; to rest
dig well and drink of the water
dig field; eat of the grain
Imperial power is? and to us what is it?

The fourth; the dimension of stillness.
And the power over wild beasts.

Canto XLIX

As long as we hear spondees and dactyls, the lack of syntactical closeness is not serious. But when the rhythm peters out and no longer carries Pound's disconnected syntax, we have this as historical narrative:

Lord North, purblind to the rights of a
continent, eye on a few London merchants . . .
no longer saw redcoat
as brother or as a protector
(Boston about the size of Rapallo)
scarce 16,000,
habits of freedom now formed
even among those who scarcely got so far as analysis
so about 9 o'c in the morning Lard Narf wuz bein'
impassible . . .

Canto LXII

We have for a prosody a tone of voice, for syntax a tangle of unconnected references.

Pound's defenders have advanced the theory of the ideogram to uncover the method and justify the coherence of the *Cantos*. Hugh Kenner tells us for the *Cantos,* "Plot, in the Dickensian sense, is obsolete." Mr. Kenner also tells us that "a philosophical system, a chronological or geographical ordering of events . . . would be no more relevant to the *Cantos* than a chain of anagrams."[27] Instead of narrative or discursive structure, an authentic syntax, the *Cantos* achieve structural unity through the ideogrammatic method. Pound does not present merely abstract words, emptied of their "thingness" and yoked together by the sterile articulations of formal grammar; he presents ideograms.

The application of the ideogram to English language and poetic frankly baffles me. Deep down, I suspect snobbery and charlatanism. Pound's disciples argue that the unity of the *Cantos* is like the unity of Chinese written characters—and so much the worse for you if you can't read Chinese. But, obviously, English poetry is not structured as the Chinese character is written. The Chinese character presumably pictures "the real thing" or "ideas in action." The ideogram signifying *man* "looks like" a man—although few Chinese immediately recognize the pictographic origins of an ideogram but conceptualize or convert the symbol into the appropriate sound. In itself the ideogram is soundless; the Chinese written language can be read by any literate Chinese, regardless of the dialect he speaks. A direct visual correspondence once existed between ideogram and thing, thought, or action, but the correspondences are now highly stylized.[28] English has no such correspondences. No English word "looks like" the thing it signifies; English orthography is a system of conventional signs for sounds. The actual *thing* a word is, is sound; as physical objects words possess only phonetic reality. The way words look on the page has no relevance to what they mean; English, after all, is not Chinese.

Yet many admirers of the *Cantos* argue their "ideogrammatic unity." It is as if the poem were written in pictures, not words. "Thinking by ideogram," as Pound actually practices it, means a poetry of vivid images and strong ideas functioning with a minimum of syntax. Ideas and images can achieve a structure of sorts through mere juxtaposition:

In a Station of the Metro

The apparition of these faces in the crowd;
Petals on a wet, black bough.

Here "ideogrammatic method" means poetry without complete sentences. The absence of verb and preposition enhances both rhythm and significance; a certain mystery evaporates if we supply the implied copula and relational word:

The apparition of these faces in the crowd
[Is like] Petals on a wet, black bough.

No harm comes if we want to see this as vaguely *analogous* to Chinese writing; the two images have spatial and emotional relationships. Grammar, however, is not missing; it is automatically supplied by the reader.

"In a Station of the Metro" comes from Pound's 1912–14 period and is often quoted as the characteristic Imagist poem. Later, when "ideogrammatic method" takes over in the *Cantos,* we see that the long poem continually breaks down into shorter Imagist poems, often no longer than one or two lines:

> a man on whom the sun has gone down
> the ewe, he said had such a pretty look in her eyes;
> and the nymph of the Hagoromo came to me,
>   as a corona of angels
> one day were clouds banked on Taishan
>   or in glory of sunset
>   and tovarish blessed without aim
> wept in the rainditch at evening
>   Sunt lumina
>
> *Canto LXXIV*

Each line or two articulates a single image; nothing, not even an implied grammar or an emotional consistency, articulates one image with another. To say that the coherence of this passage devolves on the method of Chinese writing gives assent to the notion that language can be manipulated like brightly colored bits of glass.

The "ideogrammatic method" parallels the anachronistic historiography of the *Cantos.* A programmatically anachronistic history throws events together regardless of their chronological syntax; the ideogram denies that the formal syntax of language is necessary to poetic logic. Together, ideogram and anachronism turn the *Cantos* into myth, "where past, present, and future are still tied up together; they form an undifferentiated unity and indiscriminate whole. Mythical time has no definite structure; it is still an 'eternal time.' From the point of view of the mythical consciousness the past has never passed away; it is always here and now."[29] In the undifferentiated unity and indiscriminate whole of the *Cantos,* the destruction of chronology makes all history contemporary history and all reality phantasmagorically "present."

As mythical and ideogrammatic method becomes pervasive in the *Cantos,* Pound more and more forgets that significant rhythms must have an aural shape in time. We previously noted the intermittent nature of the initial rhythmic impetus. Pound occasionally recovers the rhythm, as in sections of *The Pisan Cantos.* We find passages in Pound's loveliest "English quantities":

No glass is clearer than are the globes of this flame
what sea is clearer than the pomegranate body
holding the flame?
Pomona, Pomona . . .

Canto LXXIX

We also find Pound in one rare iambic pentameter mood, writing in the stanza and rhythm of *The Rubáiyát:*

Tudor indeed is gone and every rose,
Blood-red, blanch-white that in the sunset glows
Cries: "Blood, Blood, Blood!" against the gothic stone
Of England, as the Howard or Boleyn knows.

Canto LXXX

or blank verse with irregular rhyme:

The ant's a centaur in his dragon world.
Pull down thy vanity, it is not man
Made courage, or made order, or made grace,
Pull down thy vanity, I say pull down.
Learn of the green world what can be thy place
In scaled invention or true artistry,
Pull down thy vanity,
Paquin pull down!
The green casque has outdone your elegance.

Canto LXXXI

But these are infrequent intervals; the dominant rhythm that falters after *Canto XXXI* is undetectable after *Canto LXXXIV*. From *Canto 85* to *109* the "prosody" is oppressively visual, depending on line arrangements, spacing, and stunts. *Canto LXXV* is a page of music; *Cantos 85, 86,* and *98* are largely printed ideograms; *Cantos 93* and *97* fiddle with hieroglyphics.[30] The greater "unity" of *Section: Rock Drill (Cantos 85–95)* and *Thrones (Cantos 96–109)* lies in their orthography. What audible versification exists has little structural power because it affects the ear too faintly to set up "verbal echoes" or create a pattern of expectation.

The *Cantos,* at the time of this writing, remain unfinished. In an interview for *The Paris Review,* Donald Hall questioned Pound about the progress of his epic. Pound's replies were fuzzy, contradictory. It seems clear Pound no longer separates himself from his poem; the *Cantos* will conclude only with Pound's death:

INTERVIEWER

> Since your internment, you've published three collections of *Cantos, Thrones* just recently. You must be near the end. Can you say what you are going to do in the remaining *Cantos?* . . . Are you more or less stuck?

POUND

> Okay, I am stuck. The question is, am I dead, as Messrs. A.B.C. might wish? In case I conk out, this is provisionally what I have to do: I must clarify obscurities; I must make clearer definite ideas or dissociations. I must find a verbal formula to combat the rise of brutality—the principle of order versus the split atom. . . .
>
> I don't know. There's need of elaboration, of clarification, but I don't know that a comprehensive revision is in order. There is no doubt that the writing is too obscure as it stands, but I hope that the order of ascension in the Paradiso will be toward a greater limpidity. . . .[31]

Cantos 115 and *116,* published in the same issue of *The Paris Review,* do achieve a greater limpidity and a new measure of coherence. The ideograms and other visual contrivances have disappeared; in their place we find some of Pound's magical quantities:

> I have brought the great ball of crystal,
>   who can lift it?
> Can you enter the great acorn of light?
>
>   but the beauty is not the madness
> Tho my errors and wrecks lie about me.
>
>   and I cannot make it cohere . . .
>
> *Canto 116*

"I cannot make it cohere . . ." *Canto 116* laments Pound's inability to bring the *Cantos* into clarity and

> . . . affirm the gold thread in the pattern . . .

And no better criticism of the *Cantos* exists than these last lines with their pathos, agony, and essential honesty:

> Charity I have had sometimes,
> I cannot make it flow thru.
> A little light like a rush light
> to lead back splendour.

6

Before Pound returned to Italy, he made a recording of *Cantos I, IV, XXXVI,* and *LXXXIV.*[32] Pound is a remarkable reader: his voice is vigorously masculine and extraordinarily well modulated. He affects an Irish brogue (at least I *think* he affects it; I have never met Pound, but I assume he normally speaks the American dialect), heavily trilling the *r's* and allowing his voice to fall at the ends of lines. The effect is a beautifully stylized chant which holds firmly to metrical bedrock—when such bedrock is offered.

Pound's voice emphasizes the four-beat structure of *Canto I.* In these lines:

> Bore sheep aboard her, and our bodies also
> Heavy with weeping, and winds from sternward
> Bore us out onward with bellying canvas,
> Circe's this craft, the trim-coifed goddess . . .

he marks with slight but perceptible stresses the alliterated *b's* of the first linc and the repeated *c's* of the fourth line. He holds the caesuras for at least the length of a stressed syllable, carefully balancing the half-lines. In the line:

> Thus with stretched sail, we went over sea till day's end . . .

Pound pauses significantly on the stressed *sea* and reads the four light syllables *we went ov-er* with quick, even precision. He declaims, also with significant pauses and emphases:

> But first Elpenor came, our friend Elpenor . . .

The line startles with its unforeseen expressiveness. The labials *f* and *p* are the metrical checkpoints; Pound trills the *r's* of *first* and *friend* and pronounces Elpenor in the Greek fashion, 'Ελπήνορ, prolonging the stressed πή.

Canto IV is a suite of natural sounds. We hear a chorus of nymphs and satyrs:

> Beat, beat, whirr, thud, in the soft turf
> under the apple trees . . .

We hear the swallows crying in the tongueless voice of Procne, mourning her slaughtered son Itys. By homonymic metamorphosis *Itis* becomes *It is:*

> 'All the while, the while, swallows crying:
> Itys!
> 'It is Cabestan's heart in the dish.'
> 'It is Cabestan's heart in the dish?'

Unwitting cannibalism links the myth of Tereus and the story of Guillaume de Cabestan. Procne fed the flesh of Itys to her murderous husband Tereus; the jealous husband of Marguerite fed her the heart of Cabestan, her troubador lover. Pound's reading catches the eerie cry of the swallows:

> 'Tis. 'Tis. Ytis! . . .

Pound unvoices the *s* of *'Tis,* hissing the syllables in sharp onomatopoeia.

Two superb lines of *Canto IV* become audible rhythmic echoes as Pound's voice takes full account of their prosodic form: first the eleven syllable

> The empty armour shakes as the cygnet moves . . .

and its answer, in equal syllables twenty lines later,

> A scarlet flower is cast on the blanch-white stone . . .

In both lines the caesura follows the sixth syllable and an anapestic foot immediately follows the caesura. The two lines are completely realized Imagist poems related to each other by their rhythmic form: music for syntax once again.

Pound's delivery of *Canto LXXXIV* tries to compensate for

its prosodic disorder. Since he no longer has an audible metric to guide him—neither the strong-stress lines of *Canto I* nor the quantities of *Canto IV*—he reads dramatically. His mimicry of Senator Bankhead's Southern dialect is very funny:

> 'an'doan you think he chop an' change all the time
> stubborn az a mule, sah, stubborn as a MULE . . .'

A tone of ironic deprecation, projected by heavily falling cadences, characterizes these political and personal sallies:

> Thus the solons, in Washington,
> on the executive, and on the country, a.d. 1939 . . .
>
> and Mr Sinc Lewis has not
>   and Bartók has left us . . .
>
> and that Vandenberg has read Stalin, or Stalin, John Adams
> is, at the mildest, unproven . . .

But Pound makes no palpable satirical hits with his comic changes of voice; he sounds merely undignified and peevish. At several places he eases into the homespun accents of Lionel Barrymore playing a garrulous, daft old man. The effect is embarrassing.

Canto LXXXIV ends with an often-quoted couplet: we find relief in this sudden shift back to metrical stability:

> If the hoar frost grip thy tent
> Thou wilt give thanks when night is spent.

The music returns to Pound's voice as it briefly rediscovers formal poetic diction and the security of rhymed tetrameter. Pound descends from the soap box and once again is the poet, affirming the thread in the pattern and entering the circles of light.

VII

T. S. Eliot and the Music of Poetry

I

Eliot has given us unforgettable rhythms—rhythms which echo and re-echo in the mind's ear. We need only go to our memories for prosodical touchstones: lines grasped long ago by the "auditory imagination" and never lost. They recover an emotion from personal or racial origins, recall some shuddering gesture of the spirit, or catch the flat intonation of a bored voice. It is the heard rhythms which animate these lines:

> Where worried bodies of drowned men drift down in the
> green silence . . .
>
> Whispers and small laughter between leaves and
> hurrying feet
> Under sleep, where all waters meet.
>
> The awful daring of a moment's surrender
> Which an age of prudence can never retract
>
> Let Mr. Sweeney continue his story.
> I assure you, Sir, we are very inter*es*ted.

Eliot's rhythms, capable of such variety in movement and sonority, return us to the musical function of prosody. No modern poet has so effectively used rhythm to evoke a "knowledge of how feelings go"; no rhythms have shown such power to summon emotion to the forefront of consciousness.

Eliot has been aware of prosody-as-music. Whether he speaks, dry-mouthed and stammering,

And no rock
If there were rock
And also water
And water
A spring . . .

The Waste Land

or smoothly sings of a frozen moment, "suspended in time":

In windless cold that is the heart's heat,
Reflecting in a watery mirror
A glare that is blindness in the early afternoon . . .

Little Gidding

the patterns of stress and pause, quantity, dynamics, and syntax reach down and "make conceivable" the richness of the inner life of feeling. Eliot has quarreled with Pater's ethical notions, but Eliot's prosody—the function of the "auditory imagination"—aspires toward the condition of music.

Eliot does not approach the condition of music in order to submerge his ideas in his form or merely to create pleasing sounds. To Eliot "the music of poetry" means a great deal more than melodious verse, achieved through smooth textures and verbal tone color. The music of poetry is not "the elemental sound of brasses, strings, or wood-winds, but the intellectual and written word in all its glory—music of perfect fullness and clarity, the totality of universal relationships."[1] Alliteration and assonance, or such onomatopoeia as "Forlorn! the very word is like a bell" are not the essential music of poetry: it lies in "the totality of universal relationships."

Eliot's verse first establishes these relationships through the articulating structures of syntax. Syntax, the order of words as they arrange themselves into patterns of meaning, is the analogue to harmony in music. Like harmony, syntax generates tension and relaxation, the feelings of expectation and fulfillment which make up the dynamics of poetic life. Susanne Langer remarks:

> The tension which music achieves through dissonance, and the reorientation in each new resolution to harmony, find their equivalents in the suspensions and periodic decisions of propositional sense in poetry. Literal sense, not euphony, is the 'harmonic structure' of poetry; word melody in literature is more akin to tone color in music.[2]

Syntax gives us the arc of "literal sense," the articulations of meaning. Like harmony in music, syntax makes connections, strengthens ideas, and relates thematic material. Eliot himself emphasizes that music in poetry does not inhere in word melody and tone color, but in the harmony of meanings and connections:

> It would be a mistake, however, to assume that all poetry ought to be melodious, or that melody is more than one of the components of the music of words. . . . The music of a word is, so to speak, at a point of intersection: it arises from its relation first to the words immediately preceding and following it, and indefinitely to the rest of its context; and from another relation, that of its immediate meaning in that context to all the other meanings which it had in other contexts, to its greater or less wealth of association.[3]

The reverberation of words, their semantic resonances, are the shifting tones in the harmony of intersections and associations.

Eliot's syntax carries the bass line of his prosody. Through a deliberate and idiosyncratic use of repeated grammar and repeated words, Eliot achieves qualities common to both music and poetry—the feelings of arrest and motion, of beginnings and endings, of striving and stillness. "Musical syntax" forms a basic element in the Eliotic style and method. Although Eliot had experimented with musical forms and techniques in his earlier verse, we can hear the richest and most moving syntactical music in *Four Quartets.* I offer first the opening lines of *Burnt Norton:*

> Time present and time past
> Are both perhaps present in time future,
> And time future contained in time past.
> If all time is eternally present
> All time is unredeemable.

These lines present neither images nor metaphors, the supposed quintessential materials of poetry. Everything is handled through the silent rhythms of syntax and the audible rhythms of isochronism and strong-stress meter. We hear the echoing repetitions of individual words and phrases; we hear the more subtle repetitions of syntactical structure, the persistently unvarying grammatical forms. The syntax is static: the noun *Time,* the modifiers *past, present, future,* the copulatives *is* or *are,* all follow in strict order. We hear the literal sense modified by each repetition of word and phrase;

we hear how each repetition fits into an overall pattern of incantation.

Note the grammatical marking time in these lines:

> If all time is eternally present
> All time is unredeemable . . .

Eliot tells how time can be immovable, without direction. But there comes a *point* where Eliot must resolve his meaning, where a composer would introduce a cadence to tell us where his music is going, harmonically speaking. Then Eliot changes his syntax; he drops the copulatives and allows the movement of the preceding lines to pivot on the transitive verb *point:*

> What might have been and what has been
> Point to one end, which is always present . . .

Eliot has suspended syntactical movement by using only the verbs *is* and *are* for nine lines running. The verb *point* releases us into a new idea, and we modulate into a new syntactical unit:

> Footfalls echo in the memory
> Down the passage which we did not take
> Towards the door we never opened
> Into the rose-garden. My words echo
> Thus, in your mind . . .

Now the verbs are active; the repeated *echo* develops a special burden of sound and meaning. And we hear again a haunting syntactical melody: "Down the passage . . . Towards the door . . . Into the rose-garden. . . ."

Another kind of music is heard in the lyrical fourth section of *Burnt Norton:*

> Will the sunflower turn to us, will the clematis
> Stray down, bend to us; tendril and spray
> Clutch and cling?
> Chill
> Fingers of yew be curled
> Down on us? After the kingfisher's wing
> Has answered light to light, and is silent,
>   the light is still
> At the still point of the turning world.

We have the insistent repetitions as in the first section: "turn to us . . . bend to us . . . Down on us." These are the melodies. We have, however, an effect which, to quote Mrs. Langer again, involves "the suspense of literal meaning by a sustained ambiguity resolved in a long-awaited key word."[4] Reading the penultimate line, we briefly poise on the word *still*. Meter and rhyme (with *chill*) enforce our usual tendency to pause slightly at the end of the line, and we understand *still* as an adjective modifying *light*. Moving down to the next line, we see that *still* is more exactly an adverb whose effect is strong enough to modify the sense of both lines. The light is *even yet* at the still point of the turning world.

We realize the ambiguity here, and how the word functions as a grammatical pivot on which the movement and meaning of the lines turn. The effect is analogous to an ambiguous harmonic structure which hovers between tonalities, a structure which might take any of a number of possible directions, but which is suddenly resolved by an unexpected cadence.

In *East Coker* we note another "effect of harmony"; we might call it "the illusion of tonality." The poem opens in this key:

> In my beginning is my end. In succession
> Houses rise and fall, crumble, are extended,
> Are removed, destroyed, restored, or in their place
> Is an open field, or a factory, or a by-pass . . .

At the end of the first section, we have:

> Dawn points, and another day
> Prepares for heat and silence. Out at sea
>   the dawn wind
> Wrinkles and slides. I am here
> Or there, or elsewhere. In my beginning.

Again Eliot builds tension through repeated syntax: ". . . or in their place . . . or a factory . . . or a by-pass." This pattern is repeated, in diminution, just before Eliot restates his theme: "I am here / Or there, or elsewhere. In my beginning." The familiar, almost expected, syntax acts as a return section, preparing us for the new entrance of the theme in its initial "tonality." We stress this musical preparation through syntax. Many have recognized Eliot's use of repeated thematic material without realizing how complex Eliot's musical procedures actually are. At the end of

East Coker, we hear the same hesitant syntax announcing the theme, in inversion:

> The wave cry, the wind cry, the vast waters
> Of the petrel and the porpoise. In my end is
> my beginning.

The striking effect created by each return of the theme is not gained through simple verbal repetition or modification. It is gained through the manipulation of syntax which gives this "illusion of tonality." Eliot's procedure parallels sonata form where the principal tonality is reestablished at the end of the movement, and the main theme makes its final appearance.

We "hear" Eliot's music in the meanings of words and the structures of grammar. I qualify *hear* with quotes because the rhythms of meaning and syntax are silent; they achieve tension and resolution not in phonological but in intellectual realms. The explicit, heard music of Eliot's verse sounds in Eliot's meters and the rhythmic effects occurring within the context of formally ordered metrical patterns. I shall treat later the more technical aspects of Eliot's meters: his varied handling of syllable-stress and strong-stress meter; his uses of open rhythm and nonmetrical techniques. However, we return to *Burnt Norton* for a moment to examine the musical aspects of Eliot's explicit sound patterns and the rhythms they inspire.

The falling strong-stress lines of *Burnt Norton's* opening (see Chapter II for scansion) develop a single rhythmic idea, a motif which slowly accumulates emotional force. Individual word groups form themselves into apparent isochronic units; the four-beat strong-stress line resembles common measure (4/4) in music. If we assign note values to Eliot's word groups, we get something like this:[5]

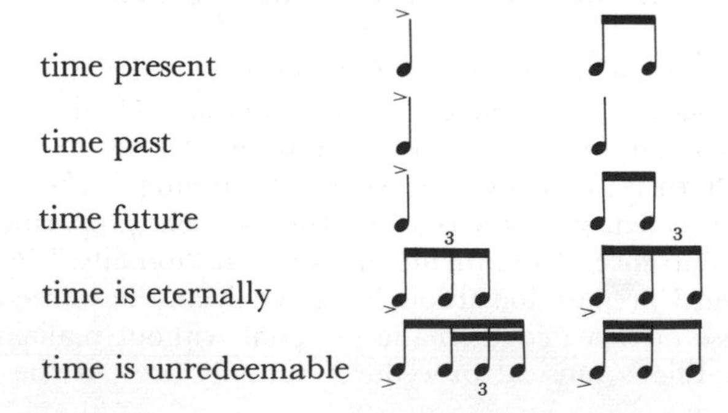

We gave earlier an example from Spender's *Vienna* (see pp. 39–40) where repeated rhythmic motifs formed "interior melodies." (Actually, Spender imitates Eliot in more than matters of technique.) Eliot's accelerating rhythm persists in our memories, modifying meaning and feeling: as the units of the phrase expand, we feel the arc of propositional sense tighten. The rhythm quickens with the thought. The statements about the nature of time in the first three lines are followed by the taut proposition of lines four and five: "If all time is eternally present, / All time is unredeemable." This is awesome; the notion challenges the imagination. We accept the opening statements as curious, teasing, the speculations of a poet with a taste for conundrums. But lines four and five have accumulated the tension (through repeated syntax as well as rhythmic expansion) appropriate to the idea: that everything we have done is still *doing,* that everything we *shall do* is already taking place. Metaphysics is implicit in the paradigms of verbs; the possibilities of human action (what might have been; what has been) are conjugated in Eliot's syntax. The whole grows to thought in slow rhythmic expansion, moving along the metric closest to musical structure. The ear hears a gently insistent four-beat line; the imagination responds to the infinitely subtle music of feeling.

2

In the latter part of this chapter, I hope to show more precisely the musicality of *Four Quartets.* The point I wish to establish is that Eliot, through prosody, and a syntax so intricately patterned that it must be reckoned a part of Eliot's prosody, evokes a complexity of feeling in ways that music evokes comparable states in the minds of sensitive listeners. Eliot extends the limitations of language by entering the domain of another art. He uses syntax and prosody like music to enlarge the available means of expression. *Four Quartets* represents Eliot's most conscious and deliberate attempt to use musical method; but from the very beginning of his career, Eliot has used sounds and rhythms in specifically musical ways.

This music has sounded in a predominantly metrical context. Some early and obviously deaf critics labeled Eliot a "free-verse poet" and since first misconceptions, like first impressions, doggedly persist, many still think of Eliot as a writer of unmetered verse.[6] Perhaps the general naiveté about matters prosodical has never been so clearly displayed as when the critics wondered at the "faintness" of the verse of *The Cocktail Party.* Some even suggested that Eliot's writing in lines was snobbish convention: *The Cocktail Party* was prose and why not write it as such? Yet *The Cocktail Party* contains lines as thumping in their metrical effect as any Eliot has written:

> PETER: I like that story.
> CELIA: I love that story.
> ALEX: *I'm* never tired of hearing that story.

Eliot has given occasional encouragement to the notion that he is, after all, really a simple fellow, unlearned in the techniques of his craft: "I have never been able to retain the names of feet and metres, or to pay the proper respect to the accepted rules of scansion."[7] But the Eliotic pose of unsophistication fools no one. In other critical writings Eliot makes clear he knows an iamb from a spondee; *Old Possum's Book of Practical Cats* displays Eliot's amazing virtuosity in rarely used, complicated meters which Eliot may not be able to name but certainly uses in accordance with whatever the "accepted rules of scansion" may be. And in an early essay, "Reflections on *Vers Libre,*" Eliot explains the principles informing his own prosodical practices.

The essay attacks *vers libre* as a negative phenomenon. Eliot points out that *vers libre,* as practiced by the Imagists, was not a verse form, but often a name used to rationalize verse that had no form. ". . . and we conclude that the division between Conservative Verse and *Vers Libre* does not exist, for there is only good verse, bad verse, and chaos." Eliot's conclusion is similar to his often-quoted, "no verse is *libre* for the man who wants to do a good job." Art allows no easy freedom. The poet, to achieve a masterly prosody, cannot abjure meter; he may work toward formal metric or away from it, but

> . . . the ghost of some simple metre should lurk behind the arras in even the "freest" verse; to advance menacingly as we doze, and withdraw as we rouse. Or, freedom is only truly freedom when it appears against the background of an artificial limitation.
>
> So much for metre. There is no escape from metre; there is only mastery.[8]

Sister Mary Martin Barry, after carefully scanning a significant body of Eliot's verse, confirms that Eliot has never escaped from meter: "... his general practice is well within the limits of metrical verse."[9] While many readers have long suspected what Sister Barry has painstakingly proven, it is good to have her statistical confirmations. Perhaps even Yvor Winters, who speaks contemptuously of Eliot's prosody, might be reassured to discover that Eliot writes scannable verse.[10]

Eliot trained himself on the meters of the late nineteenth-century poets; a stanza from "Circe's Palace," one of Eliot's undergraduate pieces, has the unmistakeable Swinburnian swing:

> Around her fountain which flows
> With the voice of men in pain,
> Are flowers that no man knows.
> Their petals are fanged and red
> With hideous streak and stain;
> They sprang from the limbs of the dead.—
> We shall not come here again.
>
> [1908]

The mixture of iambs and anapests is characteristic, as is the delicate ambiguity of stress in the last line:

We shàll ¦ nót | come hére | agáin.

Prufrock's despairing observations gain in pathos and uncertainty through similar metrical "hovering":

I dó | nòt ¦ thínk | that théy | will síng | to mé.

The metrical forms of Tennyson and Swinburne serve Eliot in his earliest volumes—with, of course, a difference. "Prufrock," "Portrait of a Lady," the "Preludes," and "La Figlia che Piange" —the most considerable pieces in the 1917 volume—have a base in the iambic verse of the later nineteenth century. But iambic pentameter exists to be evaded and approximated: "... the most interesting verse which has yet been written in our language has been done ... by taking a very simple form, like the iambic pentameter, and constantly withdrawing from it. ..."[11] The evasion and approximation of iambic pentameter define Eliot's earliest prosodic style; scansion of a short passage from "Portrait of a Lady" gives the technical essentials:

Now | that li | lacs are | in bloom
She has | a bowl | of li | lacs in | her room
And twists | one in | her fin | gers while | she talks.
'Ah, | my friend, | you do | not know, | you do | not know
What life | is, you | who hold | it in | your hands';
(Slow ly | twist ing | the li | lac stalks)
'You let | it flow | from you, | you let | it flow . . .

The passage opens in trochaics (I scan it as iambs with an initial catalexis), but the falling rhythm quickly gives way to regular iambic pentameter in the second line. The sixth line again introduces trochaics with particularly expressive effect.

The opening of "Prufrock" offers a notable example of iambic evasion:

Let us go then, you and I,
When the evening is spread out against the sky
Like a patient etherised upon a table;
Let us go, through certain half-deserted streets,
The muttering retreats
Of restless nights in one-night cheap hotels . . .

Not until the sixth line do we have unambiguous iambics. Four lines begin with two trochaic feet:

Let us | go then . . .

When the | evening . . .

Like a | patient . . .

Let us | go, through . . .

Like the passage from "Portrait of a Lady," we may read these lines of falling rhythm as iambic with initial catalexis:

Let | us go | then, you | and I . . .

Since the total metrical context is iambic, the above scansion is technically "correct," but hardly gives the rhythmic feel of the line.

Lines in "Prufrock" and "Portrait of a Lady" expand away from the pentameter; we find hexameters and even "fourteeners":

> The yellow fog that rubs its back upon the window-panes,
> The yellow smoke that rubs its muzzle on the window-panes . . .
>
> Among the smoke and fog of a December afternoon
> You have the scene arrange itself—as it will seem to do—

Evidently smoke and fog drifted in Eliot's mind to a septenary rhythm. More interesting than the long lines *per se,* are occasional "incursions of prose": lines that scansion only with difficulty can rationalize as verse:

> It is impossible to say just what I mean!
>
> Except when a street piano, mechanical and tired . . .
>
> "And so you are going abroad; and when do you return?"

Eliot seems here to escape the "artificial limitation" of metrical control. But only *seems.* The first line above is anchored by rhyme to the line which follows it:

> It is impossible to say just what I mean!
> But as if a magic lantern threw the nerves in patterns on a
> screen . . .

The secret lies in balance and tact. Eliot follows a lightly metered line (it can be scanned: It ís | im pós | si blé | to sáy | just whát | I méan) with a strong, almost ponderous line of eight feet. The delay until we hear the rhyme creates a characteristic tension, of "indecisions and revisions."

The meter of the "Preludes" is a tight iambic tetrameter. The heavily accented opening lines gain density by emphatic alliteration:

> The winter evening settles down
> With smell of steaks in passageways.
> Six o'clock.

Eliot's "evasions" of his meter consist largely of half-lines, lines of trimeter,

> Of faínt | stale sméls | of béer . . .
> One thínks | of áll | the hánds . . .

or lines where substituted feet predominate:

> And the light crept up between the shutters
> And you heard the sparrows in the gutters,
> You had such a vision of the street
> As the street hardly understands;
> Sitting along the bed's edge, where
> You curled the papers from your hair . . .

Scanning, we find in the first two lines initial trisyllabic feet and "feminine" endings; the third line is the ambiguous iambic-trochaic,

> Yóu | had ¦ súch | a ¦ ví | sion ¦ óf | the ¦ stréet . . .

which we recognize as a metrical signature in Eliot's early verse. The fourth line apparently "springs" out of syllable-stress meter; the two contiguous and nearly equal stresses of the second foot combine with the initial inverted foot to unsettle the metrical base:

> Ás the | stréet hárd | ly ún | der stánds . . .

We hear metrical echoes of this line in "La Figlia che Piange," a poem ". . . which unquestionably meant a good deal to Eliot."[12] Most readers, including myself, have always thought "La Figlia" originated in some love affair of the poet's; however, Mr. John Hayward has reassured us that ". . . 'The Weeping Girl' [is not] a real girl with whom the poet has been in love . . . [but] a statue which Mr. Eliot had looked for in a museum but had failed to find."[13] This kind of pompous and deadly criticism (for which Eliot has been partly responsible) inspires an equally sententious and self-righteous response. But the poem *is* about a lover's parting, whatever the sources of Eliot's inspiration. An essentially romantic theme is complicated by Laforguian ironies and a

Jamesian point of view. We have a triangular affair, involving the girl, her lover, and the poet-observer. The poet turns out to be the lover; he "distances" the painful parting by elaborate staging and a final rhetorical bravado: an affected irony which tries to say. "I really don't care—much!":

> Sometimes these cogitations still amaze
> The troubled midnight and the noon's repose.

The poem's metric betrays an underlying emotional intensity—so carefully concealed by the poet's disguises of attitude and setting. The observer's final "cogitations" settle into regular iambics—his "pose of repose"—but not until after significant disturbances of the meter. The excitement of the opening invocation approaches romantic violence; the third line moves toward the freedom of stress verse without losing its metrical orientation:

> ‸Wéave, | ‸wéave, | the sún | *light* ín | your háir—

Eliot's fingering of the vowels, the unaccented long syllable in the fourth foot, and the equalizing pauses disclose an ear for the music of English quantity as fully accomplished as Pound's. Quantity does not assume in Eliot's verse a point of departure; the norm which is approached or evaded is traditional syllable-stress meter. Pound, whose verse gravitates toward quantitative norms, chides Eliot for not recognizing ". . . metres depending on quantity, alliteration, etc.; Eliot writes as if all metres were measured by accent."[14] Meters measured by accent, however, bear along Eliot's half-submerged but nonetheless vehement feelings; these nervously "sprung" and counterpointed lines belie the poet's surface detachment:

> Ás the | sòul léaves | the bó | dy tórn | and brúised,
> Ás the | mínd | de sérts | the bó | dy ít | has úsed . . .
> Her háir | ó ver | her árms | and her árms fúll | of flów | ers . . .

Springing and counterpointing are possible only in syllable-stress contexts. It is significant that Pound, who prefers the suavities of a quantitative line, has rarely written verse marked by feelings in strong conflict. Pound's emotions are simple; rage and hate and love are relatively unmixed and require direct presentation.

Eliot, whose moods and passions are seldom simple, but rich, subterranean, complex, and uncertain, finds "metres measured by accent" more sensitive to the shifting and subtle movements of the inner life.

3

"Gerontion," the opening poem of Eliot's 1920 volume, ranks as a prosodic triumph. Even the metrically fastidious Yvor Winters grudgingly admires "Gerontion," although he objects on principle to Eliot's "Websterian blank-verse."[15] Actually, "Gerontion" so skillfully blends the rhythms of prose and iambic pentameter that we are unaware of the shifts into metered verse until we analyze them. The first nine lines of "Gerontion" do not define a recognizable metrical form. The old man speaks a sharply accented prose; rhythms grow out of syntactical repetitions:

> Nor fought in the warm rain
> Nor knee deep in the salt marsh, heaving a cutlass . . .

The first pentameter line is

Blís tered | in Brús | sels, pátched | and péeled | in Lón | don . . .

Eliot accurately describes the prosodic method of "Gerontion" as ". . . taking no form at all, and constantly approximating to a very simple one."[16] "Gerontion" does not, like the earlier rhymed monologues, work closely to a pentameter base; rather, it establishes a prose movement which at intense moments tightens into blank verse.

Eliot exploits the freedom of Websterian verse without damaging the poem's prosodic coherence. Websterian verse has its dangers; Winters points out that in Websterian verse,

> . . . the sense of the blank verse norm is feeble; the substitution of feet becomes meaningless because there is so much of it; there is no care for the distribution of secondary accents or lesser syllables; and there is no basic regularity which can be made to support didactic or other linking passages when they are necessary, for the Websterian poet simply does not dare revert over the long distance to formal blank verse, for fear of destroying the cohesion of the poem.[17]

Eliot is hardly feeble, pays the most meticulous attention to lesser accents and syllables, and does, in several passages, revert to blank verse. The success of a prosody may be measured by what a poet can get away with: Eliot's prosody is flexible enough to accommodate such a disorderly mouthful of labials and sibilants as *purposelessly:*

> Think at last
> I have not made this show purposelessly
> And it is not by any concitation
> Of the backward devils.

If Eliot were maintaining rigid blank verse movement, the meter would wrench *purposelessly* out of normal pronunciation, and the line would fall into a hopeless ruin. This would indeed be feeble; but Eliot avoids slackness *and* destructive regularity.

Despite Winters, Eliot's "Websterian verse" shows extreme care in its distribution of secondary accents and lesser syllables. A "rhythmic constant," constructed out of these secondary accents and syllables, develops into a prosodic tune. A grouping of two unstressed syllables followed by two stressed syllables (the Minor Ionic) recurs with obsessive frequency: "in a dry month . . . at the hot gates . . . in the warm rain . . . and the Jew squats . . . in depraved May . . . in the next room . . . of a dry brain. . . ." This repetition functions thematically and gives the poem musical coherence.

When "Gerontion" pleads for understanding, the metric tightens; it is in these passages that we hear the loosened blank verse of the Jacobean dramatists:

> After such knowledge, what forgiveness? Think now
> History has many cunning passages, contrived corridors
> And issues, deceives with whispering ambitions,
> Guides us by vanities. . . .
>
> I that was near your heart was removed therefrom
> To lose beauty in terror, terror in inquisition.
> I have lost my passion: why should I need to keep it
> Since what is kept must be adulterated?
> I have lost my sight, smell, hearing, taste and touch:
> How should I use them for your closer contact?

These great "didactic" passages fall into something less than Marlovian regularity, but they clearly establish the direction of blank verse. The movement is restless; trisyllabic feet, trochaic feet, and hypermetrical syllables occur at many points in the line. Perhaps these lines do not possess the proper firmness to please Winters. I might object to them if I felt, as Winters feels, that there is some intimate and evident connection between firm blank verse and proper literary morality. But even Winters admits that Eliot handles the Websterian verse of "Gerontion" ". . . with great skill."

"Gerontion" makes a prosodic leap; its advance over the earlier rhymed monologues is considerable. It is in "Gerontion," where Eliot abandons the plangent rhyming of "Prufrock" and "Portrait of a Lady," that his studies in the Jacobean dramatists yielded important metrical results.[18] The decision to give up rhyme is signaled in "Reflections on *Vers Libre*": "Rhyme removed, much ethereal music leaps up from the word. . . ." Rhymed verse directs attention to the ends of lines, to the obvious music of chiming sounds. Unhampered by rhyme, the mind is free to linger and construe the meanings of *juvescence,* and *concitation,* and to dwell on *History* with its *issues.* In "Gerontion" Eliot argues a position, assumes an attitude toward history. The poem makes a public statement on what we now like to call the "cultural situation." The looser prosodic form Eliot uses reduces the merely sensuous resources of language; "Gerontion" echoes with none of the music that ". . . is successful with a 'dying fall,' " easy alliteration or that legacy of the nineties, the lush hexameter:

> Afternoon grey and smoky, evening yellow and rose . . .

The music of "Gerontion" is heard as the metric releases "The word within a word. . . ." The open rhythms of conversation flow easily between the formal set speeches; prose phrasing and repeated syntax create unmistakable, characteristic "Eliotic" effects. And the whole prosodic direction of "Gerontion" is manipulated by the politic ghost "of some simple metre": the iambic pentameter lurking behind the arras.

The other English poems in the 1920 volume are all written in the Gautier stanza, urged upon Eliot by Pound. These poems are more nasty than witty, more clogged with irrelevant pedantry than flowing with gracious learning. ("Burbank with a Baedeker: Bleistein with a Cigar," a poem of thirty-two lines, contains at least twenty-one separate allusions to literature.[19]) The stanza permits epigrammatic brilliance or an ironic appraisal of Grishkin's charms:

> Grishkin is nice: her Russian eye
> Is underlined for emphasis;
> Uncorseted, her friendly bust
> Gives promise of pneumatic bliss.

Like Pound in *Mauberley,* Eliot modifies Gautier's stanza and rhymes only the second and fourth lines. (The exception, where Eliot follows Gautier's scheme exactly and rhymes *abab,* is "The Hippopotamus.") But Eliot does not use the stanza as a prosodic theme for a set of far-ranging variations; he works close to the form and brings off passages of the strictest virtuosity.

One of these passages contains perhaps the most brilliant technical stroke of all the poems in the Gautier stanza. It is the enjambment of the two final stanzas of "Burbank with a Baedeker: Bleistein with a Cigar":

> Princess Volupine extends
> A meagre, blue-nailed, phthisic hand
> To climb the waterstair. Lights, lights,
> She entertains Sir Ferdinand
>
> Klein. Who clipped the lion's wings
> And flea'd his rump and pared his claws?
> Thought Burbank, meditating on
> Time's ruins, and the seven laws.

The metrical regularity underlines the elaborate (too elaborate?) joke of the fourth and fifth lines. The strong metrical stress on the last syllable of *Ferdinand,* the special prominence of the rhyme, and the clever prosodic use of visual pause between the two stanzas, supply the element of exact comic timing. *She entertains Sir Ferdinand*—de Vere, Montague, Fitzroy? We wait to hear the appropriately aristocratic surname. *Klein* falls on the strong beat of the initial catalectic foot:

> Kléin. | Who clípped | the lí | on's wíngs . . .

The metrical stress gives a rising intonation; we pronounce the name of the parvenu Jew as a surprised question: Sir Ferdinand

Klein? The meter also makes the grammar ambiguous. If we follow the meter and stress *clipped, who* gathers strength as a relative pronoun, and the question in Burbank's mind is answered.

4

The Waste Land assimilates every prosodic advance Eliot made in his earlier verse; it also points toward newer methods, especially the strong-stress techniques of *Four Quartets* and the plays. Because of its length, *The Waste Land* raises the question of a carrying metric. If we believe Yvor Winters, *The Waste Land* fails in unity because Eliot establishes no metrical cohesiveness; the poem falls "... into lyrical fragments." I contend that Eliot succeeds in establishing a prosodic tone, a metric which is *there* and systematically a part of the poem's structure, and that this success gives *The Waste Land* what unity it has. I agree *The Waste Land* lacks the essential unity which, say, *The Rape of the Lock* possesses. My private feeling is that *The Waste Land* is too short to support its allusive and episodic structure. Pound's abridgment of the poem may not have rendered it the critical service which has been ritually applauded by most writers on Eliot and Pound.

To understand how Eliot's prosody works in *The Waste Land* means understanding the poem's dramatic structure. The symbol and myth hunters have attacked *The Waste Land* as if it had a rational narrative. We need only to unravel the images and legends and see their relationships. Then we have the story! But there is no "story" in *The Waste Land;* if we try to fit together "the broken images," we discover contradictions and discrepancies. A more fruitful approach lies in reconstructing the poem's scenario: who is speaking; when does a character shift into another character; where are we, spatially, in the poem?[20] The poem speaks with many voices; we hear monologues, dialogues, and conversations from adjacent tables and nearby rooms. Students who have the greatest difficulty in understanding *The Waste Land* as a printed poem respond to Eliot's own recorded reading.

The dramatic convention of *The Waste Land* develops out of the earlier monologues; but in "Prufrock" or "Gerontion" we hear one, or at the most, two voices. We might hear women, in the next room, "talking of Michelangelo"; or the imagined voice of one, not wishing to be misunderstood, saying, "That is not what I meant, at all." In *The Waste Land* we are assaulted by the voices and the noises of a whole civilization. The poet walks through the streets of modern London, overhearing the prophecies of Madame Sosostris or a conversation in a pub between two Cockney women. Tiresias reports a squalid sexual encounter; voices come ". . . singing out of empty cisterns and exhausted wells." At the end of the poem, the narrator is a victim of auditory hallucination; the rhythm of a children's singing game mixes with literary fragments from five languages.

Eliot meets the prosodic requirements of his complex dramatic scheme by a brilliant and simple expedient. He alternates two metrical modes; more precisely, he sets two limitations on prosodic freedom. At one pole he sets up a conversational idiom, a line of four strong stresses: this is the opening "April is the cruellest month, breeding . . ." and the succeeding seventeen lines. (See the scansion in Chapter II.) The first important passage of exhortation swings from the four-stress line of

> I réad, much of the níght, || and go sóuth in the wínter . . .

into blank verse, the other metrical pole of the poem:

> What are the roots that clutch, what branches grow
> Out of this stony rubbish? Son of man,
> You cannot say, or guess, for you know only . . .

There is no fixing of the meter in this passage; Eliot moves out of blank verse, back into stress verse:

> . . . I could not
> Spéak, and my éyes fáiled, || I was néither
> Líving nor déad, || and I knéw nóthing,
> Lóoking into the héart of líght, || the sílence . . .

Prosody shifts with the changing voices. Madame Sosostris gives way to Tiresias, who again speaks blank verse. The modulations from strong stress to iambics and vice versa are accomplished with great technical subtlety. "A Game of Chess" opens in blank verse modeled on Shakespeare's later metrical manner. Eliot wants to move from description to dialogue: the hopeless conversation between the Lady of the Dressing Table and the Man of Rats' Alley. Eliot breaks the prevailing movement with a half-line,

> And still she cried, and still the world pursues,
> 'Jug Jug' to dirty ears.

and the verse gradually loosens:

> And other withered stumps of time
> Were told upon the walls; staring forms
> Leaned out, leaning, hushing the room enclosed.
> Footsteps shuffled on the stair.
> Under the firelight, under the brush, her hair
> Spread out in fiery points
> Glowed into words, then would be savagely still.

We are now prepared, prosodically, for the neurotic rhythms of the Lady, and the sullen, mocking replies of the Man.

Eliot preserves prosodic unity by careful preparation; the movements from iambic to strong-stress are never sudden. Mister Eugenides is introduced by a line of blank verse:

> Únder | the brówn | fóg of | a wín | ter nóon . . .

The two reversed feet, especially the trochee in the third place, unsettle iambic direction so that the rest of the passage, in four-stress lines, seems scarcely different in rhythm:

> Ḿr. Eugénides, || the Smýrna mérchant
> Unsháven, || with a pócket fúll of cúrrants
> Ć.i.f. Lóndon: || dócuments at síght . . .

A dazzling instance of rhythmic modulation occurs when Tiresias works gradually into the elegiac quatrains of the typist and clerk scene. After ten preparatory lines the verse settles into the familiar stanza of Gray's *Elegy:*[21]

> The time is now propitious, as he guesses,
> The meal is ended, she is bored and tired,
> Endeavours to engage her in caresses
> Which still are unreproved, if undesired . . .

She turns and looks a moment in the glass,
Hardly aware of her departed lover;
Her brain allows one half-formed thought to pass:
'Well now that's done: and I'm glad it's over.'
When lovely woman stoops to folly and
Paces about her room again, alone,
She smoothes her hair with automatic hand,
And puts a record on the gramophone.

Prosodic tone, strengthened in pathos by the lines' alternating masculine and feminine endings, contrasts strikingly with the unpleasant subject matter. The elegiac effect adds a prosodic irony, climaxed as Eliot parodies not only the sense but the meter of Goldsmith's moral ditty:

'Well nów | that's dóne: | ánd | I'm glád | it's ó | ver.'

When lóve | ly wó | man stóops | to fól | ly ánd

Pá ces | a bóut | her róom | a gáin, | a lóne . . .

Goldsmith's original line is lengthened by a single syllable, the metrically emphatic *and. And* also receives metrical stress in the line given to the erring typist. Tiresias mimics her bored relief: his *and,* appearing conspicuously at the end of the line, echoes hers with stinging contempt.

The narrator relates the death of Phlebas the Phoenician in the more relaxed strong-stress mode. The tone here is quiet, almost understated: the four-stress line generates subdued tensions:

Phlébas the Phoenícian, || a fórtnight déad,

Forgót the crý of gulls, || and the déep sea swéll

And the prófit and lóss.

A cúrrent under séa . . .

The second line, with its final three long syllables, reconciles the opening strong-stress movement and the following iambic lines:

Picked his bones in whispers. As he rose and fell
He passed the stages of his age and youth . . .

But the four-beat line returns:

> Éntering the whírlpool.
>
> Géntile or Jéw . . .

I regard the alliterated *f's* of the first line as a deliberate prosodic atavism: Old Possum's sly hint to the reader that he is thinking in stresses rather than counting syllable-stress feet.

Tension returns in the finale of *The Waste Land.* The prosody tightens once again into blank verse as we hear the prophet's voice in three lines of ringing anaphora:

> After the torchlight red on sweaty faces
> After the frosty silence in the gardens
> After the agony in stony places . . .

The earlier dramatic scenes are replaced by disconnected, broken visions. The prophet and the protagonist are united into a single voice; the mood is one of interrogation and insanity. Iambic movement predominates, although the famous passages of spiritual thirst are set in short, hesitating lines; the Indian episode moves back into strong-stress verse:

> Gánga was súnken, || and the límp leáves
>
> Waíted for raín, || while the bláck clóuds
>
> Gáthered far dístant, || óver Hímavant.
>
> The júngle croúched, || húmped in sílence . . .

The less said about the last eleven lines of *The Waste Land* the better. I have characterized them as auditory hallucination; certainly Eliot suggests the protagonist's mental derangement. The suggestion is ironic, like the deprecating implication that Gerontion's reveries are

> Thoughts of a dry brain in a dry season.

Similarly, Eliot reminds us "Hieronymo's mad againe"—which is Eliot's way of eating his cake and having it, too. After all, *The Waste Land* may be a madman's vision of the twentieth century. But we must ponder Eliot's vision with some seriousness.

5

The carrying metric of *The Waste Land* mediates between blank verse and strong-stress meter. The poem's dramatic structure required a colloquial idiom not too far removed from prose; the poem's didactic and hortatory impulses needed the closer ordering of blank verse. Eliot wrote *Sweeney Agonistes* directly for the stage; its two brief scenes were meant as part of a longer play, *Wanna Go Home, Baby?* Eliot devised an immediately effective metric for the two *Fragments:* a metric supple enough to carry the rhythms of lower-class speech and formal enough to carry musical incantation. The style is repetitive, responsive; the subject matter, at first commonplace, later becomes sordid and comic-horrible. The metric is simplicity itself: a four-stress line sharply divided at the caesura. But unlike the strong-stress lines in *The Waste Land,* the percussive lines of *Sweeney* are carefully measured in time:

DUSTY: How about Pereira?
DORIS: What about Pereira?
I don't care.
DUSTY: You don't care!
Who pays the rent?
DORIS: Yes he pays the rent
DUSTY: Well some men don't and some men do
Some men don't and you know who

The antiphonal idiocies of Dusty and Doris follow duple time; the shifting of accents within the line gives the characteristic jazzy effect. With the appearance of Sweeney in the second part, syncopation increases. Eliot occasionally italicizes the accents in score to insure a proper performance:

DORIS: You'll carry me off? To a cannibal isle?
SWEENEY: I'll be the cannibal.
DORIS: I'll be the missionary.
I'll convert you.
SWEENEY: I'll convert *you!*

Eliot reads the *Fragment of an Agon* to an emphatic double beat—to what jazz musicians call "cut time." Over this timing, he sharply syncopates the accents; my scansion corresponds as closely as possible to Eliot's reading:[22]

DORIS: Thát's not lífe, || thát's no lífe
Whý I'd júst as sóon be déad.
SWEENEY: Thát's whát lífe is. Júst is
DORIS: Whát is?
Whát's that lífe ís?
SWEENEY: Life ís death.

Eliot heavily accents the off-beats when he delivers Sweeney's staggering revelation; my reading of the note-values is, of course, only approximate:

Í knew a man ónce || díd a girl ín—

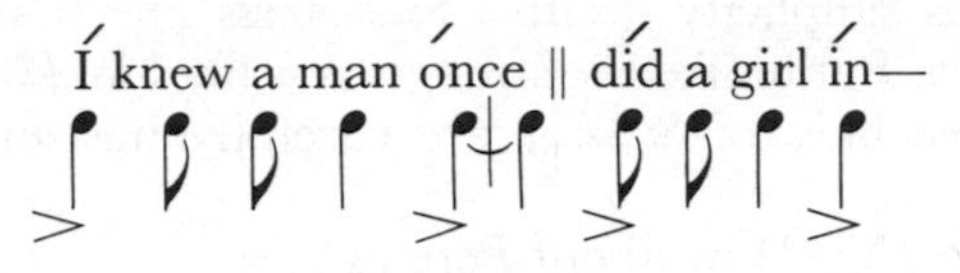

The four-stress meter is capable of great variety in tempo; we have accelerating horror in

Any man might do a girl in
Any man has to, needs to, wants to
Once in a lifetime, do a girl in.

or slow and dull-witted torpor in

These fellows always get pinched in the end.

The rhythms of *Sweeney* turn up in *The Cocktail Party.* Perhaps Eliot is perpetrating a subtle, if not exactly tasteful, joke; after all, Celia Coplestone becomes a missionary, goes among the cannibals, and if not "converted" into missionary stew, is crucified and eaten by ants. Or perhaps the similarity of rhythms derives from the ritual bases of both plays; *The Cocktail Party* elaborates the sin and atonement theme of *Sweeney.* The man-who-did-a-girl-in (who is probably Sweeney himself) suffers intolerable loneliness and delusions about what is real and imagined:

When you're alone like he was alone
You're either or neither . . .
Death or life or life or death
Death *is* life and life *is* death . . .[23]

Celia Coplestone, in language and rhythms reminiscent of *Sweeney*, wonders about love, and loneliness, and reality:

> . . . Can we only love
> Something created by our own imagination?
> Are we all in fact unloving and unlovable?
> Then one *is* alone, and if one is alone
> Then lover and belovèd are equally unreal
> And the dreamer is no more real than his dreams.
>
> Act II

More obviously Sweeney-like are passages where the speakers divide the line in stichomythia:

> JULIA: And he had a remarkable sense of hearing—
> The only man I ever met who could hear the cry of bats.
> PETER: Hear the cry of bats?
> JULIA: He could hear the cry of bats.
> CELIA: But how do you know he could hear the cry of bats?
> JULIA: Because he said so. And I believed him.
> CELIA: But if he was so . . . harmless, how could you believe him?
>
> Act I, i

A little of this goes a long way; Eliot wisely uses these rhythms thematically throughout the play: not as a carrying prosody but for heightening effects, at moments of levity or elation, or for simple conversational banter.

Eliot explains the verse-technique of his plays in a loose and puzzling way. He makes clear he employs strong-stress metric:

> What I worked out [for *The Family Reunion*] is substantially what I continued to employ: a line of varying length and varying number of syllables, with a caesura and three stresses. The caesura and the stresses may come at different places, almost anywhere in the line; the stresses may be close together or well separated by light syllables; the only rule being that there must be one stress on one side of the caesura and two on the other.[24]

Many passages in *The Family Reunion* correspond to Eliot's paradigm; especially the lyrical interchanges between Harry and Mary:

MARY

The cold spring now is the time
For the ache in the moving root
The agony in the dark
The slow flow throbbing the trunk
The pain of the breaking bud . . .

HARRY

Spring is an issue of blood
A season of sacrifice
And the wail of the new full tide
Returning the ghosts of the dead . . .

But more often than not, the verse of *The Family Reunion* settles into a four-stress line; this passage derives from a similar one in *Burnt Norton:*

HARRY

The sudden solitude in a crowded desert
In a thick smoke, many creatures moving
Without direction, for no direction
Leads anywhere but round and round in that vapour—
Without purpose, and without principle of conduct . . .

We have an undisputed three-stress line,

Without púrpose, and without prínciple of cónduct . . .

in a context largely made up of four-stress lines:

In flíckering íntervals || of líght and dárkness;
The pártial anaesthésia || of súffering without féeling
And pártial observátion || of one's ówn autómatism
While the slów stáin sinks déeper || through the skín
Táinting the flésh || and discóloring the bóne—

However, this counting of stresses seems niggling. Eliot develops a metric for his plays which is unobtrusive in the passages of low dramatic intensity and powerful in the moments of terror or exultation. Edmund Wilson has ingeniously suggested that this metric is an adaptation of the classical iambic hexameter or "trimeter": the basic meter of Roman drama:

> That this ignorance of iambic hexameter (so confusingly called 'iambic trimeter') is pretty generally prevalent in this country would seem to be indicated by the failure of writers on Eliot's plays to mention that the meter he uses is an adaptation of this. (He follows the loose Latin version—suggested to him, perhaps, by his study of Seneca—in which the line has come to depend mainly on three stresses; and he has even made a point of varying this, in the traditional Roman way, with passages written in trochaics.)[25]

Taken with Eliot's own account of his procedure, this makes good sense. Iambic trimeter consists of six iambic feet, arranged in three larger units, or dipodies. In each of these dipodies, we have a single strong accent which occurs on the first iambic foot:

> Ŏ pa | ca lin || quens Di | tis in || fer ni | lo ca
> ad sum | pro fun || do Tar | ta ri e || miss us | spe cu
> in cer | tus ut || ras od | e rim || se des | ma gis—
>
> Seneca, *Agamemnon,* 1–3

If we adapt this to English, we have, quite simply, a line of three stresses; the rhythmic effects of Latin quantity cannot be reproduced in English. We also have a line roughly divided into three major divisions or dipodies. Many such lines turn up in *The Family Reunion* and *The Cocktail Party;* many more in Eliot's most recent plays, *The Confidential Clerk* and *The Elder Statesman.* Actual Senecan influence on the prosody can be seen only in *The Family Reunion.* Like Seneca, Eliot uses a mixed metric: one line for dialogue and set speeches; another line, more fluid in movement, for choral and lyrical interludes.[26]

After *The Family Reunion* Eliot submerges obvious metrical design, abandons the formal rhyming techniques of *Murder in the Cathedral* and the intricate lyric patterns of *The Family Reunion,* and relies more and more for rhythmic interest on the repetition of phrase and the syntactical echo:

EDWARD: A common interest in the moving pictures
Frequently brings young people together.
PETER: Now you're only being sarcastic:
Celia was interested in the art of the film.
EDWARD: As a possible profession?
PETER: She might make it a profession;
Though she had her poetry.
EDWARD: Yes, I've seen her poetry—

We might note here a favorite rhythmic "tune" of Eliot's, the quadripartite

A common interest in the moving pictures

so like,

The awful daring of a moment's surrender . . .
The infirm glory of the positive hour . . .

and wickedly parodied by Edmund Wilson:

The embarrassing moment in the empty room . . .[27]

The carrying prosody of Eliot's most recent plays has achieved a rhythmic blandness, a transparency, the kindest say; a tired and nerveless prosiness, the more realistic say. We might, for a moment, refer back to some general principles for writing dramatic verse that Eliot has formulated. These are not principles a priori, but part ". . . of the self-education of a poet trying to write for the theatre. . . ."[28] The first, and earliest, caveat, was to avoid regular blank verse and its unfortunate propensity to Shakespearean echoes. Eliot's three- and four-stress line, reviving the native English, pre-Shakespearean verse tradition, "sounds nothing like" Shakespeare because it is historically unrelated to blank verse. And with its persistent and variable coincidence of rhetorical and metrical stress, the strong-stress line is endlessly adaptable to the rhythms of contemporary speech.

A second, and later, principle was ". . . the ascetic rule to avoid poetry which could not stand the test of strict dramatic utility. . . ."[29] Eliot's asceticism has led him to the verse of *The Elder Statesman,* of which the following is a fair sample:

CHARLES

And your father will come. With his calm possessive air
And his kindly welcome, which is always a reminder
That I musn't stay too long, for you belong to him.
He seems so placidly to take it for granted
That you don't really care for any company but his!

MONICA

You're not to assume that anything I've said to you
Has given you the right to criticise my father.
In the first place, you don't understand him;
In the second place, we're not engaged yet.

Compared to *Sweeney,* or even to parts of *The Cocktail Party,* this seems pretty pallid stuff. We must approve the thinning-out of the verse texture to accommodate dramatic exigency and avoid the clogging of the action. But where is the heightening, which justifies the use of verse in drama? When Lord Claverton achieves the peace which passeth all understanding, the blessed illumination of the aged Oedipus at Colonus, there is scarcely a stir of feeling; abstractions, not music, heavily move the verse along:

LORD CLAVERTON

This may surprise you: I feel at peace now.
It is the peace that ensues upon contrition
When contrition ensues upon knowledge of the truth.
Why did I always want to dominate my children?
Why did I mark out the narrow path for Michael?
Because I wanted to perpetuate myself in him.
Why did I want to keep you to myself, Monica?
Because I wanted you to give your life to adoring
The man I pretended to myself that I was . . .

Confronted with the rhythmic neutrality of this passage, we might wonder whether Eliot's dramatic verse, while having gone in the right direction, has not (as Randall Jarrell said of a rival poet) gone a great deal too far. The verse of *The Elder Statesman* and *The Confidential Clerk* has been put "on a very thin diet in order to adapt it to the needs of the stage. . . ."[30] The result has not been a lean athletic prosodic style but one displaying woeful symptoms of malnutrition.

6

When it appears, the study of the music
Of *Ash-Wednesday* should compel the minds of all
Poets; for in a hundred years no poem
Has sung itself so exquisitely well.

Karl Shapiro, *Essay on Rime*

I would be happy if my studies compelled the minds of *some* poets. Faced with Shapiro's encomium, I hesitate to submit *Ash Wednesday* to the barbarisms of metrical analysis. *Ash Wednesday* displays unsurpassed rhythmic power and control; the opening sections, all of Section III (*Al som de l'escalina*), and the concluding section convince me no metric was ever devised which so closely follows a poet's mental and emotional posture. We find occasional lapses, where Eliot yields to his own facility:

On the mainland, in the desert or the rain land,
For those who walk in darkness
Both in the day time and in the night time
The right time and the right place are not here
No place of grace for those who avoid the face . . .

Will the veiled sister between the slender
Yew trees pray for those who offend her
And are terrified and cannot surrender . . .

The obsessive interior and feminine rhyming brings these over-excited lines close to the edge of doggerel. But these are flaws occasioned not by a failure but an excess of technique.

Ash Wednesday emphatically illustrates one of Sir Donald Tovey's most brilliant generalizations: that aesthetic form is movement.[31] A variety of rhythms of "vital import" are danced out in *Ash Wednesday;* in no other poem of Eliot do we find so much ritual movement and incantatory music. We have the opening gestures of "turning"; later we find ascents and descents, climbing, walking, "stops and steps of the mind. . . ." The stiff iambics of the opening mirror an attitude of ceremony touched with despair:

Because I do not hope to turn again
Because I do not hope
Because I do not hope to turn

Desiring this man's gift and that man's scope
I no longer strive to strive towards such things
(Why should the agèd eagle stretch its wings?)
Why should I mourn
The vanished power of the usual reign?

Movement falters and direction becomes uncertain in the second and third lines: the rhythmic vacancy is the result of defeated expectation as the pentameter of the first line still echoes in our metrical memory. Eliot, moving between doubt and resolution, resembles a dancer slowly circling, stating a pattern, losing it, and finding it again. The lines of three and four feet,

Because I do not hope
Because I do not hope to turn . . .

are surprisingly resolved by the full pentameter line lifted from the Twenty-ninth Sonnet:

Desiring this man's gift and that man's scope . . .

The prosodic smoothness of this line is now contradicted by

I no lón | ger stríve | to stríve | tówards | such thíngs . . .

A monosyllabic foot springs the line at the fourth position; the wrench in rhythm mimes the striving, the hesitations of Eliot's inner struggle.

The prose movement which opens Section II interrupts the dance; the Lady, the leopards, and the bones command our eyes rather than our ears. The music and the dance resume with the song of the bones, set to the rhythms of the *Ave Maria:*

Lady of silences
Calm and distressed
Torn and most whole

Ave, Maria;
gratia plena;
Dominus tecum

A number of rhythms have now been heard as structural constants: the opening iambic; the long prose line, with its carefully placed caesural divisions,

> There, where trees flower, and springs flow, for
> there is nothing again . . .
>
> On my legs my heart my liver and that which had
> been contained
> In the hollow round of my skull . . .

and the various sections set to the liturgy of the Catholic service. There is continual shifting and interchanging of these rhythms but no sense of roughness or unprepared transition. Rhyme, used within and at the ends of lines, serves as binding material:

> At the first turning of the second stair
> I turned and saw below
> The same shape twisted on the banister
> Under the vapour in the fetid air
> Struggling with the devil of the stairs who wears
> The deceitful face of hope and of despair . . .

The stanza above introduces the third section, with its remarkable contrast between the dense, clotted rhythms of

> The same shape twisted on the banister . . .

and the untroubled iambics of

> The broadbacked figure drest in blue and green . . .

Through the ". . . slotted window bellied like the fig's fruit . . ." is glimpsed a Maytime celebration, and the poet recalls one of those aching and exalted moments of sexual experience. Eliot breaks the iambic meter and allows a characteristic repetition to supply rhythmic interest. We hear this kind of repetition as another structural constant:

> In a white gown, to contemplation, in a white gown . . .
>
> Blown hair is sweet, brown hair over the mouth blown,
> Lilac and brown hair . . .
>
> White light folded, sheathed about her, folded.

Section III concludes with an extraordinary *diminuendo;* the ascent seemingly proceeds after the last word has been uttered, into the silence of imagined time:

> Distraction, music of the flute, stops and steps
>   of the mind over the third stair,
> Fading, fading; strength beyond hope and despair
> Climbing the third stair.

Paradoxically, the rhythm *falls* as the protagonist climbs. The last words of Section III, the *Domine, non sum dignus* from the Ordinary of the Mass, are muttered in distraction as the speaker momentarily awakens from his vision.

The vision continues in Section IV but the pace has changed. The tempo is now the true *andante,* a moderate walking speed. The section is nominally iambic, with lines of varying length. Grover Smith suggests the influence of *The Faerie Queene;*[32] the lines do arrange themselves in periods resembling the Spenserian stanza, each period punctuated by longer lines. We have at least one authentic Alexandrine,

> Who then made strong the fountains and made fresh
>   the springs . . .

an approximate hexameter,

> One who moves in the time between sleep and waking,
>   wearing . . .

and Eliot's favorite septenary,

> Whose flute is breathless, bent her head and signed
>   but spoke no word . . .

However, the prosodic relevance of Spenser here is questionable; Eliot has always been fond of the long line and richly musical vowel patterns. We find, in a new and more delicate orchestration, "the music with a dying fall":

> But the fountain sprang up and the bird sang down
> Redeem the time, redeem the dream
> The token of the word unheard, unspoken

Till the wind shake a thousand whispers from the yew

And after this our exile . . .

The interior rhyming, "sprang up . . . sang down / . . . redeem the dream / . . . token . . . unspoken . . ." is exactly timed to create the tension of unfulfilled expectation. We must also note the silences indicated by the pregnant spacing between lines. These pauses for the eye, which note pauses for the ear, are like *fermata* in musical notation and are carefully observed by Eliot in his reading.[33] The absence of full stops at the conclusion of Section IV has prosodic effect; the unresolved vision remains flickering before the mind's eye, ". . . between the ivory gates."

The rhetorical clamor of Section V stands in marked contrast to the rest of the poem. Granted that Eliot intends us to hear the noise of "the unstilled world," the onomatopoeic bustle and homonymic punning of

Against the Word the unstilled world still whirled
About the centre of the silent Word . . .

is finally tedious, justifying Henry Reed's delicious parody:

The wind within a wind unable to speak for wind . . .

"Chard Whitlow"

However, we must note the rhythmic musculature of the concluding lines in Section V; they recall the classical logaoedic meter with its free mixture of anapestic and iambic feet:

And affirm before the world and deny between the rocks
In the last desert between the last blue rocks
The desert in the garden the garden in the desert . . .

The last line but one, an Eliotic hexameter, possesses two caesuras, and a violently dactylic second foot:

Of dróuth, || spít ting from | the móuth || the wíth | ered

áp | ple-séed . . .

The appropriate harshness of the inverted second foot throws the line into falling rhythm, emphasized by the final fragment, set in trochees:

O my people.

Section VI restores the iambic meter of the opening. The movements of deliberate hesitation quickly give way, and Eliot varies the metric with lines of different length and freer distribution of stresses. This modulates, almost imperceptibly, into a four-stress line:

> And the lost heart stiffens and rejoices
> In the lost lilac and the lost sea voices
> And the weak spirit quickens to rebel
> For the bent golden-rod and the lost sea smell
> Quickens to recover
> The cry of quail and the whirling plover
> And the blind eye creates
> The empty forms between the ivory gates
> And smell renews the salt savour of the sandy earth

We hear, as a kind of prosodic valediction, the rhythmic constant of

⏑ ⁄ | ⏑ ⁄ | ⏑ ⏑ | ⏑ ⁄ | ⏑ ⁄ :

The empty forms between the ivory gates . . .

echoing earlier statements of the same music:

> The vanished power of the usual reign . . .
> The infirm glory of the positive hour . . .[34]

The rhythmic animation of the four-stress lines makes vivid the sudden and intense longing for the things of this world; but "In memory only, reconsidered passion. . . ." A solemn movement of "English hexameters" preludes the concluding prayer:

> But when the voices shaken from the yew-tree drift away
> Let the other yew be shaken and reply . . .

The prayer briefly revives the two-stress *Ave Maria* meter; I venture to reset lines into their metrical periods:

> Blessèd sister,
> holy mother,
> spirit of the fountain,
> spirit of the garden . . .

An especially expressive visual *fermata* provides actual *separation* between the final line and those preceding it:

> And spirit of the river, spirit of the sea,
> Suffer me not to be separated
>
> And let my cry come unto Thee.

7

> But the abstract conception
> Of private experience at its greatest intensity . . .

Ash Wednesday is at once the most obscure and the most immediately musical of Eliot's major poems. The strain of attempting to communicate the essence of religious vision occasions an inevitable fineness in the meaning; it also occasions the music. An interval of five years separates *Ash Wednesday* (1930) from the first of the *Four Quartets, Burnt Norton* (1935). Eliot was now considering a new music, a more "transparent" medium. In a lecture delivered in 1933, Eliot remarked he wished to write poetry

> . . . which should be essentially poetry, with nothing poetic about it, poetry standing naked in its bare bones, or poetry so transparent that we should not see the poetry, but that which we are meant to see through the poetry, poetry so transparent that in reading it we are intent on what the poem *points at,* and not the poetry, this seems to me the thing to try for. To get *beyond poetry,* as Beethoven, in his later works, strove to get *beyond music.* We shall never succeed, perhaps, but Lawrence's words mean this to me, that they express to me what I think that the forty or fifty original lines I have written strive towards.[35]

"Strive towards!" The burden of *Ash Wednesday* still sang in Eliot's ears. But the music of *Four Quartets* differs from that of *Ash Wednesday*. We no longer hear the tone color, the rich intermingling of rhyme and metrical sequence which distinguish the texture and movement of *Ash Wednesday*. The music of *Four Quartets* originates at a deeper level than that of meter and rhyme; it is implicit, as we have shown in our earlier analysis, in syntax, the rhythm of thought itself.

The syntactical music of *Four Quartets* represents Eliot's highest technical achievement; hearing Eliot read the *Quartets* is as genuine a musical experience as hearing the Budapest Quartet play Beethoven's Opus 132. This is not analogical nonsense; Eliot's hint about Beethoven's later works provides an important clue to the form and substance of *Four Quartets*. J. W. N. Sullivan, whose influence on Eliot has been convincingly demonstrated by Herbert Howarth,[36] describes below Beethoven's Quartets in B Flat, Opus 130, C♯ Minor Opus 131, and A Minor, Opus 132; he is also describing, with uncanny precision, Eliot's *Four Quartets:*

> In these quartets the movements radiate, as it were, from a central experience. They do not represent stages in a journey, each stage being independent and existing in its own right. They represent separate experiences, but the meaning they take on in the quartet is derived from their relation to a dominating, central experience. This is characteristic of the mystic vision, to which everything in the world appears unified in the light of one fundamental experience. In these quartets, then, Beethoven is not describing to us a spiritual history; he is presenting to us a vision of life. In each quartet many elements are surveyed, but from one central point of view. They are presented as apprehended by a special kind of awareness, they are seen in the light of one fundamental experience. It is not any kinship between the experiences described in the separate movements themselves, but the light in which they are seen, that gives to these works their profound homogeneity.[37]

The formal prosody of *Four Quartets* grows out of this "dominating central experience" and "profound homogeneity." Each movement, in Eliot's five-movement scheme, has its characteristic metric; yet, throughout the *Quartets,* Eliot sustains an overall consistency in metrical tone. This consistency is first established by the close musical structure, derived in all probability from Beethoven's *Quartet in A Minor,* Opus 132.[38] Eliot had been using musical structures and techniques long before he composed *Four Quartets; The Waste Land* was an experiment in the use of repeated thematic material as well as being orchestral in its elaborate handling of contrasting sonorities. Eliot's methods in the *Quartets* are more strictly musical; we find the pervasive repetitions of themes, images, and rhythms. We find, in addition, devices Eliot may have absorbed in his listening to Beethoven: variation of theme, inversion, diminution, rhythmic contraction and expansion.

The metrical modes complement the musical form. The first movements of *Burnt Norton, East Coker,* and *Little Gidding* are set in Eliot's flexible strong-stress lines. Line lengths vary but the number of stresses remains close to the normative four:

> Drý the pool, || drý concréte, || brówn édged,
>
> And the póol was fílled with wáter || out of súnlight,
>
> And the lótos róse, || quíetly, quíetly,
>
> The súrface glíttered || out of heárt of líght . . .

Burnt Norton

The measure is the same in *Little Gidding,* but the alliteration gives an archaic flavor—a suggestion of *Piers Plowman:*

> Midwinter spring is its own season
> Sempiternal though sodden towards sundown,
> Suspended in time, between pole and tropic.
> When the short day is brightest, with frost and fire,
> The brief sun flames the ice, on pond and ditches,
> In windless cold that is the heart's heat,
> Reflecting in a watery mirror
> A glare that is blindness in the early afternoon . . .

The complex positioning and counterpointing of vowel length against the meter add a luster not present in the sparse lines opening *Burnt Norton.*[39] The long vowel will sometimes coincide with metrical stress, as in this line:

> A gl*á*re that is bl*í*ndness || in the *éa*rly aftern*óo*n . . .

METRICAL MODES IN *FOUR QUARTETS*

	I Landscape	II Lyric	III Didactic	IV Lyric	V Didactic
BURNT NORTON	Four-stress line	1. Irregularly rhymed tetrameter 2. Hexameters and septenaries 3. Loose blank verse and four-stress line	1. Four-stress 2. Three-stress	1. Irregular iambic, rhymed	1. Four-stress 2. Three-stress
EAST COKER	Four-stress line	1. Irregularly rhymed tetrameter 2. Four-stress	1. Hexameter 2. Irregular five- and four-stress	1. Regular tetrameter stanzas	1. "Hexameters" 2. Four-stress
THE DRY SALVAGES	1. Five-stress anapestic/dactylic 2. Four-stress	1. Adapted sestina 2. Probably non-metrical, merging into four-stress	1. "Hexameters" 2. Four-stress	1. Five-line stanza unrhymed; falling rhythm	1. Four-stress 2. Three-stress
LITTLE GIDDING	1. Four-stress 2. Irregular blank verse; four-stress	1. Regular trimeter and tetrameter stanzas 2. Blank verse in "*terza rima*"	1. "Hexameters" 2. Three-stress	1. Regular tetrameter and trimeter stanzas	1. Four-stress with irregular blank verse 2. Three-stress

The vowel may be duplicated at the analogous metrical position:

> When the shórt day is bríghtest, || with fróst and fíre . . .

Long and short vowels may be inverted and balanced, short, long followed by long, short:

> Susp*e*nded in t*i*me, between p*o*le and tr*o*pic . . .

Or the long vowels may occur on the off-beats, cross-rhythmically:

> Sempitérnal th*ou*gh sódden t*owa*rds súnd*ow*n . . .

A rhythmic crescendo marks the fifth line of our passage from *Little Gidding,*

> The bríef | sun flámes | the íce, | on pónd | and dít | ches . . .

and we see the line falls into blank verse. The next line moves back into the four-stress mode,

> In wíndless cóld || that is the héart's héat . . .

with a crowding together of the two final stresses. Again we discover that the principle of Eliot's metric resides in ". . . the contrast between fixity and flux, this unperceived evasion of monotony, which is the very life of verse."[40] The opening of *The Dry Salvages* skillfully avoids the monotony usually occasioned by triple meter in English; although the lines move in almost regular trisyllabic feet, anapests and dactyls, there is neither the solemn torpor of *Evangeline* nor the galloping frenzy of *The Destruction of Sennacherib:*

> I do not know much about gods; but I think that the river
> Is a strong brown god—sullen, untamed and intractable,
> Patient to some degree, at first recognized as a frontier;
> Useful, untrustworthy, as a conveyer of commerce;
> Then only a problem confronting the builder of bridges . . .

Each line has five principal stresses and a strongly felt caesura; the meter is anapestic pentameter with dactylic and spondaic substitutions. But the ear is not assaulted by anapests and dactyls;

it hears the slow and primitive music of the Mississippi as it flows through past and present, recalling Eliot to childhood memories. The ear hears the infinitely subtle inflections of human feeling.

The second movement of each quartet opens with a rhyming lyric. The precision of the natural order is "figured" in regular tetrameter,

> We move above the moving tree
> In light upon the figured leaf
> And hear upon the sodden floor
> Below, the boarhound and the boar
> Pursue their pattern as before
> But reconciled among the stars . . .
>
> *Burnt Norton*

as are the disturbances of the spring, "not in time's covenant":

> Comets weep and Leonids fly
> Hunt the heavens and the plains
> Whirled in a vortex that shall bring
> The world to that destructive fire
> Which burns before the ice-cap reigns . . .

The second movement of *The Dry Salvages* introduces a variation on sestina form. The pattern is complicated, and as it unfortunately turns out, clumsy and self-defeating. The end-rhymes of the first stanza

> Where is there an end of it, the soundless *wailing,*
> The silent withering of autumn *flowers*
> Dropping their petals and remaining *motionless;*
> Where is there an end to the drifting *wreckage,*
> The prayer of the bone on the beach, the *unprayable*
> Prayer at the calamitous *annunciation?*

undergo an increasingly desperate metamorphosis until we get *sailing* and *bailing,* and *devotionless, oceanless,* and *erosionless.* The ineffable *weariness* here brings to mind Eliot's own parody of this mood;

O when will the creaking heart cease?
When will the broken chair give ease?
Why will the summer day delay?
When will Time flow away?

Lines to a Persian Cat

A longer section, of greater philosophic density, follows the lyrical interludes. In *Burnt Norton* Eliot penetrates to the unity of all experience; these lines, among all that Eliot has written, certainly approach the *poetry beyond poetry:*

At the still point of the turning world. Neither flesh
    nor fleshness;
Neither from nor towards; at the still point, there the
    dance is,
But neither arrest nor movement. And do not call it fixity,
Where past and future are gathered. Neither movement from
    nor towards,
Neither ascent nor decline. Except for the point,
    the still point,
There would be no dance, and there is only the dance . . .

Though the lines contain six and seven principal stresses, they move with all the ease and grace of the celestial dance they describe. Equally remarkable is the parallel section of *Little Gidding,* the "Inferno" episode. Eliot's adaptation of Dante's stanza avoids rhyme but alternates masculine and feminine endings to achieve the interlocking effect of *terza rima:*

In the uncertain hour before the morning
  Near the ending of interminable night
  At the recurrent end of the unending
After the dark dove with the flickering tongue
  Had passed below the horizon of his homing
  While the dead leaves still rattled on like tin . . .

The first five lines follow Dante's *endecasillabo,* even to observing the ellision of a final vowel before *h*:

Had passed below *th' horizon* of his homing . . .

We are not dealing, however, with syllabic meter but blank verse. Eliot's "familiar compound ghost" speaks in grave, measured pentameter:

> Let me disclose the gifts reserved for age
>   To set a crown upon your lifetime's effort.
>   First, the cold friction of expiring sense
> Without enchantment, offering no promise
>   But bitter tastelessness of shadow fruit
>   As body and soul begin to fall asunder . . .

The final allusion to *Hamlet* reminds us that Eliot's versification owes as much to Shakespeare as to Dante; it may also be Old Possum's little joke that the "compound ghost," ingeniously fashioned from a dozen literary sources,[41] is only that sad spook, the ghost of Hamlet's father:

> The day was breaking. In the disfigured street
>   He left me, with a kind of valediction,
>   And faded on the blowing of the horn . . .

Some readers have been dismayed by Eliot's weariness, his repetitive circling of ideas, and his flaccid rhythms in the *Quartets*. Karl Shapiro complains

>   Eliot
> Himself in the *Quartets* (in my opinion
> His most depressing prosody) makes shift
> Of rhythms one thought he had exhausted ten
> Or fifteen years before. Symptoms of doubt
> Lie in reiteration; we sense confusion,
> The anxiety of the sensitive to mistakes.
>
> *Essay on Rime*

Donald Davie, in a devastating analysis of *The Dry Salvages,* speaks of its ". . . stumbling, trundling rhythms . . . inarticulate ejaculations of reach-me-down phrases . . . debased currency of the study circle. . . ."[42] Exhaustion and even clumsiness certainly mar passages in *East Coker* and *The Dry Salvages;* the two inner *Quartets* suffer the most from Eliot's bemused prosiness and the grinding futility of disillusion chasing its tail. We are often dulled by purposeless rhythms or bored by

> The loud lament of the disconsolate chimera.

I agree with Mr. Davie that these lines are dismal in every respect:

> It seems, as one becomes older,
> That the past has another pattern, and ceases to be
> a mere sequence—
> Or even development: the latter a partial fallacy
> Encouraged by superficial notions of evolution . . .

Eliot allows too many weak syllables to intervene between strong stresses:

> En cour aged by su per fi cial no tions of e vo lu tion . . .

Since it is nearly impossible to tell which syllables are dynamically strong, the metrical checkpoints are obscured. The obsessive parenthetical qualification disrupts syntactical movement,

> Which becomes, in the popular mind . . .

> The moments of happiness—not the sense of well-being . . .

> I sometimes wonder if that is what Krishna meant—
> Among other things—or one way of putting the same thing . . .

and there are sections of *The Dry Salvages* when Eliot, usually so precise, loses control of his grammar.

But we need not judge the *Quartets* by their arid or tired moments. The vigorous opening of *The Dry Salvages* (quoted above), the section beginning,

> The river is within us, the sea is all about us;

continuing with the magnificent,

> The sea has many voices,
> Many gods and many voices.
> The salt is on the briar rose,
> The fog is in the fir trees . . .

and concluding with the sonorous and mysterious,

> And the ground swell, that is and was from the beginning,
> Clangs
> The bell . . .

redeem the weak sestina and the unilluminated metaphysics of "what Krishna meant."

Far from containing Eliot's "most depressing prosody," *Little Gidding* concludes the *Quartets* with a consistently strong and unbroken rhythmic impulse. While the other *Quartets* struggle with definition and direction, *Little Gidding* reaches a resolution of both technique and idea. The large formal rhythm (the five-movement divisions of landscape, lyric, didactic, lyric, didactic) is firmly settled as a pattern; the *Gestalt* of the other three *Quartets* is impressed on our minds. The expected sequence of metrical modes (see the chart on p. 207) now seems inevitable; we react with a sense of prepared surprise to the changes from four-stress verse to regular iambics, and from irregular pentameter to regular three-stress verse. Within each movement Eliot achieves his surest rhythms against an always discernible controlling meter.

The opening, with its balance between strong-stress and pentameter verse, offers these superb lines:

> And glow more intense than blaze of branch, or brazier,
> Stirs the dumb spirit: no wind, but pentecostal fire
> In the dark time of the year. Between melting and freezing
> The soul's sap quivers. There is no earth smell
> Or smell of living thing. This is the spring time
> But not in time's covenant.

The lines at first expand toward five stresses and blank verse; as the overall rhythm turns downward, reaching toward conclusion, the line turns back to four stresses:

> But this is the nearest, in place and time,
> Now and in England.
>
> If you came this way . . .
>
> Is England and nowhere. Never and always.

The lyrics of Sections II and IV have the simple regularity of songs; their mixture of iambic with trochaic and anapestic feet derives largely from the examples of Blake and Tennyson—and *their* great example, the Shakespearean song:

> Ásh on | an óld | man's sléeve
>
> Is áll | the ásh | the burnt ró | ses léave.
>
> Dúst in | the áir | sus pén | ded
>
> Márks | the pláce | where a stó | ry én | ded . . .

As in many of Shakespeare's songs, the iambic line begins on the strong syllable (trochaic or monosyllabic substitution): where the musical beat would naturally fall.

A hiatus, indicated by a visual pause, intervenes between the two strophes of Section V:

> So while the light fails
> On a winter's afternoon, in a secluded chapel
> History is now and England.
>
> With the drawing of this Love and the voice
> of this Calling
>
> We shall not cease from exploration
> And the end of all our exploring
> Will be to arrive where we started
> And know the place for the first time.

The break is charged with silent energy; the poet stops, catches his breath for his final statement. The concluding movement (in three-stress lines) draws together motifs from all the *Quartets;* the falling rhythm of

> Quick now, here, now, always—

is transformed upward:

> When the tongues of flame are in-folded
> Into the crowned knot of fire
> And the fire and the rose are one.

As God's testing fire merges with the Rose of His Love, the rhythm slowly rises and ends the sequence of the *Quartets* in quiet triumph.

VIII

Hart Crane and Wallace Stevens

I make no strong case for pairing these two poets other than that they both possess the "American sensibility." As poets they are as different in technique and temperament as Tennyson and Browning. Their dissimilarity, in fact, may serve critical generalization; in the dialectic of extreme opposition, Red and White, Left and Right, often exhibit comparable qualities. Hart Crane represents the American writer brutally scarred by his experience, and critics call him alienated; Wallace Stevens kept a fastidious distance between himself and "real life." He has also been called alienated. We may often wish Crane could submerge his turbulence and allow the poetry to sing through, unencumbered by the mud and silt dredged up from the sunless bottoms of rivers and seas. We may often wish that Stevens' poetry were less fictive, less of the sun and the moon, of "the formulations of midnight"; that it admit a subject larger than poetry itself. But the wishes of critics, set against the achievement of Crane and Stevens, are paltry things; the poets gave themselves magnificently, and it is ungrateful to ask for something else. If the wishes of critics were horses, all poets would be riding Shakespeare's Pegasus.

On one matter Crane and Stevens do approach each other; neither had a gift for the "plain style"; each sought after the incantatory power of words, the authority of rich and rhythmic language. In attempting to characterize the style of both poets, the word "rhetorical" comes immediately to mind. Although rhetoric has fallen into disrepute—many poets misunderstood Pound to have said poetry should be as *flatly* written as prose—twentieth-century poetry has often made use of resounding rhetoric; Yeats,

Thomas, Eliot, when occasion and need make it appropriate, do not avoid Shakespearean or even Miltonic vividness. Too much has been made of "verse as speech" and the "conversational idiom"; it is not the low-keyed poems in gray language which raise the hairs on the back of the neck and set the stimulus singing along the ganglia.

The implications for prosody are clear. Rhetoric can only be sustained by consummate rhythmic control; the great masters of rhetoric in English, Shakespeare and Milton, have also been the greatest masters of metric. Rhetoric is language with more sensuous surface than conceptual substance; it becomes the job of prosody, then, to keep rhetoric from flowing into pure sound or dissolving into pure image. Rhythm, the container in which time is contained, tells us how an idea feels; rhythm will rescue for cognition what may never receive articulate verbal expression, what rhetoric may overstate or conceal.

Crane's rhetoric is often self-defeating. It stems from injured sensibility, from a stupendous reaction to experience, or from simple ignorance. When Crane is in control of his rhythm, however, we can overlook rhetorical excess and exalt with him in the joyous use of language. Stevens' rhetoric is not often amazed reaction to experience and never ignorance; rather, it is diffidence: an effort to bring, without philosophical pompousness, the indefinable to definition. Stevens' purest rhetoric, his infamous use of nonsense syllables, has irritated many; but it is precisely here that we frequently discover Stevens bringing the subtlest thought and feeling into view:

> We say: At night an Arabian in my room,
> With his damned hoobla-hoobla-hoobla-how,
> Inscribes a primitive astronomy
>
> Across the unscrawled fores the future casts
> And throws his stars around the floor. By day
> The wood-dove used to chant his hoobla-hoo
>
> And still the grossest iridescence of ocean
> Howls hoo and rises and howls hoo and falls.
> Life's nonsense pierces us with strange relation.

Notes toward a Supreme Fiction

Stevens' rhetoric, the hoobla-hoobla of "life's nonsense," forms part of his meaning, piercing us "with strange relation." Stevens' rhetoric does not always come off; the relations may remain persistently, stubbornly strange as they do in the opening lines of "Credences of Summer":

> Now in midsummer come and all fools slaughtered
> And spring's infuriations over and a long way
> To the first autumnal inhalations, young broods
> Are in the grass . . .

But so gripping are the rhythms here, so compelling the movement, that we almost forget our syntactical bafflement (is *come* noun or verb?), and our wonder about what particular fools were slaughtered and why. The rhythm affects our inner perception with a feeling of ripeness and fullness of time and that sense of continual change which penetrates all life, all reality.

I

> . . . after the erection of the Chinese Wall of Milton,
> blank verse suffered not only arrest but
> retrogression.
>
> T. S. Eliot, "Marlowe"

The distinction of Eliot's prosody erected its own "Chinese Wall." A poet, coming under its shadow, could write his heart out, strain to clamber over the wall—as did Hart Crane. The tone and texture of Crane's verse are notably uneven; we are frequently jarred by the crudity of his rhythms, his inability to discover the appropriate metrical form for his feelings. Much that is rhythmically bad in Crane's poetry has its origin in Eliot's unassimilated influence: Crane never learned to master the delicate balance between "fixity and flux" which sets Eliot apart from the large numbers of his imitators. Crane did discover a metrical idiom congenial to his talent, but he first broke his head against The Chinese Wall.

Here is Crane's version of Eliotic ennui and urban despair:

> Behind
> My father's cannery works I used to see
> Rail-squatters ranged in nomad raillery,
> The ancient men—wifeless or runaway
> Hobo-trekkers that forever search
> An empire wilderness of freight and rails.

Each seemed a child, like me, on a loose perch,
Holding to childhood like some termless play.
John, Jake or Charley, hopping the low freight
—Memphis to Tallahassee—riding the rods,
Blind fists of nothing, humpty-dumpty clods.

"The River" from *The Bridge*

And here is the passage Crane was, consciously or otherwise, using as his model:

A rat crept softly through the vegetation
Dragging its slimy belly on the bank
While I was fishing in the dull canal
On a winter evening round behind the gashouse
Musing upon the king my brother's wreck
And on the king my father's death before him.

The Waste Land, 187–192

Crane maintains a steady iambic beat; the lines are clinched with resonant rhymes. Crane's language intends to express something of *Waste Land*-ish hopelessness and horror, of the desolate landscapes behind the gashouse and the cannery works, but the couplets almost bounce with good-humored vitality. We wonder if Crane's intention might not be parody here: as if he were deliberately trying to show there is life and energy behind the gashouse yet!

The Bridge gives other evidence of Crane's struggle against the Eliotic mode. Occasionally Crane gets close to the spirit of Eliot's technical discoveries, but his discomfort with freer rhythms leads him into awkward rhyming and odd locutions:

So memory that strikes a rhyme out of a box
Or splits a random smell of flowers through glass—
Is it the whip stripped from the lilac tree
One day in spring my father took to me,
Or is it the Sabbatical, unconscious smile
My mother almost brought me once from church
And once only, as I recall—?

"Van Winkle" from *The Bridge*

The third line is beautifully sprung by the trochaic third foot; the next line, with its doggerel meter and rhyme, wrecks the passage.

Again I offer a corresponding passage from *The Waste Land,* not for odious comparison, but to show how intensely personal Eliot's rhythms are:

> *Dayadhvam:* I have heard the key
> Turn in the door once and turn once only
> We think of the key, each in his prison
> Thinking of the key, each confirms a prison . . .
>
> *The Waste Land,* 412–415

Crane knew what he was up against, playing Eliot's gambits. In letters to Allen Tate and Gorham Munson, he assesses his situation, vis-à-vis Eliot:

> I have been facing [Eliot] for *four* years,—and while I haven't discovered a weak spot yet in his armour, I flatter myself a little lately that I have discovered a safe tangent to strike which, if I can possibly explain the position, —goes *through* him toward a *different goal.* You see it is such a fearful temptation to imitate him that at times I have been almost distracted. . . . In his own realm Eliot presents us with an absolute *impasse,* yet oddly enough he can be utilized to lead us to, intelligently point to, other positions and 'pastures new.' Having absorbed him enough we can trust ourselves as never before, in the air or on the sea.[1]

> However, I take Eliot as a point of departure toward an almost complete reverse of direction. His pessimism is amply justified in his own case. But I would apply as much of his erudition and technique as I can absorb and assemble toward a more positive, or (if [I] must put it so in a skeptical age) ecstatic goal. I should not think of this if a kind of rhythm and ecstasy were not (at odd moments, and rare!) a very real thing to me.[2]

Crane quarrels with Eliot's temperament; he could not *feel* what Eliot felt but suggests that Eliot's techniques might be used to express his own more exuberant, more violent nature. Unfortunately Eliot's metrical techniques, his subtle and limpid rhythms, were hardly suited to Crane's emotional make-up and even less suited to Crane's subjects. And Crane did not have Eliot's ear for conversation, the gift for rendering contemporary speech. The overheard conversations and interpolated monologues in *The Bridge* are fashionable pastiche effects and now sound dated. The distance between Crane and verse-as-speech was considerable; note the unevenness of tone and uncertain rhythm in this passage:

> "I ran a donkey engine down there on the Canal
> in Panama—got tired of that—
> then Yucatan selling kitchenware—beads—
> have you seen Popocatepetl—birdless mouth
> with ashes sifting down—?
>
> and then the coast again . . ."

"Cutty Sark" from *The Bridge*

Crane does not maintain convincing speech cadence; the last line shifts suddenly into formal hexameter, breaking cleanly at the sixth syllable:

> with ásh | es síft | ing dówn—? ||
>
> and thén | the cóast | a gáin . . .

The final lines of "Cape Hatteras" explode down the page in fine Imagist disorder; it looks like authentic visual prosody:

> Yes, Walt,
> Afoot again, and onward without halt,—
> Not soon, nor suddenly,—No, never to let go
> My hand
> in yours,
> Walt Whitman—
> so—

The fermatas for the eye function aurally, but the lines scan as regular iambics. We have the curious case of a perfectly conventional syllable-stress meter masquerading as the wildest free verse. Crane's prosodic posing conceals a pedestrian rhythm and an embarrassingly maudlin sentiment.

The example of Crane underlines a continuing assertion of this book: that prosody has neither decorative nor semantic functions apart from the work it does as a conveyer of feeling. As long as Crane used, or tried to use, Eliot's rhythms, he was expressing feelings inimical to his own temperament. He could not adapt Eliot's loosened metric to what he had to say. His view of the world did not include Eliot's particular horror and despair. Crane's gift, like Whitman's, was ceremonious and rhetorical; his true poetic *métier* was the apostrophe, the classic form of lyric celebration. His best works are set pieces: the "Proem: To Brooklyn Bridge," the "Voyages," and the magnificent conclusion to "The River."

In these poems we observe a sureness of prosodic technique; the rhythms neither falter nor prove embarrassing to the concepts. The meter Crane settles on is a traditional pentameter which lends itself to the cadences of invocation. The form may seem limiting; it restricts Crane to only a few octaves of feeling. But Crane's development as a poet, up to the time he leaped from the S. S. "Orizaba," was perfectly congruent with the meter in which he accomplished his best work. Actually, he had absorbed from Eliot and others more technique than his sensibility and experience could possibly transmute into first-rate poetry. Or, to put it differently, he possessed metrical knowledge which his emerging powers as a poet could not put to use.

Crane's true metrical idiom was the unashamedly rhetorical line of the Elizabethans. If Eliot at a crucial point in his career found the relaxed blank verse of Jacobean dramatists suited to his moods, so Crane discovered in Marlowe and Jonson rhythms consonant with his exuberance and awe. Here Crane celebrates the Brooklyn Bridge:

> O harp and altar, of the fury fused,
> (How could mere toil align thy choiring strings!)
> Terrific threshold of the prophet's pledge,
> Prayer of pariah, and the lover's cry,—
>
> Again the traffic lights that skim thy swift
> Unfractioned idiom, immaculate sigh of stars,
> Beading thy path—condense eternity:
> And we have seen night lifted in thine arms.
>
> Under thy shadow by the piers I waited;
> Only in darkness is thy shadow clear.
> The City's fiery parcels all undone,
> Already snow submerges an iron year . . .

O Sleepless as the river under thee,
Vaulting the sea, the prairies' dreaming sod,
Unto us lowliest sometime sweep, descend
And of the curveship lend a myth to God.

"Proem: To Brooklyn Bridge"

Earlier we suggested that the success of a prosody might be measured by what a poet can get away with. Crane's rhythm minimizes his uncertain, almost haphazard syntactical progression. Perhaps, by definition, the apostrophe requires no explicit grammar; the understood subject of every sentence is The Bridge, and every verb links the poet to his love. But without the binding meter, the omission of verbs and uncertain use of reference would be destructively apparent.

Crane's "mighty line" also overrides his flawed diction and conceals his queer metaphorical mixtures; carried along by the excited movement, we are not disposed to wonder what *unfractioned idiom* means, what precisely is intended by the image *Vaulting the sea,* or whether a neologism such as *curveship* is defensible. Similarly, possessed, even drugged by Crane's rhythms, we are apt to overlook obvious errors in the choice of words; *wrapt* in the fifth line below (from *Voyages II*) has grotesque connotations:

And yet this great wink of eternity,
Of rimless floods, unfettered leewardings,
Samite sheeted and processioned where
Her undinal vast belly moonward bends,
Laughing the wrapt inflections of our love . . .

Crane meant *rapt*—his misspelling may be a case of homonymic confusion. Again, the sounding rhythms conceal an ill-contrived syntax: every line is a shifted construction; images drift and float off, cut from their grammatical moorings. Crane's derangement of language is the result of his Dionysiac methods of composition, the raging of his personal demon, and his commitment to Symbolist practice. But the flaring heat of Crane's rhythm, the absolute energy of his genius, fuses the second stanza of *Voyages II:*

Take this Sea, whose diapason knells
On scrolls of silver snowy sentences,

The sceptered terror of whose sessions rends
As her demeanors motions well or ill,
All but the pieties of lovers' hands . . .

In three lines we find compacted grammatical ambiguity (is *knells* verb or noun?), a wild synaesthesia (*diapason* is *seen* on scrolls of snowy sentences), and Shakespearean cliché (*sceptred terror*).

These two stanzas appear to live on their prosody alone; the emotional force and solemn dignity of their rhythms seem, on first impact, independent of what the language is saying. But the metrical craft surprises with its sudden relevance; eternity's wink is felt as the spasmodic tremor of an inverted third foot:

And yét | this gréat | wínk of | e tér | ni tý . . .

We note other prosodical details. With few exceptions the lines are heavily end stopped. Crane unconsciously feels for rhymes: *bends* in the first stanza is echoed by *rends* and *hands* in the second stanza; *knells* is echoed by *ill.* The last two stanzas modulate into new clarity; aided now by syntactical closeness, a grammatically precise handling of imperatives, the metrical pressure forces the poet into prophetic lucidity as he foretells his own death by water:

Mark how her turning shoulders wind the hours,
And hasten while her penniless rich palms
Pass superscription of bent foam and wave,—
Hasten, while they are true,—sleep, death, desire,
Close round one instant in one floating flower.

Bind us in time, O Seasons clear, and awe.
O minstrel galleons of Carib fire,
Bequeath us to no earthly shore until
Is answered in the vortex of our grave
The seal's wide spindrift gaze toward paradise.

Perhaps Crane's greatest sustained passage is the concluding section of "The River." Syntax and meter are exactly suited here to Crane's feelings of relentless movement and religious awe:

Down, down—born pioneers in time's despite,
Grimed tributaries to an ancient flow—
They win no frontier by their wayward plight,
But drift in stillness, as from Jordan's brow.

You will not hear it as the sea; even stone
Is not more hushed by gravity . . . But slow,
As loth to take more tribute—sliding prone
Like one whose eyes were buried long ago

The River, spreading, flows—and spends your dream.
What are you, lost within this tideless spell?
You are your father's father, and the stream—
A liquid theme that floating niggers swell.

Damp tonnage and alluvial march of days—
Nights turbid, vascular with silted shale
And roots surrendered down of moraine clays:
The Mississippi drinks the farthest dale.

O quarrying passion, undertowed sunlight!
The basalt surface drags a jungle grace
Ochreous and lynx-barred in lengthening might;
Patience! and you shall reach the biding place!

Over De Soto's bones the freighted floors
Throb past the City storied of three thrones.
Down two more turns the Mississippi pours
(Anon tall ironsides up from salt lagoons)

And flows within itself, heaps itself free.
All fades but one thin skyline 'round . . . Ahead
No embrace opens but the stinging sea;
The River lifts itself from its long bed,

Poised wholly on its dream, a mustard glow
Tortured with history, its one will—flow!
—The Passion spreads in wide tongues, choked and slow,
Meeting the Gulf, hosannas silently below.

If, as Eliot points out, Marlowe "commenced the dissociative process which drew [blank verse] farther and farther away from the rhythms of rhymed verse,"[3] it was Crane who worked blank verse back into the rhythms of rhymed verse, and then attempted to revive rhymed verse as a major form. In these "heroic quatrains" from "The River" Crane discovers the prosodic form most congenial to his genius. His failures in freer rhythms and unrhymed verse point to the unformed, highly uneven quality of his genius—he had nowhere attained full powers before his death—and to a striking conflict of *Zeitgeist* and sensibility. Crane wanted to follow the "conversational mode" and prose syntax which Pound and Eliot espoused as *the* twentieth-century prosody (though their individual practice diverged widely from their professed ideals); he found himself, like those post-Miltonic writers of blank verse, Thomson and Warton, behind the unscalable Chinese Wall.

2

"A source of trumpeting seraphs in the eye,
"A source of pleasant outbursts on the ear.

"A Primitive Like an Orb"

"Music falls on the silence like a sense,
"A passion that we feel, not understand.

Notes toward a Supreme Fiction

Stevens had dealings with the Imagists, but what he bought from them he invested at considerable profit. *Harmonium* contains a number of poems in short lines which might be labeled "imagist"; they concentrate on presenting a single effect of sound or sight. But the "imagist" poem in *Harmonium* adds metaphysical depth to Imagist descriptive brilliance; we must pursue meaning down elusive symbolic ways. An Imagist poem usually has height and width, the image and its accompanying or resultant aura of feeling:

OREAD

Whirl up, sea—
Whirl your pointed pines.
Splash your great pines
On our rocks,
Hurl your green over us—
Cover us with your pools of fir.

H. D.

H. D. renders rather than describes her feelings; we sense the violence as we see the scene.

Stevens' three-dimensioned "imagist" poem may be illustrated by the brief and tantalizing "Valley Candle" (from *Harmonium*):

My candle burned alone in an immense valley.
Beams of the huge night converged upon it,
Until the wind blew.
Then beams of the huge night
Converged upon its image,
Until the wind blew.

The poem states in highly condensed and elliptical fashion what was to become Stevens' perennial theme: the interaction of the poetic mind with the creative imagination and final reality. As I read this poem, the candle symbolizes Coleridge's Imagination which "dissolves, diffuses, dissipates in order to recreate . . ."; the huge night is unilluminated reality—chaos, in effect. The candle—the poet's imagination—burns in isolation; it only partially illuminates, for the beams of unimagined reality threaten the flickering light. The coming of the wind marks the cessation of imaginative activity. First the candle, then its image vanish—and reality vanishes with both. The poem expresses a deep and characteristic pessimism; with the extinguishing of imagination, chaos extends its sinister dominion and brings oblivion both to mind and its imaginative constructs.

This paraphrase is more than usually inadequate; an extended analysis would reveal an even greater complexity of idea and feeling. But positive dangers lurk in extended analysis. So elusive are Stevens' meanings, so various the possible interpretations, that further exegesis only discovers contradiction. Stevens' method, with its coy use of open symbols, creates its own inevitable discrepancies. The candle may represent imagination, but also "mind" (in the philosophical or psychological sense?), or simple perception. Depending on how we read the symbols, the poem explores epistemological or ontological landscapes.

The only sure approach toward Stevens is through his other poems. "Valley Candle" is a sketch, a prelude in the sense that Chopin's *Préludes* make use of material elsewhere exploited. Stevens tells us that

One poem proves another and the whole,
For the clairvoyant men that need no proof:
The lover, the believer and the poet.

"A Primitive Like an Orb"

Poetry, like religion and love, is self-justifying; one's God, one's mistress, and one's experience of poetry need no explanation other than that gods, mistresses, and poems form essential parts of our comprehended reality. This may seem to resemble the doctrine of art for art's sake, but Stevens makes no dichotomy between poem and world, imagination and reality. For the art-for-art's-saker the poem builds a reality apart from experience; for Stevens *all* experience is aesthetic experience:

It is
As if the central poem became the world,
And the world the central poem, each one the mate
Of the other, as if summer was a spouse,
Espoused each morning . . .

"A Primitive Like an Orb"

The process of insight is circular [*Like an Orb*]; we come to know "The essential poem at the centre of things" by means of "lesser poems." Every act of speech creates a world; the smaller poems explain the larger; the larger poems form

. . . a poem of
The whole, the essential compact of the parts,
The roundness that pulls tight the final ring.

And so we have our *Orb.* We are reminded that a "lesser poem" in *Harmonium* bears the opulent title, "Frogs Eat Butterflies. Snakes Eat Frogs. Hogs Eat Snakes. Men Eat Hogs."

Given his theme, then, "The essential poem at the centre of things," we might expect to find Stevens a most delicate and elegant master of prosody. We return to "A Primitive Like an Orb" for further enlightenment; no one explains Stevens better than Stevens himself. The essential poem, "the miraculous multiplex of lesser poems," appears as

A giant, on the horizon, glistening,

IX

And in bright excellence adorned, crested
With every prodigal, familiar fire,

And unfamiliar escapades: whirroos
And scintillant sizzlings such as children like,
Vested in the serious folds of majesty,
Moving around and behind, a following,
A source of trumpeting seraphs in the eye,
A source of pleasant outbursts on the ear.

Obviously, for Stevens the "plain style" of poetry does not exist; its rhythms must sound with

Whirroos
And scintillant sizzlings such as children like . . .

Stevens captures exactly what children like, especially in those elegantly nonsensical and compactly meaningful poems like "The Ordinary Women":

Then from their poverty they rose,
From dry catarrhs, and to guitars
They flitted
Through the palace walls.

They flung monotony behind,
Turned from their want, and, nonchalant,
They crowded
The nocturnal halls.

The lacquered loges huddled there
Mumbled zay-zay and a-zay, a-zay.
The moonlight
Fubbed the girandoles.

Another "piece of sophisticated looniness" (to quote Theodore Roethke[4]) which we cherish for its delicious music is the "Cortège for Rosenbloom." The rhythmic theme, stated in the first stanza, derives from the two heavy stresses in the name of the departed:

Now, the wry Rosenbloom is dead
And his finical carriers tread,
On a hundred legs, the tread
Of the dead.
Rosenbloom is dead.

This processional music turns oriental, and the meter settles into two strong beats as the feet of "the finical carriers" rise and fall:

> To a chirr of gongs
> And a chitter of cries
> And the heavy thrum
> Of the endless tread
> That they tread;
>
> To a jangle of doom
> And a jumble of words
> Of the intense poem
> Of the strictest prose
> Of Rosenbloom.

Stevens' absolute delight in sound led early critics into curious excesses. We have this impressionist outburst of Paul Rosenfeld, much in the James Huneker manner:

> The playing of a Chinese orchestra. On a gong a bonze creates a copper din. The most amazing cacophony amid dissolving labials and silkiest sibilants. Quirks, booms, whistles, quavers. Lord, what instruments has he there? Small muffled drums? Plucked wires? The falsetto of an ecstatic eunuch?[5]

Rosenfeld makes no attempt to penetrate the surface music; he credits Stevens with ". . . a music signaled as vain, an exaltation, not so much 'without sound' as without object, a bland, curiously philosophical movement of the soul without signification. What he has to say appears too useless for him to say it out."[6]

Subsequent criticism has, of course, taken Stevens more seriously; a recent essay by Geoffrey Moore is called "Wallace Stevens: A Hero of Our Time." This is a long way from Rosenfeld —and Gorham Munson's "The Dandyism of Wallace Stevens."[7] A world of preoccupation has been discovered beneath the "scintillant sizzlings" of Stevens' highly finished poetic surfaces. It should not have taken so long to discover. "Le Monocle de Mon Oncle" is as successful a poem about a self-mocking middle-aged lover as "Prufrock"; "Sunday Morning" deals as significantly with the problems of religious belief as *The Waste Land.* And Stevens is a master, to the same high degree as Eliot, of the "auditory imagination": the ability to probe beneath the pia mater of consciousness, to evoke, by means of rhythm, states of feeling so subtle that they forever defy paraphrase in conceptual language.

We might match tropes from "Le Monocle de Mon Oncle" and "Prufrock" to show Stevens as Eliot's prosodic equal.[8] The thematic material of both poems is similar:

> And so I mocked her in magnificent measure.
> Or was it that I mocked myself alone?
> I wish that I might be a thinking stone.

———

> I should have been a pair of ragged claws
> Scuttling across the floors of silent seas.

———

> Shall I uncrumple this much-crumpled thing?
> I am a man of fortune greeting heirs;
> For it has come that thus I greet the spring.
> These choirs of welcome choir for me farewell.

———

> Shall I part my hair behind? Do I dare to eat a peach?
> I shall wear white flannel trousers, and walk upon the beach.
> I have heard the mermaids singing, each to each.
>
> I do not think that they will sing to me.

In the anguish of his embarrassment, the protagonist of "Le Monocle de Mon Oncle" wishes to be a "thinking stone"; Prufrock prefers the complete obliteration of his acute self-consciousness. The mermaids snub Prufrock; the spring choirs farewell to the aging uncle.

If anything, Stevens achieves greater subtlety in his exact iambics than Eliot in his more elastic metric. The most memorable lines of both poets, however, fall into quite close pentameters. Eliot's pentameter lines follow some anapestic stretching; the couplet of the ragged claws, and the stiffly iambic

> I do not think that they will sing to me . . .

afford a marked change of pace. The prosody is also aided by the self-consciously portentous visual isolation of the lines. Stevens maintains a more homogeneous texture, though he will occasionally invert feet and add hypermetrical syllables:

And só | I mócked | hér in | mag ní | fi cent méa | sure . . .

3

The prosody of "Valley Candle" is based on simple repetitions and parallelisms. "Anecdote of the Prince of Peacocks" has a delicately varied two-stress line; I quote the final strophe:

> I knew from this
> That the blue ground
> Was full of blocks
> And blocking steel.
> I knew the dread
> Of the bushy plain,
> And the beauty
> Of the moonlight
> Falling there,
> Falling
> As sleep falls
> In the innocent air.

How "free" this highly controlled verse actually is we leave to the reader's judgment; note the use of rhythmic constants (That the blue ground . . . Of the moonlight), the occasional rhyme, and the diminuendo indicated by the gradual shortening of line length:

> Of the moonlight
> Falling there,
> Falling . . .

This use of line "shape" suggests Imagist practice. The first stanza of "Tattoo" (*Harmonium*) moves outward toward the margin, then pulls itself in:

> The light is like a spider.
> It crawls over the water.
> It crawls over the edges of the snow.

It crawls under your eyelids
And spreads its webs there—
Its two webs.

A more formal prosodic scheme orders the rhythms of "Peter Quince at the Clavier." The title and the opening image,

Just as my fingers on these keys
Make music, so the selfsame sounds
On my spirit make a music, too . . .

signal an explicit musical organization. Stevens comments on his own method, and on the function of prosody as we conceive it, when he meditates

Music is feeling, then, not sound . . .

Phoneticians, please take note!

The four movements of "Peter Quince" offer contrasts in tempo, and critics have recognized affinities to the four-movement form of the classical symphony. We make no positive point for point identifications other than noting that the third section might be considered a scherzo, *allegro molto vivace.* The first movement is *moderato,* the second *andante,* and the last *andante* again. This does not correspond to the movements of classical sonata-symphony form (Allegro-Andante-Minuet-Allegro) and it reverses the scheme of the baroque sonata (slow-fast-slow-fast). However, the obvious juxtaposition of contrasting movements and the use of repeated themes justify naming the structure of "Peter Quince" a musical one.

The meter of movements I, III, and IV is iambic tetrameter; Stevens gets fabulous variety in this traditional line. Two significant sources of metrical interest are the initial trochee,

Júst as | my físng | ers ón | these kéys . . .

Músic | is féel | ing, thén, | not sóund . . .

Hére in | this róom, | de sír | ing yóu,

Thínk ing | of yóur | blùe-shá | dowed sílk . . .

and the slight tension of a metrically stressed syllable nudging a nonmetrically but rhetorically stressed syllable:

. . . the sélf | sàme sóunds . . .

And thús | it ís | thàt whát | I féel . . .

. . . of yóur | blùe-shá | dowed sílk . . .

A rising Ionic marks a shift in the poet's thought when he forgets the object of his own desire and remembers Susanna:

Of a gréen éve | ning, cléar | and wárm . . .

Alliteration emphasizes the mounting blood pressure of the lecherous elders:

The red-eyed elders watching, felt

The basses of their beings throb
In witching chords, and their thin blood
Pulse pizzicati of Hosanna.

Again we have the delicate crowding of metrically and rhetorically stressed syllables:

The réd- | èyed él | ders . . .

and théir | thìn blóod . . .

The second movement alternates a slow two-and-one-stress line; it also introduces a tender, sensuous feminine rhyming. The last three lines of the second movement serve as an *attacca,* indicating that the third movement follows without a break:

She turned—
A cymbal crashed,
And roaring horns.

Stevens' musical vocabulary underscores his intentions. A mention of horns and cymbals lead us into dance rhythms, although the meter remains four-stress iambic:

Soon with a noise like tambourines,
Came her attendant Byzantines.

They wondered why Susanna cried
Against the elders by her side;

And as they whispered, the refrain
Was like a willow swept by rain.

Lengthened vowels and tinkling rhymes reach across the meter in lightly accented cross-rhythms; dotted lines show bar lines and note-values show approximate syllabic length:

$\frac{2}{4}$ Soon with | a noise | like ¦ tam | bour ¦ ines

In the final movement the music returns to the meditative pace of the opening. But there are important prosodic changes. The obsessive feminine rhyming,

So evenings die, in their green going,
A wave, interminably flowing.
So gardens die, their meek breath scenting
The cowl of winter, done repenting.
So maidens die, to the auroral
Celebration of a maiden's choral.

contains reminiscences of the second movement; the repetitions of words and rhythms suggest Romantic, cyclical, rather than eighteenth-century sonata form. These quiet feminine endings give a "dying fall," a vanishing quality to the whole passage. I know of few passages so thoroughly suggestive of gentle fading away, flowing away, as this one.

Less professedly musical than "Peter Quince," "Sea Surface Full of Clouds" is actually a theme and a set of four variations. Stevens uses the variation-form elsewhere in *Harmonium;* we have the brief "Nuances of a Theme by Williams" and the more elaborate "Thirteen Ways of Looking at a Blackbird." But nothing Stevens ever wrote equals the sheer technical bravura of "Sea Surface Full of Clouds."

The overall design shows a classical symmetry. There are five sections, each made up of six three-line pentameter stanzas. This iambic triad proved an especially felicitous discovery for Stevens; in it he composed his important longer poems, the *Notes toward a Supreme Fiction,* and the *Auroras of Autumn,* as well as a number of his finest shorter pieces, the "Final Soliloquy of the Interior Paramour" and the late, extraordinarily moving "The World as Meditation." Unlike these great, final works, "Sea Surface Full of Clouds" chimes with rhyme and interior consonances and alliterations. No mere listing of its technical features does the work justice; no quoting of examples explains the way the poem uses repetition, ornamentation, and variation. The musical analogues to "Sea Surface Full of Clouds" are Mozart's piano variations where theme and structure remain clearly delineated in each variation. Mozartean, too, is that combination of gaiety and formal perfection: an almost otherworldly joy carried by a technique at once astonishing and effortless.

Theme-and-variation stand at the very center of Stevens' poetic method. It is no exaggeration to say that all his work after *Harmonium* represents variations on a single theme: a theory of poetry which would also be a theory of reality. This is, of course, a large order; it limited Stevens no more than James's obsession with innocence and evil limited him. Stevens set a high value on developing a theory of poetry. Something of his passion about aesthetic matters can be felt in these excerpts from *The Necessary Angel:*

> The theory of poetry, as a subject of study, was something with respect to which I had nothing but the most ardent ambitions. It seemed to me to be one of the great subjects of study.[9]
>
> Yet hypotheses relating to poetry, although they may appear to be very distant illuminations, could be the fires of fate, if rhetoric ever meant anything.[10]

Stevens believed that poetry's mode of operation lay in the recognition of resemblances. Metaphor, not imitation, formed the basis of poetic knowledge; quarrelling with that rattling old skeleton Aristotle, Stevens wittily observed "An imitation may be described as an identity *manqué.*"[11] "Sea Surface Full of Clouds" is a poetic rendering of what the sea and the sky resembled on five successive mornings, of what "they made one think of. . . ." Now here exists the perfect opportunity for a prosody based on musical form; the theme-and-variation technique keeps the musical idea in mind (in ear) while continually changing its mode of resemblance. And the variations ultimately assume a greater importance than the theme—which may be trivial, or as in Beethoven's *Diabelli Variations,* neutral fuel for the blaze of imagination.

"The proliferation of resemblances extends an object."[12] In a late composition, "Analysis of a Theme," Stevens extends and varies a previous theme:

> It was when the trees were leafless first in November
> And their blackness became apparent, that one first
> Knew the eccentric to be the base of design.
>
> "Like Decorations in a Nigger Cemetery"

"Analysis of a Theme" changes the object and the tone; the theme exuberantly illustrates rather than gravely theorizes:

THEME

> How happy I was the day I told the young
> Blandina of three-legged giraffes . . .

The stanzas which follow explore first "the conscious world" where there is no "true tree," where resemblances are between parts of unimagined reality. The concluding two stanzas show resemblances among imagined things. We delight in fabulous beasts; poetic knowledge creates its special happiness, the joys of eccentric design:

> The knowledge of bright-ethered things
> Bears us toward time, on its
> Perfective wings.
>
> We enjoy the ithy oonts and long-haired
> Plomets, as the Herr Gott
> Enjoys his comets.

Stevens uses a shortened three-line stanza; the texture and rich iambic music of "Sea Surface Full of Clouds" have disappeared. We find an apparent casualness of rhyme and functional, rather than formal, rhythms. But the prosodic ease is deceptive. The shift from iambs to anapests in the first line of the last stanza is "accidental" in the way that such "accidents" happen to poets of genius and long experience.

4

It would require a small book to assay the prosodic gold which shines in Stevens' blank verse. He is the superlative modern master of the form. Marianne Moore's commendation, "Not infrequently Wallace Stevens's 'noble accents and lucid, inescapable rhythms' point to the universal parent, Shakespeare,"[13] is not a reviewer's compliment; it is a simple truth. Yvor Winters has also approvingly noted "Sunday Morning" "to contain . . . a sweetness and . . . an illusory simplicity which . . . are scarcely less than Shakespearean. . . ."[14]

In surveying the development of Stevens' blank verse, "Sunday Morning" stands as our point of departure. The opening lines define iambic movement without maintaining a clear metrical norm. The first and third lines have only three rhetorical stresses; the second line has eleven syllables, the fourth has a trochaic third foot,

> Complacencies of the peignoir, and late
> Coffee and oranges in a sunny chair,
> And the green freedom of a cockatoo
> Upon a rug mingle to dissipate
> The holy hush of ancient sacrifice.

and not until the fifth line does the verse settle down into regular iambic pentameter. Throughout the rest of the poem, scansion shows the usual departures from the traditional blank verse "code": the inverted initial foot; the caesura after the fourth, fifth, or sixth syllable; the maintenance of the decasyllabic line. The trisyllabic foot, common to Websterian blank verse, is rare, and can be usually rationalized in elision:

> The skýˊ | will béˊ | much fríˊend | li‿er thénˊ | than nóˊw . . .
> The tréˊes, | like séˊ | ra fíˊn, | and éˊch | o‿ing híˊlls . . .

Still rarer is the inverted final foot; we find one example, however, in "Sunday Morning,"

> E láˊ | tions whénˊ | the fórˊ | est blóˊoms; | gúˊs ty . . .

and another in a later poem, "A Primitive Like an Orb":

And ín | brìght éx | cel lénce | a dórned, | crés ted . . .

Numerous lines contain only four strong rhetorical stresses with the fifth metrical accent falling variously on syllables of low dynamic quality. We find the typically Shakespearean,

Of men that perish and of summer morn . . .

A part of labor and a part of pain . . .

where four-stress structure peers through the pentameter. There is little cross-rhythmical tension, however; Stevens is controlling rather than releasing feeling. The position of the light metrical stress varies; it sometimes falls on *and,*

The bough of summer *and* the winter branch . . .

Deer walk upon our mountains, *and* the quail . . .

and occasionally on an auxiliary or a preposition,

Does ripe fruit never fall? Or *do* the boughs . . .

Alone, shall come fulfilment *to* our dreams . . .

By the consummation *of* the swallow's wings . . .

The last line above begins with a trisyllabic foot; this eleven-syllable line is an obvious exception to the usual elision of the extra syllable.

The music of "Sunday Morning" is not Shakespearean throughout; we hear other harmonies, Tennyson's, for example:

Winding across wide water, without sound.
The day is like wide water, without sound,
Stilled for the passing of her dreaming feet . . .

The unbroken sentence concluding "Sunday Morning," with its energetic verbs and active syntax, suggests the last stanza of Keats's *Ode to Autumn:*

Deer walk upon our mountains, and the quail
Whistle about us their spontaneous cries;
Sweet berries ripen in the wilderness;
And, in the isolation of the sky,
At evening, casual flocks of pigeons make
Ambiguous undulations as they sink,
Downward to darkness, on extended wings.

We feel here that pulse of meditation which quickens the Keatsian sublime: a physical sense of thought dramatized for the eyes and ears of the reader. The deer *walk,* the quail *whistle,* the berries *ripen,* the pigeons *sink;* these actions are bound together by the sounding rhythms of superlative blank verse aided by recurring patterns within the metrical structure. The final line, by way of valediction, shows the characteristic rhythmic constant of the whole poem: four strong rhetorical stresses, here pointed up by alliteration.

The blank verse of "The Idea of Order at Key West" is pitched higher than the verse of "Sunday Morning"; it has a surface hardness, a more emphatic drive to its rhythms. While the opening of "Sunday Morning" is quiet and metrically evasive, "The Idea of Order" opens with strident precision:

She sang beyond the genius of the sea.
The water never formed to mind or voice,
Like a body wholly body, fluttering
Its empty sleeves; and yet its mimic motion
Made constant cry, caused constantly a cry,
That was not ours although we understood,
Inhuman, of the veritable ocean.

We find less delicacy than in "Sunday Morning" but considerably more energy. Occasional rhymes and repetitions punctuate the line endings:

Even if what she sang was what she heard,
Since what she sang was uttered word by word.
It may be that in all her phrases stirred
The grinding water and the gasping wind;
But it was she and not the sea we heard.

Perhaps nowhere in Stevens' poetry does his central theme achieve such luminously clear expression. The singer represents the mind which creates the reality it contemplates—the imagination which orders the world into being, knowledge, and, ultimately, value:

> She was the single artificer of the world
> In which she sang. And when she sang, the sea,
> Whatever self it had, became the self
> That was her song, for she was the maker. Then we,
> As we beheld her striding there alone,
> Knew that there never was a world for her
> Except the one she sang and, singing, made.

The volume *Ideas of Order* (1935) contains several poems in three-line stanzas. We notice a change in prosodic style, a shift away from blank-verse firmness and resonance to a newer kind of transparence and rhythmic freedom. "Anglais Mort à Florence" retains the foot structure of blank verse, but the grand rhetoric of "The Idea of Order at Key West" and the Shakespearean cadences of "Sunday Morning" have both disappeared. In their place we find elements of the style which receives apotheosis in *Notes toward a Supreme Fiction* and the superb valedictory poems of *The Rock*. Individual sentences tend to be short, the rhythms clipped, and the texture thinned out:

ANGLAIS MORT À FLORENCE

> A little less returned for him each spring.
> Music began to fail him. Brahms, although
> His dark familiar, often walked apart.
>
> His spirit grew uncertain of delight,
> Certain of uncertainty, in which
> That dark companion left him unconsoled . . .

Compare these lines with "Sad Strains of a Gay Waltz":

> The truth is that there comes a time
> When we can moan no more over music
> That is so much motionless sound.
>
> There comes a time when the waltz
> Is no longer a mode of desire, a mode
> Of revealing desire and is empty of shadows.

Stevens breaks up iambic structure without rendering his rhythms flaccid. We observe a further development toward the rhythmic form of *Notes toward a Supreme Fiction* in "Of Hartford in a Purple Light." The lines are four or five stressed but without a strict sense of blank verse motion:

OF HARTFORD IN A PURPLE LIGHT

A long time you have been making the trip
From Havre to Hartford, Master Soleil,
Bringing the lights of Norway and all that.

A long time the ocean has come with you,
Shaking the water off, like a poodle,
That splatters incessant thousands of drops . . .

Stevens never turned completely away from traditional blank verse. He returns to it again and again, often in moods of celebration, of rhetorical pomp, or expansive love:

What more is there to love than I have loved?
And if there be nothing more, O bright, O bright,
The chick, the chidder-barn and grassy chives

And great moon, cricket-impresario,
And, hoy, the impopulous purple-plated past,
Hoy, hoy, the blue bulls kneeling down to rest.

"Montrachet-le-Jardin"

Our previous example from "A Primitive Like an Orb,"

And in bright excellence adorned, crested
With every prodigal, familiar fire,
And unfamiliar escapades . . .

is Miltonic, a high style though one which also admits suppleness and conversational ease. The final stanza of "A Primitive Like an Orb" departs from blank verse with numerous trisyllabic feet and internal pauses. We hear thought becoming music, not a man thinking in meter:

That's it. The lover writes, the believer hears,
The poet mumbles and the painter sees,
Each one, his fated eccentricity,
As a part, but part, but tenacious particle,
Of the skeleton of the ether, the total
Of letters, prophecies, perceptions, clods
Of color, the giant of nothingness, each one
And the giant ever changing, living in change.

5

The line and stanza patterning of *Notes toward a Supreme Fiction* would delight a medieval poet's sense of the power and significance of number. Three, seven, ten, and their related sums and multiplications figure in the poem's organization. The three largest sections are called, "It must be abstract; It must change; It must give pleasure." Each large section is subdivided into ten smaller sections; each of these smaller sections is made up of seven three-line stanzas.

We have no difficulty scanning the verse of *Notes toward a Supreme Fiction;* the usual "rules" work well enough. Most of the lines are five-stressed, though less than half the lines contain ten syllables.[15] The rhythm of blank verse surges forward at times, then fades and dissolves into other cadences. Stability and change are not, however, poles of absolute dramatic contrast but elements interfused in the overriding rhythms of the poem. The following section begins with marked metrical irregularities which modulate at the seventh line into closer pentameter. The rhythm actually *contracts* from a rhetorical flow, controlled by a figure of grammar ("To sing . . . To be crested . . . to exult," etc.) to lines controlled by precisely metrical feet:

To sing jubilas at exact, accustomed times,
To be crested and wear the mane of a multitude
And so, as part, to exult with its great throat,

To speak of joy and to sing of it, borne on
The shoulders of joyous men, to feel the heart
That is the common, the bravest fundament,

This is a facile exercise. Jerome
Begat the tubas and the fire-wind strings,
The golden fingers picking dark-blue air:

For companies of voices moving there,
To find of sound the bleakest ancestor,
To find of light a music issuing

Whereon it falls in more than sensual mode . . .

"It Must Give Pleasure"

The meter impresses itself upon the meaning with considerable ingenuity. The first two stanzas speak of actual human emotions: praise, the sharing of communal feelings, joy, and exultation. The second pair of stanzas turn toward feeling as it is transformed into music, into the "more than sensual mode." An emphatic antithesis is clarified by the metrical stressing of *That* and *This:*

Thát is | the cóm | mon, the brá | vest fún | da mént,
Thís is | a fá | cile éx | er císe. | Je róme . . .

Our "facile exercise" proceeds with facility in clearest pentameter:

Be gát | the tú | bas ánd | the fíre- | wìnd stríngs,
The gól | den fín | gers píck | ing dárk- | blùe aír:
For cóm | pa níes | of vóí | ces móv | ing thére . . .

Feelings of the heart, however, move in quite different, less obviously "artificial" rhythms:

To síng | jú bi las | at ex áct, | ac cús | tomed tímes,
To be crés | ted and wéar | the máne | of a múl | ti túde . . .

Stevens never wrenches his tone to accommodate the meter. He never omits syllables to achieve a more precise beat, but allows the movement of conversation to take over whenever the argument of the poem demands it. Often the rhythm shifts in midline, from rising to falling:

On her trip around the world, Nanzia Nunzio
Confronted Ozymandias . . .

The rising iambic rhythm is occasionally confuted by an inverted final foot, a metrical mannerism of Stevens,

> The first idea was not our own. *Adam* . . .

> To speak of joy and to sing of it, *borne on* . . .

or by reversing the highly susceptible second foot,

> The book, *hot for* another accessible bliss . . .

> The spent *feeling* leaving nothing of itself . . .

A syllable which would ordinarily have been omitted by an earlier poet will intrude in an otherwise regular passage:

> It might and might have been. But as it was,
> A *dead* shepherd brought tremendous chords from hell
>
> And bade the sheep carouse. Or so they said.
> Children in love with them brought early flowers
> And scattered them about, no two alike.

This *dead* Saintsbury would have certainly named a "perversity." But in Stevens' metrical context the extra syllable scarcely stirs a ripple.

The metrical form of *Notes toward a Supreme Fiction* dominates the important poems of Stevens' two final volumes, *The Auroras of Autumn* and *The Rock*. The three-line stanza, the open rhythms approaching blank verse, and a new clarity of texture mark the final evolution of Stevens' prosody. The stanza itself, the triad, enters more actively into rhythmic structure; it retards, connects, holds over, or looks ahead:

> Farewell to an idea . . . A cabin stands,
> Deserted, on a beach. It is white,
> As by a custom or according to
>
> An ancestral theme or as a consequence
> Of an infinite course. The flowers against the wall
> Are white, a little dried, a kind of mark
>
> Reminding, trying to remind, of a white
> That was different, something else, last year
> Or before, not the white of an aging afternoon,

Whether fresher or duller, whether of winter cloud
Or of winter sky, from horizon to horizon.
The wind is blowing the sand across the floor.

The Auroras of Autumn, II

Stevens uses the caesura not only as a metrical comma, a breathing pause in the middle of the line, but also as an integral element in rhythmic phrasing. Interior pausing conceals the metrical pulse and heightens the normal tensions of meaning: the resolutions of syntactical expectation and the logic of grammar. In the lines below the caesuras continually delay our full apprehension of the sense; the syntactical cadence is held off until we nearly lose the grammatical thread:

The flowers against the wall
Are white, a little dried, a kind of mark

Reminding, trying to remind, of a white
That was different, something else, last year
Or before, not the white of an aging afternoon . . .

Each caesural pause affects the dynamics of the phrasing; the repeated hesitations build up in a minor crescendo, a steadily rising curve of intensity. Stevens phrases his lines as a musician might phrase a melody.

The stylistic development evident in these two final volumes approaches that ultimate *poetry beyond poetry* envisioned by Eliot.[16] The poems of *The Rock* come close to achieving the transcendence of "poetry standing naked in its bare bones." We mention two of the finest of these last poems: "To an Old Philosopher in Rome" and "The World as Meditation." They decline all deliberate effects; what exists as music in these poems is completely absorbed in what they say. If we recognize that these lines possess a blank verse base and prose rhythm, we recognize what is both obvious and nearly irrelevant:

The bed, the books, the chair, the moving nuns,
The candle as it evades the sight, these are
The sources of happiness in the shape of Rome,
A shape within the ancient circles of shapes,
And these beneath the shadow of a shape . . .

"To an Old Philosopher in Rome"

We find further refinements in "The World as Meditation." Specific phonetic values, the densities of consonant and vowel hardly exist as "prosody"—though we may hear, sounding like a string quartet playing in some distant room, the music of blank verse:

> The trees had been mended, as an essential exercise
> In an inhuman meditation, larger than her own,
> No winds like dogs watched over her at night.
>
> She wanted nothing he could not bring her by coming alone.
> She wanted no fetchings. His arms would be her necklace
> And her belt, the final fortune of their desire.
>
> But was it Ulysses? Or was it only the warmth of the sun
> On her pillow? The thought kept beating in her like her heart.
> The two kept beating together. It was only day.

Neither sensuous immediacy nor deliberate organization distracts us "from what the poem *points* at."[17] Stevens maintains his three-line stanza; an occasional pentameter line flickers across the page:

> No winds like dogs watched over her at night . . .

But prosody has dissolved into meaning; technique has become both thought and expression. We may exclaim, as Thomas Mann's Wendell Kretschmar exclaimed over the second movement of Beethoven's *Sonata Opus 111,* "Here—the appearance—of art is thrown off—at last—art always throws off the appearance of art."[18]

IX

The Generation of Auden

We conclude our prosodic studies with a group of poets born in the decade 1907–17: the "second generation" of modern poets. The selection of poets indicates no canon, no conferring of "great" or "best." Criticism, especially of living writers, cannot be hagiography. The major figure in this section is Auden; the other poets, English and American, have written work of prosodic interest and value, and are now old enough to have shown a course of stylistic development.

Auden's work set new fashions in prosody. Nearly half the poems in his first book, *Poems* (1930), are in regular stanzaic forms. Hopkins, whose work was published too late to have had any significant effect on Pound and Eliot, is prosodically very much in evidence. It is largely through Auden and Dylan Thomas that Hopkins' techniques became common currency during the thirties and forties. Auden also made good use of some of Wilfred Owen's experiments in off-rhyme and assonance. Other of Auden's interests, especially in Anglo-Saxon poetry, have borne important fruit; the current generation of poets are, in a real sense, his technical heirs. One critic, A. Alvarez, credits Auden with reversing the trend initiated by Eliot and Pound and returning English poetry to its proper tradition:

> English literature now, in the 1950s, is safely back on the track that seemed to have been abandoned when *Prufrock and Other Observations* appeared in 1917; it is back in the old way of traditional forms, traditional language and more or less traditional sentiments. It has got there . . . by way of the

work of Auden and his poetic colleagues. Auden himself, as an undergraduate poet, was obviously influenced by Eliot, but there is essentially almost nothing in common between them.[1]

The discerning of trends is especially dangerous when poets are still taking bearings and setting courses: it is not *essentially* true that with Auden twentieth-century poetry suddenly turned back to traditional metric. After Auden prosodic style veered sharply away from unmetered and loosely metered verse. The trend still more or less holds; the poets of the late forties and fifties have shown an almost religious devotion to iambic pentameter, intricate stanzas, and close formal arrangements. In two representative first volumes, W. S. Merwin's *A Mask for Janus* (1952) and Anthony Hecht's *A Summoning of Stones* (1954), we find several sonnets, a rare double sonnet, a couple of sestinas, a half-roundel, and one poem of seven stanzas built on two rhymes and a refrain.

But a reaction to the reaction has unquestionably set in. We find in Roethke's *Words for the Wind* (1958) a wealth of poems written in traditional meters, but also the magnificent "Elegy for Jane," composed in unmetered, Whitmanesque lines of varied length. Robert Lowell's first major collection, *Lord Weary's Castle* (1946), written entirely in rhymed syllable-stress meters, has been followed by *Life Studies* (1959), whose verse is sharply stressed but rarely metrical. Certainly, the poetry of the sixties is turning away from the technical influence of Auden; it is, however, too soon to say whether we are moving into a new period of relaxed meters and looser rhythms.

We conclude our inquiry at a point where prosodic trends initiated by Auden in 1930 now seem to have run their course of development. It may be that prosody will continue to shift from right to left, from the restraint of the traditional meters to the freedom of the nonmetrical prosodies; it may be that an entirely new period style will emerge from the current trends. Or some dominating figure, such as Pound or Auden, will exert a major influence and urge *his* prosodic discoveries on a new generation of poets.

1 W. H. Auden

Auden would trust implicitly a critic who could say "yes" to this query:

> "Do you like, and by like I really mean like, not approve of on principle:
>
> Complicated verse forms of great technical difficulty, such as Englyns, Drott-Kvaetts, Sestinas, even if their content is trivial?"[2]

Auden may be indulging in some good-natured critic-baiting. Only students of Old Norse are apt to have developed an affection for *drott-kvaett* ("court measure"), the intricate stanza of Skaldic poetry. But the query is not facetious. The most ingenious explicator of texts will neglect to name the meter and stanza of a poem from which he has extracted fourteen levels of meaning. To most critics prosody is simply not "meaning"; metrics and versification are deemed contemptible studies. Poets are afflicted with similar ignorance; Auden, in his "Daydream College for Bards," requires the study of Greek, Hebrew, rhetoric, comparative philology, and prosody.

Auden's work reflects his fascination with prosodic techniques. He has used the sestina, the villanelle, the canzon; he has invented or adapted many complicated stanzas; he is a master of assonance, rhyme, pararhyme, and refrain. He writes songs and sonnets with the fluency of an Elizabethan; he has revived the ballad. To many this makes him a poet's poet, or worse, a prosodist's poet! Admittedly, Auden's poetry presents a prosodist's feast—but, at least to me, a feast not unlike that offered a musical analyst by the ingenuity and wealth of Bach's fugues and canons. I do not know whether Auden is a great poet; I suspect he has, paradoxically, too much to say. His language lacks resonance, and the imagination behind the language is frequently commonplace. We rarely marvel at a poem of Auden's before we fully understand it, as we marvel at:

> And all their eyes still fixed, hoping to find once more,
> Being by Calvary's turbulence unsatisfied,
> The uncontrollable mystery on the bestial floor.

But if we accept Eliot's reasons for ascribing greatness to Tennyson, "abundance, variety, and complete competence,"[3] we must, at least, admit Auden into the pantheon of important poets.

Our first example is the title poem from *Look, Stranger* (1936), a fine illustration of Auden's lyric manner:

> Look, stranger at this island now
> The leaping light for your delight discovers,
> Stand stable here
> And silent be,
> That through the channels of the ear
> May wander like a river
> The swaying sound of the sea.
>
> Here at the small field's ending pause
> Where the chalk wall falls to the foam, and its
> tall ledges
> Oppose the pluck
> And knock of the tide,
> And the shingle scrambles after the suck-
> ing surf, and the gull lodges
> A moment on its sheer side.
>
> Far off like floating seeds the ships
> Diverge on urgent voluntary errands;
> And the full view
> Indeed may enter
> And move in memory as now these clouds do,
> That pass the harbour mirror
> And all the summer through the water saunter.

The wealth of prosodic detail, including interior rhymes and a variety of metrical feet, does not impede its iambic music. The first line, with its initial falling Ionic,

Lóok, strán ger at | this ís | land nów

is balanced by the next line, with its quick iambs and delightful inner rhyme,

The léap | ing líght | for yóur | de líght | dis cóv | ers . . .

The rhyming deserves special notice. The mixture of conventional rhymes and consonantal half-rhyme (sometimes called *pararhyme*) derives from Wilfred Owen.[4] The jamming together of strong stresses, the programmatic alliteration, and the minor mannerism of splitting a rhyme word between two lines

> And the shingle scrambles after the suck-
> ing surf, and the gull lodges . . .

are familiar features of Hopkins' idiom.

Hopkins-like alliterative and assonantal patterns distinguish our next example; the entire poem from which it is taken is disappointing (XV from *Look, Stranger*), but the first two stanzas are brilliant in imagery and exciting in rhythms:

> The chimneys are smoking, the crocus is out in the border;
> The mountain ranges are massive in the blue March day;
> Like a sea god the political orator lands at the pier;
> But, O, my magnet, my pomp, my beauty
> More telling to heart than the sea,
> Than Europe or my own home town
> To-day is parted from me
> And I stand on our world alone.
>
> Over the town now, in for an hour from the desert
> A hawk looks down on us all; he is not in this;
> Our kindness is hid from the eye of the vivid creature;
> Sees only the configuration of field,
> Copse, chalk-pit, and fallow,
> The distribution of forces,
> The play of sun and shadow
> On upturned faces.

The stanza consists of three five-stress lines followed by five lines of three or four stresses. The five-line section is rhymed either "straight" (*sea / me*) or obliquely (*forces / faces; fallow / shadow*). Trisyllabic feet preponderate in the long lines; the rhythm falls. The rhythm of the short lines runs counter, in rising iambs:

> But, Ó, | my mág | net, my pómp, | my béau | ty

The complexity of prosodic means and the whole rhythmic *élan* bring it very close to sprung rhythm; we are not surprised to discover a minor theft from Hopkins' *The Loss of the Eurydice:*

> And you were a liar, O blue March day.
> Bright sun lanced fire in the heavenly bay;
> But what black Boreas wrecked her? he
> Came equipped, deadly-electric . . .

In *Another Time* (1940) Auden moves away from his early masters and writes a number of his most characteristic pieces. A new style is apparent; we find none of the articleless mannerism and Old English primitivism of

> Save him from hostile capture,
> From sudden tiger's spring at corner;
> Protect his house
> His anxious house where days are counted
> From thunderbolt protect . . .

11, from *Poems* (1930)

but a more personal, more unadorned speech. Auden emigrated to America in 1939; his new style, with its eschewal of the deliberately literary and its sloughing off of obvious influences, has the appearance of a symbolic gesture to his adopted country. The prosody shows diminished contrivance and a greater operating efficiency. The first three lines of "Musée des Beaux Arts" are decasyllabic, but only roughly iambic:

> A bóut | súf fer | ing théy | were né | ver wróng,
> The Óld | Más ters: | how wéll | they ún | der stóod
> Its hú | man po sí | tion; ∧ | how it tákes pláce . . .

The unsettling trochee in the second foot of the first two lines and the anomalous third line pull the rhythm away from blank verse. Succeeding lines amble into prose:

> While someone else is eating or opening a window or just
> walking dully along;
> How, when the aged are reverently, passionately waiting
> For the miraculous birth, there always must be
> Children who did not specially want it to happen, skating . . .

Rhyme serves to punctuate, to either separate or link sections of the poem. The final lines *fall* in approximate dactyls, suggesting, perhaps, Icarus' spiraling descent:

> Sóme thing a | máz ing, a | bóy fal ling | óut of the | skу́,
>
> Had | sóme where to | gét to and | sáiled calm ly | ón.

The metric of "The Unknown Citizen" urges along the poem's ironic implication. Bland officialese, the language of the Social Worker's Report, is undercut by mincing anapests; the effect is like a sneer:

> He was found by the Bureau of Statistics to be . . .
>
> And all the reports on his conduct agree . . .
>
> Except for the War till the day he retired
> He worked in a factory and never got fired,
> But satisfied his employers, Fudge Motors, Inc.
> Yet he wasn't a scab or odd in his views,
> For his Union reports that he paid his dues . . .

Auden changes the line when the Public Opinion Researchers give their report:

> When there was peace, he was for peace; when there was
> war, he went.
> He was married and added five children to the population,
> Which our Eugenist says was the right number for a
> parent of his generation,
> And our teachers report that he never interfered with
> their education.

Auden crams the line with more syllables than the meter can comfortably contain. The sequence of rhymes suggests Calypso or Ogden Nash; the lines hurry, trying fruitlessly to avoid metrical disaster, toward the deliberately clumsy triple rhymes. The final couplet swings into double iambics: the tripping meter of Gilbert's patter songs ("If you're anxious for to shine, in the high aesthetic line . . ."):

> Was he free? Was he happy? The question is absurd:
> Had anything been wrong, we should certainly have heard.

How well the silly lilt of the meter demolishes the glib certainty and smug authority of the final statement!

Another Time contains the two superb elegies on Yeats and Freud. (I analyze "In Memory of Sigmund Freud" in Chapter 11.) "In Memory of W. B. Yeats" falls into three contrasted sections: the first in Eliotic unmetered verse; the second in regular blank verse; the third, a dirge in heavily accented trochaic stanzas. Syntactical repetition, the use of refrain, the elaboration of metaphor by grammatical symmetry direct the rhythm of the first section:

> The provinces of his body revolted,
> The squares of his mind were empty,
> Silence invaded the suburbs,
> The current of his feeling failed: he became
>   his admirers.

The trochaic tetrameters of the last section move with the measured tread of a *marcia funebre* or the Celtic *Coronach:*

> Earth, receive an honoured guest;
> William Yeats is laid to rest:
> Let the Irish vessel lie
> Emptied of its poetry.

Auden's *Collected Poetry* (1945) merits the accolade Eliot bestowed on Pound's *Selected Poems:* "This book would be, were it nothing else, a textbook of modern versification." Auden's range of stanzaic forms is tremendous; we are tempted to arrange and classify, to note ingenuities and acclaim the sheer virtuosity of an effortless technique. Within the stanzas the meters may be free or strict; they may follow traditional syllable-stress patterns; they may move according to syllabic or strong-stress principles. Auden gives the lie to the notion that the more intricate forms may only be used for trivial themes, that "A dainty thing's the Villanelle / It serves its purpose passing well." One of Auden's gifts to his own generation, and the succeeding one, is that a difficult metric and a complex stanza need not signify merely Petrarchan elaboration; the modern villanelle may be a poem of serious wit, like Auden's "Time will say nothing but I told you so," a powerful and terrifying incantation, like Dylan Thomas' "Do not go gentle into that good night," or a somber lament on the expense of spirit, like Empson's "Missing Dates."

Auden goes further than either Pound or Eliot toward solving the technical problems of the English sestina. An early example of this difficult Provençal form, "Hearing of harvests rotting in the valleys," follows the traditional paradigm; Auden even meets the ancient requirement that each end-word be a noun of two syllables:[5]

> Hearing of harvests rotting in the valleys,
> Seeing at end of street the barren mountains,
> Round corners coming suddenly on water,
> Knowing them shipwrecked who were launched for islands,
> We honour founders of these starving cities,
> Whose honour is the image of our sorrow.

The trochaic form of the end word gives flexibility to the prevailing iambic meter; the line is blank verse but hendecasyllabic. A later sequence of four sestinas, "Kairos and Logos," does not use the traditional order of end-words—where the last word of the sixth line is picked up by the first line of the succeeding stanza; rather Auden devises what I take is an original sequence, 123456, 315264, 536142, etc. This arrangement mutes the insistence of the end-words and allows greater syntactical freedom. In another sestina, from *The Sea and the Mirror*, Auden experiments with still a different order of end-words.[6] Auden chooses these end-words with great care. He generally uses either neutral and tractable abstractions, *death, love, time, world;* or simple concrete nouns, *child, home, garden, forest.* He thus avoids the clatter and bang of Pound's "Altaforte" with its *crimson, clash,* and *opposing;* and the strait-jacketed somnolence of Eliot's modified sestina in *The Dry Salvages* with its *wailing* and *bailing* and *motionless* and *erosionless.*

The systematic complexity of the sestina is only infrequently justified by real poetic merit. However, at least one of Auden's sestina's, "Quite suddenly her dream became a word," rises above the ingenuity of the form. Because the sestina is essentially a set of variations on six words and the lines keep circling back to the same concepts, the form resists progression and development. But "Quite suddenly her dream became a word" retells, as a *Märchen,* the story of The Loss of Innocence; the poem has a tight little plot. There is no sense, as in most sestinas, that the poet is treading water. The end-words, *word, child, one, garden, home,* and *forest,* accumulate symbolic values; reading the envoy,

> Of course the forest overran her garden,
> Yet, though, like everyone, she lost her home,
> The Word still nursed Its motherhood, Its child.

we know, of course, that the *garden* is our Edenic Home, the *word* The Logos.

We turn to Auden's longer poems. No single prosodic mode carries *The Sea and the Mirror* and *For the Time Being;* each is a suite of lyrics with interspersed free verse and prose, "a medley composed of meters of all kinds."[7] These poems are cast in dramatic form, and the prosodic modes adjust themselves to both characters and chorus. The *Narrator* in *For the Time Being* speaks matter-of-fact unmetered verse:

> If, on account of the political situation,
> There are quite a number of homes without roofs, and men
> Lying about in the countryside neither drunk nor asleep,
> If all sailings have been cancelled till further notice,
> If it's unwise now to say much in letters, and if,
> Under the subnormal temperatures prevailing,
> The two sexes are at present the weak and the strong,
> That is not at all unusual for this time of year.

The rhythm is syntactical; Auden delays the resolution of the conditional clause until the eighth line and builds tension through the persistently repeated *if.* The *Chorus* follows with a tail-chasing stanza of five lines:

> Alone, alone, about a dreadful wood
> Of conscious evil runs a lost mankind,
> Dreading to find its Father lest it find
> The Goodness it has dreaded is not good:
> Alone, alone, about a dreadful wood.

(This is the stanza of Baudelaire's *Lesbos.*) The great variety of stanzaic forms in *For the Time Being* recalls Romantic closet drama with its elaborate lyrical interludes and continued suggestion of musical setting. Of course, Auden has music in mind; *For the Time Being* is subtitled *A Christmas Oratorio.*

The prosodic music of *The Age of Anxiety* makes greater pretensions; I doubt, however, whether the highly contrived alliterative strong-stress line of this poem succeeds as a carrying metric. Perhaps the form too much suggests the heroic strictness of *Beowulf;* perhaps the continual consonantal clang (it is easy to fall into) drowns out any nuance that might be effected by other and subtler prosodic means.

The demand for alliteration undoubtedly serves an aesthetic end; the most apt words are often brought into play by technical requirements:

> Behold the infant, helpless in cradle and
> Righteous still, yet already there is
> Dread in his dreams at the deed of which
> He knows nothing but knows he can do,
> The gulf before him with guilt beyond,
> Whatever that is, whatever why
> Forbids his bound; till that ban tempts him;
> He jumps and is judged: he joins mankind,
> The fallen families, freedom lost,
> Love become Law. Now he looks at grown-ups . . .

Jumps . . . judged . . . joins; fallen families, freedom; Love . . . Law; the words seem inevitable as their declension retells Auden's favorite story, The Fall of Man. On other occasions the requirements of alliteration force the poet into unintended irrelevancy or grotesque pedantry:

> High were those headlands; the eagles promised
> Life without lawyers. Our long convoy
> Turned away northward as tireless gulls
> Wove over water webs of brightness
> And sad sound. The insensible ocean,
> Miles without mind, moaned all around our
> Limited laughter, and below our songs
> Were deaf deeps, denes of unaffection . . .

It is not surprising that Auden's meter can move with the rise and fall of the sea, that it urges lines as lovely as these:

> Wove over water webs of brightness
> And sad sound.

He is, after all, using the meter of the *Seafarer* and the *Wanderer*. But we also have, "Life without lawyers . . ." and "denes of unaffection . . ."; the first an example of grabbing the first word that fits the pattern (why not *labor, lovers,* or *lust?*), the second an absurd inkhorn term.

The imprecision in the above examples is that of accidental irrelevancy. The alliterative line proves exactly right for, and indeed encourages, the intended irrelevancies of Auden's surrealistic tomfooleries:

> Thank God I was warned
> To bring an umbrella and had bribes enough
> For the red-haired rascals, for the reservoir guard
> A celluloid sandwich, and silk eggs
> For the lead smelters; for Lizzie O'Flynn,
> The capering cowgirl with clay on her hands,
> Tasty truffles in utopian jars,
> And dungarees with Danish buttons
> For Shilly and Shally the shepherd kings.

The character here wanders in a visionary landscape; he is drunk, and the "word salad" effect is appropriate. In a more serious vein, the alliterative line's impulse toward free association is exploited in interior monologue and passages of psychoanalytic introspection. Rosetta, the eclogue's feminine voice, muses on her relationship with her inadequate father:

> . . . I shan't find shelter, I shan't be at peace
> Till I really take your restless hands,
> My poor fat father. How appalling was
> Your taste in ties. How you tried to have fun,
> You so longed to be liked. You lied so . . .
> Did you ever love
> Stepmother Stupid? You'd a strange look,
> Sad as the sea, when she searched your clothes.
> Don't be cruel and cry. I couldn't stay to
> Be your baby. We both were asking
> For a warmth there wasn't, and then wouldn't write.

Since the alliterative line has long been associated with gnomic utterance, nearly everything said in *The Age of Anxiety* is heavily colored with unearned *significance.* It is difficult to use the line for passages of low intensity, bridge sections, and those other parts of a long poem which Coleridge points out cannot be all poetry.

Auden's last three volumes, *Nones* (1951), *The Shield of Achilles* (1955), *Homage to Clio* (1960), contain an abundance of merely occasional pieces. We have the hilarious "Under Which Lyre," the best spoof of Academia yet written. We must all keep well the Hermetic Decalogue:

> Thou shalt not do as the dean pleases,
> Thou shalt not write thy doctor's thesis
>   On education,
> Thou shalt not worship projects nor
> Shalt thou or thine bow down before
>   Administration.
>
> Thou shalt not answer questionnaires
> Or quizzes upon World Affairs,
>   Nor with compliance
> Take any test. Thou shalt not sit
> With statisticians nor commit
>   A social science.

These lines place Auden among the great comic rhymers, Byron, Gilbert, and Ogden Nash—to whom they are obviously indebted. The stanza is borrowed from Chaucer's *Sir Thopas,* itself a burlesque of the tail-rime stanza of fourteenth-century metrical romance.

In these latest volumes Auden gives way to some of his more unfortunate inclinations: the publication of superficially clever, embarrassingly cute verse; the persistent, almost dogged use of a slangy, off-the-cuff idiom; and, concomitantly, an aggressive antipoetic stance which hardly excuses frequent carelessness. Many pieces in these volumes should never have been published; limericks, for instance, are only meant for oral transmission, and I have never read any, including those given full-page presentation in *Homage to Clio,* which stand up in print. I have never been one to turn up my nose at good clean colloquial fun in modern poetry, but I find this sort of thing arch and obnoxious:

> So pocket your fifty sonnets, Bud;
>   tell Her a myth
> Of unpunishable gods and all the girls
>   they interfered with . . .

Brother, you're worse than a lonesome Peeper
or a He-Virgin
Who nightly abhors the Primal Scene
in medical Latin:
She mayn't be all She might be but
She *is* our Mum.

"Dame Kind," in *Homage to Clio*

Auden is trying too hard to be one of the boys; the attempt at American tough-talk does not come off. *Bud, brother,* and *peeper* maintain a consistent, if offensive, tone, but an American would say *Mom,* not *Mum.*

Prosodically, we find a general loosening of the line; the rhythms tend to run slack—effortlessly, to be sure—but their very relaxation has become a mannerism. Two pieces in prose, "Vespers" (*The Shield of Achilles*) and "Dichtung and Wahrheit" (*Homage to Clio*), are symptomatic of Auden's desire to break free of prosodic regulation and abandon obvious device. Like Eliot in the *Quartets,* he wants to sublimate technical skill and release the pure concept, the naked emotion.

But Auden does his best work under the supervision of stanzaic form and precise metrical cadence. The title poem from *The Shield of Achilles* is one of his most powerful performances to date: a clear and crushing prophecy of life in the cheerless Utopian world. Instead of scenes of Arcadian joy, Thetis sees in the handicraft of Hephaestos

A million eyes, a million boots in line,
Without expression, waiting for a sign.

Thetis' Arcadian expectations are set in three-stress lines, eight lines to the stanza:

She looked over his shoulder
For athletes at their games,
Men and women in a dance
Moving their sweet limbs
Quick, quick, to music,
But there on the shining shield
His hands had set no dancing-floor
But a weed-choked field.

The Utopian reality follows in iambic pentameter, arranged in the rime-royal stanza:

> A ragged urchin, aimless and alone,
>   Loitered about that vacancy; a bird
> Flew up to safety from his well-aimed stone:
>   That girls are raped, that two boys knife a third,
>   Were axioms to him, who'd never heard
> Of any world where promises were kept
> Or one could weep because another wept.

The contrast between Arcadian grace and Utopian misery is admirably served by the alternation of the eight and seven line stanzas. Consonant with the poem's theme and subject, the rhythms move with hard precision in the scenes of Utopian desolation and with greater fluidity and variety in the scenes of Arcadian abundance and freedom. Three of the four eight-line stanzas conclude with the same pattern of stress,

> And a sky like lead . . .
>
> But a weed-choked field . . .
>
> Who would not live long . . .

forming a punctuating rhythm constant to each section, and finally, to the entire poem.

2 *Stephen Spender and Louis MacNeice*

The reputation of the three leading members of the "Auden group," Spender, Day-Lewis, and MacNeice, faded in the post-war period. Reasons are not hard to find. The hegemony of the New Criticism, with its rigid ontological bureaucracy, was not sympathetic to any poetry fiercely committed to "subject"; and the poetry of the thirties was crying for political action. Guilt-stricken liberals are apt to be embarrassed by poems like Spender's, "Oh young men oh young comrades," and feel such effusions belong more to the history of lost causes than to poetry. As for myself, I agree with William Empson:

> Besides, I do not really like
>   The verses about "Up the Boys,"

> The revolutionary romp,
> The hearty uproar that deploys
> A sit-down literary strike . . .

The best work, from the prosodist's point of view, that came from the group has little to do with Popular Front communism or The Defence of the Spanish Republic. Which is to say that whatever survives as good poetry has lasted because the poet exercised due technical care and wrote with appropriate sensibility and concern for language. Spender had great gifts for language and for rhythm; only Eliot has surpassed, in matters of music and reverberation, such a poem as "I Think Continually of Those Who Were Truly Great":

> I think continually of those who were truly great.
> Who, from the womb, remembered the soul's history
> Through corridors of light where the hours are suns,
> Endless and singing. Whose lovely ambition
> Was that their lips, still touched with fire,
> Should tell of the Spirit, clothed from head to foot
> in song.
> And who hoarded from the Spring branches
> The desires falling across their bodies like
> blossoms. . . .
>
> Near the snow, near the sun, in the highest fields,
> See how these names are fêted by the waving grass
> And by the streamers of white cloud
> And whispers of wind in the listening sky.
> The names of those who in their lives fought for life,
> Who wore at their hearts the fire's centre.
> Born of the sun, they travelled a short while toward
> the sun
> And left the vivid air signed with their honour.

Here, as he was unable to do in the more ambitious *Vienna,* Spender masters that elusive principle of "fixity and flux" which gives power and resonance to Websterian blank verse. A number of other poems in the same measure show comparable prosodic splendor. "The Express," "The Landscape near an Aerodrome," and especially the conclusion of "An Elementary School Classroom in a Slum,"

Break O break open till they break the town
And show the children to green fields, and make
their world
Run azure on gold sands, and let their tongues
Run naked into books, the white and green leaves open
History theirs whose language is the sun.

are deservedly well-anthologized examples of Spender's best work.

MacNeice is a tidier craftsman than Spender but without Spender's moments of genuine eloquence. We all remember "The Sunlight on the Garden," a prosodic tour-de-force; I give the two final stanzas:

The sky was good for flying
Defying the church bells
And every evil iron
Siren and what it tells:
The earth compels,
We are dying Egypt, dying

And not expecting pardon,
Hardened in heart anew,
But glad to have sat under
Thunder and rain with you,
And grateful too
For sunlight on the garden.

The head-rhymes, *flying-defying, iron-siren,* etc., produce a peculiarly sweet and astringent melody.

A fine classical scholar, MacNeice has experimented with pseudo-quantitative meters. His version of *Solvitur Acris Hiems* (Horace, *Ode 1, 4*) approaches and departs from Horace's metrical scheme, illustrating the tantalizing difficulties in adapting quantitative meter to the incorrigible stresses of English. Horace uses the so-called Fourth Archilochian Strophe, a four-line stanza:

Solvitur acris hiems grata vice veris et Favoni,
trahuntque siccas machinae carinas,
ac neque iam stabulis gaudet pecus aut arator igni,
nec prata canis albicant pruinis.

The first line, a Greater Archilochian, belongs to the Latin dactylo-trochaic verses; the line consists of four dactyls followed by three trochees, seven feet in all:

Solvitur | acris hi | ems gra | ta vice | veris | et Fa | voni . . .

The alternating lines are iambic hexameters (the catalectic kind):

tra hunt | que sic | cas ma | chi nae | ca ri | nas ∧

MacNeice writes Horace's meter this way:

Win ter to | Spring: ∧ the | west wind | melts the | frozen
rancour,
The wind | lass drags | to sea | the thir | sty hull;
Byre is no | lon ger | wel come to | beast or | fire to |
plough man
The field | re moves | the frost | cap from | his
skull.

The Latin lines are each reduced by one foot; the long line becomes a hexameter, the short line an iambic pentameter. MacNeice attempts to preserve the general rhythmic outline of the Latin: a falling line (dactylo-trochaic) followed by the rising iambic. There is noticeable conflict between stress and quantity; if we scan by stresses alone, MacNeice's first line rises in a syllable-stress hexameter:

Win ter | to Spring: | the west | wind melts | the fro | zen
ran | cour . . .

But in some details MacNeice comes surprisingly close to the Latin. The contrast between the longer and shorter half of the first and third lines, the preservation of the spondee in the third foot of the first line and the second foot of the third line, the pleasing alternation of falling and rising rhythm—all are happy inspirations from Horace's original.

MacNeice's Sapphics, in the poem "June Thunder," make no pretense at exact adherence to the paradigm. Three lines set in falling rhythm are followed by the shorter fourth line:

Blackness at half-past eight, the night's precursor,
Clouds like falling masonry and lightning's lavish
Annunciation, the sword of the mad archangel
    Flashed from the scabbard.

If only now you would come and dare the crystal
Rampart of rain and the bottomless moat of thunder,
If only now you would come I should be happy
    Now if now only.

One line corresponds to the Lesser Sapphic:

Clōuds lĭke | fāllĭng | māsŏnrӯ ănd | līghtnĭng's | lāvĭsh . . .

And the fourth lines are acceptable Adonics:

Flāshed frŏm thĕ | scābbărd . . .
Nōw ĭf nŏw | ōnlӯ . . .

MacNeice infuses his Sapphics with those qualities of yearning and wonder which characterize the great examples of the form.

3 Dylan Thomas

Dylan Thomas had no personal intimacy with Auden's Oxford Movement, but he shared its ancestry. Thomas read Hopkins and Wilfred Owen; he experimented with a great variety of prosodic shapes and forms and devised some of the most intricate stanzas to be found in poetic literature. The effect of Auden was chiefly technical; Thomas' poetry, from the very first, was unpolitical and unpreachy: aggressively unconcerned with "ideas" and revolutionary only in the sense that it was temperamentally in agreement with all revolution.

The nature of Thomas' poetry demanded severe prosodic regulation. A typical Thomas poem does not move by careful grammatical articulation but is carried headlong by highly formal rhythmic patterns. Rhythm in a Thomas poem is a *sounding* rhythm—rarely the unheard music of authentic syntax. We are hardly aware that the opening stanza of "Poem in October" proceeds along a series of shifted constructions; the images are separated by a very acute sense of metrical timing. Typography, syllable count, and a texture of interior rhymes and alliteration allay the feeling of incompleteness occasioned by the lack of exact grammatical relationships.

We see the extreme of Thomas' poetic method in the ten sonnets from *Twenty-Five Poems* (1936). I attempt no exegesis of these poems; none is probably possible. But a comparison between Sonnet IV and George Herbert's *Prayer* offers a clue to the kind of poetic structure Thomas had in mind and how well Thomas succeeds in handling associative progression:

PRAYER

Prayer the Churches banquet, Angels age,
    Gods breath in man returning to his birth,
The soul in paraphrase, heart in pilgrimage,
    The Christian plummet sounding heav'n and earth;

Engine against th'Almightie, sinners towre,
    Reversed thunder, Christ-side-piercing spear,
The six-daies world transposing in an houre,
    A kinde of tune, which all things heare and fear;

Softnesse, and peace, and joy, and love, and blisse,
    Exalted Manna, gladnesse of the best,
    Heaven in ordinarie, man well drest,
The milkie way, the bird of Paradise,

    Church-bells beyond the starres heard, the souls bloud,
    The land of spices; something understood.

IV

What is the metre of the dictionary?
The size of genesis? the short spark's gender?
Shade without shape? the shape of Pharaoh's echo?
(My shape of age nagging the wounded whisper).
Which sixth of wind blew out the burning gentry?
(Questions are hunchbacks to the poker marrow).
What of a bamboo man among your acres?
Corset the boneyards for a crooked lad?
Button your bodice on a hump of splinters,
My camel's eyes will needle through the shroud.
Love's reflection of the mushroom features,
Stills snapped by night in the bread-sided field,
Once close-up smiling in the wall of pictures,
Arc-lamped thrown back upon the cutting flood.

from *Twenty-Five Poems*

Herbert's poem accumulates power with each successive brilliant phrase; image and metaphor are spaced by rhythmic pauses, and syntactical completeness is suspended until the end of the poem. The grammatical structure is appositive: the body of the poem follows the suppressed copula *is*. However, the images and abstractions do not ride free; even the striking and often-quoted "Church-bells beyond the starres" makes its full effect only in context. On this point Austin Warren remarks, "It remains true, however, that the verse which, in its context and as climax, moves the reader cannot be detached; for it is by virtue of its position in the whole poem and is pervaded by what has gone before that it acquires light and warmth."[8] We add that Herbert provides a severe logic of context, a syntax of clearly defined categories: the terms of each appositive phrase belong to theology, music, Biblical reference, and the well-understood language of religious discourse.

We discover no clear linkages among Thomas' gnomic questions. According to one exegete, the child Dylan is asking his mother "embarrassing questions about sex and obstetrics."[9] Maybe; but more likely Thomas was freely associating on the lines of

> Goe, and catche a falling starre,
> Get with child a mandrake roote,
> Tell me, where all past yeares are,
> Or who cleft the Divels foot . . .

without bothering to drop the referential thread and bind up the seeming irrelevancies into a meaningful bundle. The sonnet form, by itself, does not supply sufficient connective power to compensate for Thomas' abjuration of logical syntax. Nor is iambic verse strongly rhythmical enough to space out Thomas' images; there are no significant pauses loaded with surging emotional content.

To represent Thomas by one of his earlier, image-clotted sonnets does him an injury. His best work lies in those spacious stanzas where the long-breathed rhythms can rise and fall, move up to a climax, and dwindle to silence. The stanza of "Poem in October" is a beautiful prosodic mechanism:

> It was my thirtieth year to heaven
> Woke to my hearing from harbour and neighbour wood
> And the mussel pooled and the heron
> Priested shore

The morning beckon
With water praying and call of seagull and rook
And the knock of sailing boats on the net webbed wall
Myself to set foot
That second
In the sleeping town and set forth.

Thomas counts syllables (in analogous lines of succeeding stanzas), but unlike Marianne Moore whose anecdotal rhythm has close affinities with prose, he weights each line with strong stresses. His model here is Hopkins' "The Wreck of the Deutschland"; like Hopkins he often crowds his stresses together:

And the knock of sailing boats on the *net webbed wall* . . .

Beyond the border and under the *lark full cloud* . . .

And the *twice told fields* of infancy . . .

Although Thomas truculently denied any knowledge of Welsh and its highly formal metrical systems,[10] his lines chime with internal consonantal correspondence, or *cynghanedd,* a prescribed feature of Welsh versification:

*W*oke to my *h*earing from *h*arbour and neighbour *w*ood . . .

The correspondence in this line forms *cynghanedd croes:* a pattern of alliterated syllables in symmetrical arrangement (*w* . . . *h:h* . . . *w*).[11] "Fern Hill" abounds in such permutations:

Above the lilting *h*ouse and *h*appy as the *g*rass was *g*reen . . .
And once below a *t*ime I *l*ordly had the *t*rees and *l*eaves . . .
And *g*reen and *g*olden I was *h*untsman and *h*erdsman . . .
And *h*onoured among *f*oxes and *ph*easants by the gay *h*ouse . . .

Another feature of Welsh versification is the rich use of internal rhyme and assonance. Thomas often rhymes from the middle of one line to the middle of the next, or from middle to end. The rhyming here is approximate:

Now as I was young and *easy* under the apple boughs
About the lilting house and *happy* as the grass was green,
The night above the dingle *starry* . . .

"The Conversation of Prayers" systematically rhymes end and middles in a crisscross pattern:[12]

> The conversation of *prayers* about to be *said*
> By the child going to *bed* and the man on the *stairs*
> Who climbs to his dying *love* in her high *room,*
> The one not caring to *whom* in his sleep he will *move*
> And the other full of *tears* that she will be *dead*...

Such trickiness may be scorned, but the rhyme scheme actually mirrors the theme of the poem. The poem expounds the old Protestant "... idea of the reversibility of grace."[13] The prayers of the child and the man cross in night; the child, praying for quiet rest,

> Shall drown in a grief as deep as his made grave...

the man, "Who climbs to his dying love in her high room,"

> Tonight shall find no dying but alive and warm
>
> In the fire of his care his love in the high room...

Through the mysterious efficacy of prayer, the boy assumes the burden of the man's grief; through prayer their situations suffer a spiritual reversal. As the poem develops, certain lines and half-lines are repeated but their positions are shifted:

> By the child going to bed and the man on the stairs...
>
> From the man on the stairs and the child by his bed...

This may be a howling example of "imitative form," but we can scarcely deny its effectiveness.

Similarly, in one of Thomas' greatest poems, "Do Not Go Gentle into That Good Night," the formal demands of the villanelle enhance the meaning. Thomas makes the most of his form: I can think of no other villanelle in the language which seems so little contrived. The refrain lines of most villanelles bear scant relationship to the poetic argument; their function is usually decorative. But Thomas manages his syntax cannily; the repetition of the refrain completes the grammatical sense of each tercet:

Do not go gentle into that good night,
Old age should burn and rave at close of day;
Rage, rage against the dying of the light.

Though wise men at their end know dark is right,
Because their words had forked no lightning they
Do not go gentle into that good night.

Good men, the last wave by, crying how bright
Their frail deeds might have danced in a green bay,
Rage, rage against the dying of the light. . . .

The lines are, without exception, decasyllabic; Thomas varies the rhythm with contiguous heavy stressing, an occasional trochee, or an Ionic:

Ráge, ráge | agáinst | the dý | ing óf | the líght . . .

Though wíse | mén at | their énd | know dárk | is ríght . . .

And yóu, | my fá | ther, thére | on the sád héight . . .

The meter of one splendid line makes a crucial semantic choice for the reader:

Curse, bléss, | me nów | with yóur | fierce téars, | I práy . . .

If we resist the temptation to read the first and fourth feet as emphatic accentual spondees, we understand that blessing outweighs the cursing and the ferocity.

Toward the end of his life, especially in the poems of *In Country Sleep,* Thomas' prosody hardens into a set of predictable mannerisms. The rhythms become more emphatic but less subtle and various; upward and downward cadences often repeat themselves to the point of monotony. What once seemed excited and energetic now becomes forced; very Hopkinsesque lines are ugly with unconvincing onomatopoeia:

Flash, and the plumes crack,
And a black cap of jack-
Daws Sir John's just hill dons, and again the gulled
        birds hare
To the hawk on fire, the halter height, over Towy's
        fins,
In a whack of wind.

"Over Sir John's Hill"

We hear the violence of Hopkins' strong-stressing and dislocated grammar; the jar of cross-accents and the crunch of rhymes and consonants generate more noise than feeling. Whole stanzas of "In Country Sleep" seem only mouthfuls of vowels and consonants; sheer, beautiful, but nearly meaningless sound:

> The haygold haired, my love asleep, and the rift blue
> Eyed, in the haloed house, in her rareness and hilly
> High riding, held and blessed and true, and so stilly
> Lying the sky
> Might cross its planets, the bell weep, night gather her eyes,
> The Thief fall on the dead like the willynilly dew . . .

These last poems were written for declamation; their metrical idiom shaped by Thomas' oracular, incantatory style of reading aloud. Thomas admitted he found the public platform "the place on which to give the poem the works."[14] His magnificently sonorous voice imposed similar rhythms on any poetry he read; it was the besetting weakness of his delivery. As a result, the last poems are static, rich in bombast and ecstatic rant, impressive as runes, charms, or chants. But they show that Thomas had been listening too closely to the sound of his own voice.

4 *William Empson, Vernon Watkins, and Henry Reed*

A number of fine English poets came to maturity with Auden and Thomas. No single figure has exerted Auden's influence or achieved Thomas' status; it is nearly impossible to single out a representative poet or even group of poets. I content myself with the examination of poems selected from William Empson, Vernon Watkins, and Henry Reed. These men scarcely make up a "school." Empson has something of the early Eliot's hard-boiled intellectualism but is largely his own man. Watkins, though older than Dylan Thomas, sometimes reminds us of him. However, what we recognize as Thomas in Watkins' verse is, perhaps, only their common bardic and Welsh ancestry. Henry Reed, who has published sparingly, seems to me the most considerable poet of the three; he has worked out his own individual romantic-ironic style, and he has something to say. The prosodical fashion of close stanzas and controlled meters holds with most of these poets; Watkins and Reed also favor a long line, something between Websterian blank verse and English hexameter.

Empson writes the strictest meters. Wisely mistrusting his ear, he counts out his lines on his fingers. The following stanzas are from his "This Last Pain"; the extreme compression of thought and the constricted, muscle-bound couplets well exemplify "a style from a despair":

Thorns burn to a consistent ash, like man;
A splendid cleanser for the frying-pan:
    And those who leap from pan to fire
    Should this brave opposite admire.

All those large dreams by which men long live well
Are magic-lanterned on the smoke of hell;
    This then is real, I have implied,
    A painted, small, transparent slide . . .

Imagine, then, by miracle, with me,
(Ambiguous gifts, as what gods give must be)
    What could not possibly be there,
    And learn a style from a despair.

These end-stopped epigrammatic couplets, with their stylized syntactical inversions, suggest an unmusical Pope: the brilliance and the intelligence are there, but the harmonies are missing. Empson makes a virtue of his deficiency. His genuine metrical awkwardness ("And learn a style from *a* despair") gives his lines a bleak, unlovely, but dreadfully honest quality. He works *against* prosody as a sculptor in steel cuts emotional forms out of the highly resistant metal. The recalcitrance of the material provides part of the artistic result.

Not, however, always to advantage. Empson cannot manage the relaxed movement of blank verse; his lines in unrhymed pentameter are thumpingly end-stopped, like James Thomson's "unrhymed couplets":

Stevenson says they wake at two o'clock
Who lie with Earth, when the birds wake, and sigh;
Turn over, as does she, once in the night;
Breathe and consider what this quiet is,
Conscious of sleep a moment, and the stars.

"Sleeping Out in a College Cloister"

The handfuls of metrically mis-stressed syllables pave a very bumpy prosodical road—which gets worse as the poem rambles on:

> There is a nightmare period between
> (As if it were a thing you had to swallow)
> When it engulfs the sky, and remains alien,
> When the full size of the thing coming upon you
> Rapes the mind, and will not be unimagined.

There is no flow, no sustaining rhythm. Unless we can discover charm in Empson's dogged indifferencc to the sound of his verse, we must judge these lines prosodically bad.

The work of thc Welsh poet Vernon Watkins offers a musical contrast to Empson's crabbed lines. Earlier (see Chapter 11) we noticed his "Ophelia" with its Sapphic stanza and strong-stress meter. The same solemn music governs "Thames Forest" which reads like a Druidic charm:

> Years are divine rings: moments are immortal.
> The months are saplings, centuries are oakenshaws.
> Lightfoot the soul goes. Impressive is the shadow
> Cast by those time-groves.
>
> Darkness of the sycamore flies across the river.
> From a pattern of foliage see the spirit struggling
> Through meshes like memories, woven of their terror
> Wondering, emerging. . . .
>
> Stilled on the charmed world, upward the life looks,
> Stunned by that oracle speaking from the tree's root:
> 'One that is strange-born, one that dies tomorrow
> Dances today here.'

A falling meter (dactylic-spondaic) arranged in eleven-and-five syllable lines controls this haunting rhythm; the meter, however, is counterpointed against a four-stress alliterative pattern. Double accents mark the principle stresses:

> Years are di | vine rings: || mo ments are im | mor tal.
>
> The months are | sap lings, || cen tu ries are | oak en shaws.
>
> Light foot the | soul goes. || Im | pres sive is the | shad ow
>
> Cast by those | time-groves.

A rich liquidity characterizes Watkins' prosodic style; he handles quantity and alliteration with near Swinburnian facility. We always catch the music in his lines, though the music sometimes has more easiness than depth.

A lush Oriental sensuality is suggested by the slow hexameters of "Cantata for the Waking of Lazarus":

> There sang a fountain in a Syrian courtyard leaping
> Near to the place where Lazarus, the loved of Jesus, lay,
> Lazarus, four days dead, alone in the shadow sleeping.
> Some say that in the sepulchre where mute he lay
> There on the burning rose of resurrection-day
> His eyes were sleeping fixed, although his veins were cold.

The secret of this prosodic mastery lies in the placing of the caesura. To avoid monotony Watkins often divides the line at three points:

> Lazarus, || four days dead, || alone in the shadow || sleeping . . .

The final section of the poem breaks into an ecstatic prayer. In these lines the caesura always comes after the sixth syllable; the rhythm is trance-like and ceremonious as the poet calls on His Redeemer to descend:

> Love, newly born, come down: for you the fountain playing
> Leaps into light, then spills, and fills the basin's brim.
> Water gives life to stone, and light renews our saying:
> For you thc sages wait, and listening cherubim
> Support the fountain's weight around its marble base.
> For you the ages wait, old prophets are not still
> Around this font of birth; they strain to see your face.

Inner rhyming and hieratic repetition strengthen the evocation and insistence of these magical lines.

Less ornamented, starker and simpler in metric, are the three-stress lines of Watkins' "The Death Bell." We catch a familiar movement in the beat, a memory of Yeats:

> I that was born in Wales
> Cherish heaven's dust in scales
> Which may at dusk be seen
> On every village green

Where Tawe, Taff, or Wye
Through fields and woods goes by . . .

How can a stone bell teach
To all men or to each
The ascending fall of those
In whom heaven's scales repose?
Not even the full-starred night
Can put conception right
Till bone be knit with bone.
Then shall their loss be known.

Henry Reed's *A Map of Verona* (1946) is among the slimmest of slim volumes, yet its pieces have been widely anthologized; two poems, "Naming of Parts" and "Chard Whitlow," have the status of modern classics. "Chard Whitlow" parodies Eliot's *Quartets* and the limp, hesitating line of Eliot's bemused and woolly moments:

As we get older we do not get any younger.
Seasons return, and to-day I am fifty-five.
And this time last year I was fifty-four,
And this time next year I shall be sixty-two.

Like all good parodies Reed's little spoof renders criticism and offers appreciation. "Chard Whitlow" might be taken as an expression of gratitude as well; Reed has learned from Eliot the secret of the free blank-verse line and the delicate balance which keeps the line from either decaying into prose or from stiffening into regular metrical cadences. The following lines, from Reed's "Philoctetes," could be included in "Chard Whitlow" without seriously disturbing the metrical texture and, perhaps, without gravely affecting the sense:

I can only point to one time and speak of it,
And point to another which is different.
One is the buildings of hell, when over a crime
We plaster darkness on darkness, and pray for silence,
While the light grows louder above the disordered days,
The bells with their loud ringing pull down the tower,
And the walled-up entry of death lies exposed and broken.

An exemplary handling of Eliotic blank verse is displayed in Reed's dramatic monologue "Chrysothemis." The tone is both tense and subdued; the line modulates between a dignified hexameter and a sharper, terser five-stress unit:

> I cannot follow them into their world of death,
> Or their hunted world of life, though through the house,
> Death and the hunted bird sing at every nightfall.
> I am Chrysothemis: I sailed with dipping sails,
> Suffered the winds I would not strive against,
> Entered the whirlpools and was flung outside them.
> Survived the murders, triumphs and revenges.

The rhythm is extraordinarily steady, though without the nervous energy of "Gerontion." Chrysothemis must hold precariously to her sanity as the lines she speaks clutch metrical bedrock. Reed uses the trisyllabic foot, that enemy of "firmness," very cautiously; the norms are the syllable-stress hexameter,

> I cán | not fól | low thém | in tó | their wórld | of déath . . .
> Í am | Chry só | the mís: | I saíled | with díp | ping saíls . . .

and the normal iambic pentameter:

> Súf fered | the wínds | I wóuld | not stríve | a gaínst . . .

When Chrysothemis remembers the murder of Agamemnon, an anapestic foot quickens the pace of each line:

> This was the yawn of time while a murder
> Awaited another murder. I did not see
> My father's murder, but I see it now always around me,
> And I see it shapeless: as when we are sometimes told
> Of the heroes who walk out into the snow and blizzard
> To spare their comrades' care, we always see
> A white direction in which the figure goes,
> And a vague ravine in which he stumbles and falls.
> My father rises thus from a bath of blood,
> Groping from table to chair in a dusky room
> Through doorways into darkening corridors,
> Falling at last in the howling vestibule.

The stumbling rhythm of two anapests unsteadies the dying Agamemnon:

Gró ping | from tá | ble to cháir | in a dús | ky róom . . .

The suggestion here is subtle enough, but hardly can be missed. Whether instinct or deliberate craft prompted Reed to use consecutive anapests does not matter; the technical fact has its aesthetic consequences.

The three poems included under the title "Lessons of the War" are written in formal six-line stanzas. These poems explore, with keen metaphysical wit, the ironic implications which arise when the artificialities of war clash with the natural order. "Naming of Parts" maintains a double discourse; the brisk instructions of the gunnery instructor mingle with the wandering thoughts of a new recruit. In the fourth line below, the mind of the spring-infatuated recruit makes comically obscene metaphorical connections:

> And this you can see is the bolt. The purpose of this
> Is to open the breech, as you see. We can slide it
> Rapidly backwards and forwards: we call this
> Easing the spring. And rapidly backwards and forwards
> The early bees are assaulting and fumbling the flowers:
>   They call it easing the Spring.

The lines are deftly metered in anapests and dactyls; the long lines have a norm of five stresses, the shorter sixth line, only three:

For to dáy | we have nám | ing of párts . . .

In appropriate lines the prevailing anapests back up to dactyls:

> Ráp id ly | báck wards and | fór wards: we | cáll this∧
> Éas ing the | spríng.∧ And | ráp id ly | báck wards
>   and | fórwards . . .

Only the very innocent can miss how the slight shift in rhythm so delightfully helps to ease the Spring!

Reed has published in *Encounter*[15] "The Auction Sale," a splendid narrative poem of some three hundred lines. The poem tells, with irony and pathos, of a rural auction and the bidding for an unsigned Renaissance painting—a Titian-like "Venus and

Mars." "The Auction Sale" is composed in irregularly rhymed octosyllabics; the opening lines swing along in catchy tetrameter singsong:

> Within the great grey flapping tent
> The damp crowd stood or stamped about;
> And some came in, and some went out
> To drink the moist November air;
> None fainted, though a few looked spent
> And eyed some empty unbought chair.

The lines glow with Elizabethan ardor when Reed describes the warmly erotic picture set before the rural crowd:

> *Effulgent in the Paduan air,*
> *Ardent to yield the Venus lay*
> *Naked upon the sunwarmed earth.*
> *Bronze and bright and crisp her hair,*
> *By the right hand of Mars caressed,*
> *Who sunk beside her on his knee,*
> *His mouth towards her mouth inclined,*
> *His left hand near her silken breast.*

Reed plays off the ironic discrepancies between the mythical, amorous subject of the painting, and the tense, restrained atmosphere of the auction tent. The behavior of Mars and Venus is uninhibited and stands in humorous contrast to the decorous conduct and strongly suppressed emotions of the three men bidding for the painting. The rhythms artfully control the shifts of feeling; in the narrative sections the lines progress dryly with the stresses predictable. Many lines relax into folksy doggerel and fit the meter with deliberate carelessness:

> It is a picture which though unsigned
> Is thought to be of the Superior kind,
> So I am sure you gentlemen will not mind
> If I tell you at once before we start
> That what I have been asked to say
> Is, as I have said, to say:
> *There's a reserve upon this number . . .*

But in the descriptive passages (set by Reed in italics for aesthetic distance, a "framing" device) the meter is fluid and suave:

In ritual, amorous delay,
Venus deposed her sheltering hand
Where her bright belly's aureate day
Melted to dusk about her groin;
And, as from words that Mars had said
Into that hidden, subtle ear,
She turned away her shining head.

This rarely beautiful poem owes much of its success to its carrying meter. Reed can make his octosyllabics behave with Shakespearean sweetness of melody, with Wordsworthian naiveté, or with Hudibrastic colloquial roughness. None of the shifts in rhythm and tone, however, disrupts the narrative progression eased steadily forward by seemingly limited but actually enormously abundant prosodic resources.

5 *Stanley Kunitz, Theodore Roethke, and Robert Lowell*

A high order of technical accomplishment distinguishes the poetry of three American poets who emerged in the early forties: Stanley Kunitz, Theodore Roethke, and Robert Lowell. Excuses for this selection are surely unnecessary, but explanations may be in order. Although his first poems appeared in the late twenties, Kunitz went virtually unrecognized until the publication of his *Selected Poems 1928–1958*. Roethke, slightly younger than Kunitz, has enjoyed a steadily growing postwar reputation, but his work, until quite recently, was missing from the most popular anthology of contemporary poetry.[16] Lowell may belong to the "younger" generation of American poets which includes Richard Wilbur and Howard Nemerov; since all these poets are now past forty, the distinction may be academic. Nor is it my intention to embalm any poet or group of poets in chronology; all of the men mentioned are living, producing workers and first-rate craftsmen.

Kunitz' acknowledged masters are Donne, Baudelaire, and Eliot. He pays each the formal compliment of allusion or translation; in the blank-verse poem "The Class Will Come to Order" a celebrated line from *The Relique,*

A bracelet of bright hair about the bone

appears in witty paraphrase:

> Absurd though it may seem,
> Perhaps there's too much order in this world;
> The poets love to haul disorder in,
> Braiding their wrists with her long mistress hair,
> And when the house is tossed about our ears,
> The governors must set it right again.
> How wise was he who banned them from his state!

A great variety of movement and tone shades the feeling in these lines. The only outstanding metrical departure is the shortened first line (trimeter rather than pentameter), but Kunitz' ear for quantity and monosyllabic harmonies is nearly unmatched among American poets. The quality of sinuous beauty which inheres in the fourth line,

> Braí ding | their wrísts | with her lóng mís | tress haír

is produced by the strategically placed short *i*'s as well as by the reversed first foot and the double foot standing in the third and fourth positions.

Especially worthy of commentary are the monosyllabic lines, "the glory of our verse and language." "The Class Will Come to Order" ends with two delicately ambiguous lines, one of eight, the other of ten syllables:

> I smiled but I did not tell them,
> I did not tell them why it was I smiled.

The gentle tug between speech stress and metrical stress teases the meaning first one way, then another. Emphasizing the metrical pattern,

> I smiled but *I* did not tell *them*

we get an antithesis between *I* and *them;* the poet *I*, kept his secret from *them,* the class. If we let rhetorical stress override the metrical pattern,

> I smiled but I did *not tell* them

the strong *tell* enforces the act of *not* telling. The whole assertion is further modified in the last line where *not* and *them* now appear in metrically unstressed positions, and *tell* and *why* receive the emphasis:

I díd | not téll | them whý | it wás | I smíled.

Our next example, also in blank verse, comes from "The Thief." Again, we note an extraordinary refinement of language and feeling singing through a much varied music:

Pick-pocket, pick-thank music plucks the strings
For the rag-madonna with perdurable babe
Most dolorously hallowing the square
Where Caesar walks three steps to meet Bernini,
Whose sumptuous art runs wild
From gate to gate, pausing in tiptoe-joy
Only to light a torch of fountains, to set
His tritons dancing, or at a blest façade
To cast up from his wrist a flight of angels,
Volute on volute, wing on climbing wing.
In the middle of my life I heard the waters playing.

This long verse-paragraph winds through many syntactical delays, holding back a full stop until the tenth line. The last line, with its echo from Dante and its lengthened meter (irregular hexameter), stabilizes the rhythmic flow of the previous lines.

Kunitz is as deft in stanza and rhyme as he is in blank verse. A measured tetrameter and wire-tight irony hold in balance compassion, fury, chagrin, amusement—and a final resolution of all these:

I thought of Judith in her tent,
Of Helen by the crackling wall,
Of Cressida, her bone-lust spent,
Of Catherine on the holy wheel:
I heard their woman-dust lament
The golden wound that does not heal.

What a wild air her small joints beat!
I only poured the raging wine
Until our bodies filled with light,
Mine with hers and hers with mine,
And we went out into the night
Where all the constellations shine.

from "She Wept, She Railed"

In another mood and stanza the qualities are lyric grace and Arcadian serenity; the somewhat "medieval" imagery is complemented by a stiff, archaic trimeter movement:

> The lily and the swan
> Attend her whiter pride,
> While the courtly laurel kneels
> To kiss his mantling bride.
>
> Under each cherry-bough
> She spreads her silken cloths
> At the rumor of a wind,
> To gather up her deaths,
>
> For the petals of her heart
> Are shaken in a night,
> Whose ceremonial art
> Is dying into light.

from "When the Light Falls"

"Ceremonial art" well describes Kunitz' meticulously realized poems.

The earlier poems of Roethke show the sustaining influence of Auden. This brief poem, from *Open House* (1941), with its deceptively easy doggerel meter, has the unmistakable Auden touch:

ACADEMIC

> The stethoscope tells what everyone fears:
> You're likely to go on living for years,
> With a nurse-maid waddle and a shop-girl simper,
> And the style of your prose growing limper and limper.

We note the wobbly anapests (mixed with an occasional iamb) and zany feminine rhyming of Auden:

> The poet reciting to Lady Diana
> While the footmen whisper 'Have a banana',
> The judge enforcing the obsolete law,
> The banker making the loan for the war,

The expert designing the long-range gun
To exterminate everyone under the sun,
Would like to get out but could only mutter;—
'What can I do? It's my bread and butter.'

XVIII, *Look, Stranger!*

The steady trimeter of Roethke's "Night Journey" also suggests Auden's handling of traditional meter; if anything, these lines have a purity of language and firmness of rhythm Auden rarely achieves:

Beyond the mountain pass
Mist deepens on the pane;
We rush into a rain
That rattles double glass.
Wheels shake the roadbed stone,
The pistons jerk and shove,
I stay up half the night
To see the land I love.

In a brief prose excursion, "Some Remarks on Rhythm,"[17] Roethke allows us a theoretical glimpse into his prosodic methods. The essay begins with the modest question, "What do I like?" and continues with carefully detailed prosodic analyses of nursery rhymes, his own poems, and poems by Blake, Janet Lewis, D. H. Lawrence, and others. The analyses are extraordinarily fine, as we might expect from a poet with Roethke's rhythmic sensitivity. His first example, from Mother Goose, is a mysterious precursor of *symboliste* significances:

Hinx, minx, the old witch winks.
The fat begins to fry,
There's nobody home but Jumping Joan,
And Father and Mother, and I.

Roethke remarks:

Now what makes that catchy . . . For one thing, the rhythm. Five stresses out of a possible six in the first line. Though maybe 'old' doesn't take quite as strong a stress as the others. . . . Notice the second, 'The fat begins to fry,' is absolutely regular metrically. It's all iambs, a thing that

> often occurs when previous lines are sprung or heavily counterpointed. The author doesn't want to get too far from his base, from his ground beat. The third line varies again with an anapest and variations in the 'O' and 'U' sound. . . .[18]

From "Hinx, minx" and other nursery rhymes, Roethke generalizes, "that while our genius in the language may be essentially iambic, particularly in the formal lyric, much of memorable or passionate speech is strongly stressed, irregular, even sprung, if you will."[19] Of course Roethke's nursery rhyme examples, written when English verse was moving from strong-stress to syllable-stress meters, tend to confirm his generalization.

It is only a short hop from Roethke's speculations to his practice—a hop backwards, since it is obvious his theories are based on what he has done in his own work. The love poem, "Words for the Wind," opens with "Hinx, minx" rhythms:

> Love, love, a lily's my care,
> She's sweeter than a tree.
> Loving, I use the air
> Most lovingly: I breathe;
> Mad in the wind I wear
> Myself as I should be,
> All's even with the odd,
> My brother the vine is glad.

The second line, regularly iambic, occurs after a heavily stressed opening line. Other lines vary with trochaic and anapestic substitutions. Later in the poem, Roethke moves further from his iambic base:

> The sun declares the earth;
> The stones leap in the stream;
> On a wide plain, beyond
> The far stretch of a dream,
> A field breaks like the sea;
> The wind's white with her name,
> And I walk with the wind.

The measure now sounds familiar: the irregularly metered three-stress line we find in Yeats's mature poems. Roethke acknowledges his ancestor, in some lines from his "Four for Sir John Davies":

> I take this cadence from a man named Yeats;
> I take it, and I give it back again:
> For other tunes and other wanton beats
> Have tossed my heart and fiddled through my brain.

While the counterpointed iambic line remains a mainstay of Roethke's prosody, he has listened closely to "other tunes and wanton beats." He has himself parsed the music of his moving "Elegy for Jane,"—certainly one of his best performances in unmetered verse. I quote the first strophe:

> I remember the neckcurls, limp and damp as tendrils;
> And her quick look, a sidelong pickerel smile;
> And how, once startled into talk, the light syllables
> leaped for her,
> And she balanced in the delight of her thought,
> A wren, happy, tail into the wind,
> Her song trembling the twigs and small branches.
> The shade sang with her;
> The leaves, their whispers turned to kissing;
> And the mold sang in the bleached valleys under
> the rose.

Roethke's analysis of these lines explains how he maintains restraint and balance without the control of regular meter. He comments on the "Elegy":

> . . . let me indicate one or two technical effects in my little piece. For one thing, the enumeration, the favorite device of the more irregular poem. We see it again and again in Whitman and Lawrence. 'I remember,' then the listing, the appositions, and the absolute construction. 'Her song trembling,' etc. Then the last lines in the stanza lengthen out . . . There is a successive shortening of the line length, an effect I have become inordinately fond of, I'm afraid. This little piece indicates in a way some of the strategies for the poet writing without the support of a formal pattern—he can vary his line length, modulate, he can stretch out the line, he can shorten.[20]

Enumeration and varying the line length—these dominate the prosody of those wild, free-associating poems collected in

Praise to the End (1951). "The successive shortening of line length" does indeed become a mannerism, almost a signature:

See what the sweet harp says.
Should a song break a sleep?
The round home of a root,—
Is that the place to go?
I'm a tune dying
On harsh stone.
An Eye says,
Come.

I keep dreaming of bees.
This flesh has airy bones.
Going is knowing.
I see; I seek;
I'm near.
Be true,
Skin.

"O, Thou Opening, O"

It would be a misnomer to call this "free verse": to paraphrase Eliot, no verse could be free which so successfully captures such awareness exploding from underground. Or to bring Roethke to bear on himself again:

> We must permit poetry to extend consciousness as far, as deeply, as particularly as it can, to recapture, in Stanley Kunitz' phrase, 'what it has lost to some extent to prose.' We must realize, I think, that the writer in freer forms must have an even greater fidelity to his subject matter than the poet who has the support of form. He must keep his eye on the object, and his rhythm must move as a mind moves, must be imaginatively right, or he is lost.[21]

"His rhythm must move as a mind moves. . . ." This is especially pertinent when the poet's mind turns inward, when he greets his "thingy spirit" and deliberately abandons the logic of usual relationships:

Reason? That dreary shed, that hutch for grubby
schoolboys!
The hedgewren's song says something else.

> I care for a cat's cry and the hugs, live as water.
> I've traced these words in sand with a vestigial tail;
> Now the gills are beginning to cry.
> Such a sweet noise: I can't sleep for it.
> Bless me and the maze I'm in!
> Hello, thingy spirit.
>
> "I Cry, Love! Love!"

The irrelevancy here is not like Auden's often kitschy surrealism; Roethke writes the phylogeny of the subconscious. The rhythms *are* imaginatively right. As in Whitman, each line comprises the prosodic unit; each line draws exactly enough breath to sustain it. Regular meter would destroy the sense of improvisation, the sense that the movements of the poem trace an ontogony which repeats racial history.

"Meditations of an Old Woman"—the five-part poem concluding *Words for the Wind*—has been noted critically as a response to *Four Quartets.*[22] Roethke was certainly thinking of Eliot; we find in the "Meditations" many echoing passages, many lines which pick up Eliot's words for refutation or amplification. A comparison of two passages shows what Roethke owes Eliot; the first is from *The Dry Salvages,* the second from the "First Meditation":

> When the train starts, and the passengers are settled
> To fruit, periodicals and business letters
> (And those who saw them off have left the platform)
> Their faces relax from grief into relief,
> To the sleepy rhythm of a hundred hours.
> Fare forward, travellers! not escaping from the past
> Into different lives, or into any future;
> You are not the same people who left that station
> Or who will arrive at any terminus . . .

> All journeys, I think, are the same:
> The movement is forward, after a few wavers,
> And for a while we are all alone,
> Busy, obvious with ourselves,
> The drunken soldier, the old lady with her peppermints;
> And we ride, we ride, taking the curves
> Somewhat closer, the trucks coming
> Down from behind the last ranges,
> Their black shapes breaking past;

And the air claps between us,
Blasting the frosted windows,
And I seem to go backward,
Backward in time . . .

The bases of the prosody are the same: we discover enumeration, a gradual narrowing of line length and rhythmic period, and the repeated use of "verbal forms that keep the action going."[23] Roethke's rhythm is tauter, charged with fiercer energy. Eliot sprawls, his line runs slacker, and his self-conscious use of clichés subverts verbal excitement. Prosodically, Roethke improves upon his original—although he cannot approach Eliot when the Old Master has his magic firmly in control:

Their faces relax from grief into relief,
To the sleepy rhythm of a hundred hours.

Most of the "Meditations" are written in unmetered verse. However, Roethke frequently turns to a lyrical, unrhymed stanza of three beats,

What lover keeps his song?
I sigh before I sing.
I love because I am
A rapt thing with a name.

or to a highly personal blank verse:

By swoops of bird, by leaps of fish, I live.
My shadow steadies in a shifting stream;
I live in air; the long light is my home;
I dare caress the stones, the field my friend;
A light wind rises: I become the wind.

This short-breathed line, characterized by the nervous end-stopping, is an identifying feature of Roethke's style. It is especially effective in those exclamatory passages of sudden association and rapt discovery—passages that resemble the speech of a verbally gifted and extraordinarily sensitive five-year-old:

How sweetly I abide. Am I a bird?
Soft, soft, the snow's not falling. What's a seed?
A face floats in the ferns. Do maimed gods walk?

Of course, the last question could have been asked only by a sophisticated five-year-old who had read *The Golden Bough!*

The best parts of the "Meditations" approach the transcendence and ecstasy of *Four Quartets.* Roethke affirms the natural life, a world of the sentient body as well as a world of spiritual exaltation. When Eliot tells us,

> Sin is Behovely, but
> All shall be well, and
> All manner of thing shall be well.

Roethke answers, with some acidity,

> It is difficult to say all things are well,
> When the worst is about to arrive;
> It is fatal to woo yourself,
> However graceful the posture.

For Eliot, all things will be well in the next world; but Roethke prefers, "Instead of a devil with horns . . . a serpent with scales." For Eliot, ends are beginnings and the road up is the road down; Roethke—or his persona in the poem—cries:

> I'm released from the dreary dance of opposites.

Paradoxically, Eliot's influence is also Roethke's release; the final strophe of "What Can I Tell My Bones" (the fifth and last "Meditation") is written in "free" meter that Roethke characterizes in nearly Eliotic terms:

> I agree that free verse is a denial in terms. There is, invariably, the ghost of some other form, often blank verse, behind what is written, or the more elaborate rise and fall of the rhythmical prose sentence.[24]

More than "the ghost" of blank verse haunts this passage:

> The sun! The sun! And all we can become!
> And the time ripe for running to the moon!
> In the long fields, I leave my father's eye;
> And shake the secrets from my deepest bones;
> My spirit rises with the rising wind;
> I'm thick with leaves and tender as a dove,

> I take the liberties a short life permits—
> I seek my own meekness;
> I recover my tenderness by long looking.
> By midnight I love everything alive.
> Who took the darkness from the air?
> I'm wet with another life.
> Yea, I have gone and stayed.
>
> What came to me vaguely is now clear,
> As if released by a spirit,
> Or agency outside me.
> Unprayed-for,
> And final.

Like Eliot, Roethke has great gifts for modulation, for loosening the meter without audible creaks and bumps. The first six lines are stable blank verse; the change in movement comes with the seventh line:

> I take the liberties a short life permits . . .

The line is sprung by an extra monosyllabic foot, *life;* the sprung line serves as a rhythmic junction for the freer lines which follow. And we note again the long *morendo* as the line length shortens. Such prosodic manipulation is exemplary "imitative form." Release and resignation, an end to searching, and the resolution of spirit with nature find their expressive container in the slowly diminishing rhythm.

Robert Lowell's first two volumes, *Land of Unlikeness* (1944) and *Lord Weary's Castle* (1946) stride in a "Goliath's armor of brazen metric."[25] His recent poems walk relatively unarmed. The change in Lowell's prosody, from a strict convention of carefully worked stanzas and rhyming couplets to his recent mode of nearly naked speech, has not come easily. Lowell admits, "I never dared write [free verse] until I was almost forty. If it doesn't work, if the rhythm isn't right and the experience isn't right, you have nothing, I think." The crux is *experience:* Lowell affirms, "I'm sure the rhythm is the person himself."[26]

The person behind the drama and violence, the *Schrei,* of *Land of Unlikeness* is obscurely realized. Lowell's muscular Catholicism exercises itself in dense, harsh language; the prosody, as Allen Tate points out in his brief *Introduction,* seems *willed* on the language. The result is often a poetry of religious exhibitionism;

not always, as Tate suggests, a poetry of strong religious struggle which attempts to recover Christian symbolism for a world gone rotten with material progress. Struggle, as well as a complex, even burlesqued symbolism are present; but the defects and distortions of these first poems emerge as much out of confusion and bad taste as out of Lowell's religious agonies.

In "Christ for Sale" Lowell attempts the recovery of that seventeenth-century "integrated sensibility" and presents the doctrine of The Redemption in language and images that willfully disgust:

> In Greenwich Village, Christ the Drunkard brews
> Gall, or spiked bone-vat, siphons His bilged blood
> Into weak brain-pans and unseasons wood:
> His auctioneers are four hog-fatted Jews.
> In furs and bundlings of vitality,
> Our ladies, ho, swill down the ichor in this Dye.
>
> Drying upon the crooked nails of time,
> Dirty Saint Francis, where is Jesus' blood,
> Salvation's only Fountainhood and Flood?
> These drippings of the Lamb are Heaven's crime.
> Queens, Brooklyn and Manhattan, come and buy:
> Gomorrah, had you known the wormwood in this Dye!
>
> Us still our Savior's mangled mouth may kiss
> Although beauticians plaster us with mud:
> Dog of the veins, your nose is stopped with blood;
> Women are thirsty, let them lap up this:
> The luncher's stop to spit into Christ's eye.
> O Lamb of God, your loitering carrion will die.

Neither the forced language and the imagery of *emesis,* nor the strident rhythms do much to clarify the poet's blasphemies. (I understand, of course, that Lowell is blasphemous in the modern sense: in the way that Baudelaire and Joyce are Catholic blasphemers and hence deeply, though paradoxically, religious.) The second line is sprung by strong-stressing:

> Gáll, or spíked bóne-vát, síphons His bílged blóod . . .

The emotional intention, white-hot anger, is lost in the incoherent splutter of consonants.

Lowell omitted "Christ for Sale," along with ten other poems from *Land of Unlikeness,* in his actual *début* volume *Lord Weary's Castle.*[27] Those poems reprinted from the earlier book were revised, a few heavily. Many of the revisions entail only the change of a single line or a single word, but all the changes offer prosodic improvements. Thus the final couplet of "Children of Light"

> And light is where the ancient blood of Cain
> Is burning, burning the unburied grain . . .

becomes in *Lord Weary's Castle*

> And light is where the landless blood of Cain
> Is burning, burning the unburied grain.

Landless alliterates with *light;* it also removes the unpleasantly nasal *an-* and its unfortunate rhyme with *Cain.* The change of a single word strengthens the opening of "The Crucifix":

> How dry Time screaks in its fat axle-grease,
> As sure November strikes us through the ice . . .
>
> *Land of Unlikeness*

> How dry time screaks in its fat axle-grease,
> As spare November strikes us through the ice . . .
>
> *Lord Weary's Castle*

Extensive revisions improve the rest of the poem; lines five through eight are both verbally and metrically strengthened:

> It's time: the worldly angels strip to tease
> And wring out bread and butter from their eyes,
> To wipe away the past's idolatries;
> Tomorrow's seaways lurch through Sodom's knees.
>
> *Land of Unlikeness*

> It's time: the old unmastered lion roars
> And ramps like a mad dog outside the doors,
> Snapping at gobbets in my thumbless hand.
> The seaways lurch through Sodom's knees of sand
> Tomorrow . . .
>
> *Lord Weary's Castle*

Lowell expunges the tasteless Clevelandisms of an angelic strip-tease and the ocularly expressed bread and butter; he varies the level iambic meter with a rising Ionic and an initial trochee:

> And rámps | like a mád dóg | out síde | the dóors,
> Snáp ping | at gób | bets ín | my thúmb | less hánd.

The striking feature of the metric of *Lord Weary's Castle* is its overwhelming physicality. Lines clang and grind; the movement stops dead and resumes with a shudder; stress jams against stress until lines break under the tension:

> With flat glass eyes pushed at him on a stick . . .
>
> "Between the Porch and the Altar"

It is an exciting workout for both ear and eye to read "The Quaker Graveyard in Nantucket"—as exciting as to read "Lycidas": a poem it resembles, thematically and prosodically.[28] Note the even roll of the enjambed lines after the full stop of the first descriptive fragment:

> A brackish reach of shoal off Madaket,—
> The sea was still breaking violently and night
> Had steamed into our North Atlantic Fleet,
> When the drowned sailor clutched the drag-net. Light
> Flashed from his matted head and marble feet,
> He grappled at the net
> With the coiled, hurdling muscles of his thighs . . .

Note Lowell's penchant for the double foot of two light and two heavy stresses; these lines are from the second strophe of "The Quaker Graveyard:"

Sea-gulls blink their heavy lids
Seaward. The wind's wings beat upon the stones,
Cousin, and scream for you and the claws rush
At the sea's throat and wring it in the slush
Of this Old Quaker graveyard where the bones
Cry out in the long night for the hurt beast
Bobbing by Ahab's whaleboats in the East.

This Ionic rhythm is obsessive: "and the claws rush . . . at the sea's throat . . . in the long night for the hurt beast." The rhythm of the gracefully expressive slow line

Cry out in the long night for the hurt beast

shows a tremendous advance in feeling and technique over the strained awkwardness of,

Us still our Savior's mangled mouth may kiss . . .

Lowell's thematic rhythms and the repetition of metrically similar lines give "The Quaker Graveyard" a powerful stylistic consistency; Moby Dick rises and menaces us in constant Ionics:

The bones cry for the blood of the white whale . . .

The occasional alternation of a short line (usually trimeter) with the prevailing pentameters adds another "rhythmic constant." Lowell owes this metrical suggestion to Milton; a comparison of lines from "Lycidas" and the first strophe of "The Quaker Graveyard" shows the extent of Lowell's debt and how expertly he has adapted Milton's rhythm to his own use:

Begin then, Sisters of the sacred well,
That from beneath the seat of *Jove* doth spring,
Begin, and somewhat loudly sweep the string.
Hence with denial vain, and coy excuse;
So may some gentle Muse
With lucky words favor my destin'd urn,
And as he passes turn,
And bid fair peace be to my sable shroud.

> The corpse was bloodless, a botch of reds and whites,
> Its open, staring eyes
> Were lustreless dead-lights
> Or cabin-windows on a stranded hulk
> Heavy with sand. We weight the body, close
> Its eyes and heave it seaward whence it came...

Acting as his own critic, Lowell remarks, "... this is a poem by someone who's read Milton very carefully, and yet it's not very Miltonic."[29]

Lowell's awareness of English metrical tradition crops up everywhere in *Lord Weary's Castle.* The nine-line stanzas of "The Ghost" and "Mr. Edwards and the Spider," while not corresponding exactly to a specific pattern in the *Songs and Sonnets,* are unmistakably Donne-like. The stanza of "The Drunken Fisherman" comes from Marvell's *The Garden:*

> Wallowing in this bloody sty,
> I cast for fish that pleased my eye
> (Truly Jehovah's bow suspends
> No pots of gold to weight its ends);
> Only the blood-mouthed rainbow trout
> Rose to my bait. They flopped about
> My canvas creel until the moth
> Corrupted its unstable cloth.

The run-on couplet, "with its rhymes buried," of "Between the Porch and the Altar" and "After the Surprising Conversions" "is very much like the couplet Browning uses in 'My Last Duchess,' in *Sordello*..."[30] Lowell also inherits from Browning the unbeautiful mannerism of beginning a new sentence with the last foot of the line:

> Time runs, the windshield runs with stars. The past
> Is cities from a train, until at last
> Its escalating and black-windowed blocks
> Recoil against a Gothic church. The clocks
> Are tolling. I am dying. The shocked stones
> Are falling like a ton of bricks and bones...
>
> "Between the Porch and the Altar"

The two finest poems of Lowell's third book, *The Mills of the Kavanaughs* (1951), are hammered into the close-fitting armor of the run-on couplet. But Lowell is now a master of the form; the two poems "Falling Asleep Over the Aeneid" and "Mother Marie Therese" are little hampered by the requirements of rhyme and meter. Lowell achieves a controlled freedom where "any sort of compression or expansion is possible."[31] The necessity of rhyme does not force Lowell into those embarrassments which mar "Between the Porch and the Altar":

> But my dishonor makes him drink. Of course
> I'll tell the court the truth for his divorce . . .
>
> One
> Must have a friend to enter there, but none
> Is friendless in this crowd, and the nuns smile.
> I stand aside and marvel; for a while
> The winter sun is pleasant . . .

Of course / divorce, One / none, and *smile / for a while* are neutral rhymes of convenience which betray Lowell's struggle to get on with the poem.

The rhyming of "Falling Asleep Over the Aeneid" has rich semantic resonance; the rhyming words put out pseudopods of meaning which reach back and grip each other. Thus the connotations of *fire / pyre, rod / God,* and *files / miles* in the opening lines do not form random movements of meaning but are organic, purposive:

> The sun is blue and scarlet on my page,
> And *yuck-a, yuck-a, yuck-a, yuck-a,* rage
> The yellowhammers mating. Yellow fire
> Blankets the captives dancing on their pyre,
> And the scorched lictor screams and drops his rod.
> Trojans are singing to their drunken God,
> Ares. Their helmets catch on fire. Their files
> Clank by the body of my comrade—miles
> Of filings!

This rhyming continues with almost undiminished brilliance to the poem's conclusion. Lowell displays a new prosodic skill in "Falling Asleep Over the Aeneid": the ability to modulate his tone with lines pitched at a dynamic level lower than *double forte*. We find lyric delicacy and gentleness easing the powerful rhetoric:

> The plumes blow;
> The beard and eyebrows ruffle. Face of snow,
> You are the flower that country girls have caught,
> A wild bee-pillaged honey-suckle brought
> To the returning bridegroom—the design
> Has not yet left it, and the petals shine;
> The earth, its mother, has, at last, no help:
> It is itself.

We already see in "Thanksgiving's Over," the last poem in *The Mills of the Kavanaughs,* some of the prosodic flexibility and close personal rhythm of Lowell's more recent work. "Thanksgiving's Over" is phantasmagoric, fevered; Michael, the narrator, dreams of his mad wife who committed suicide. She speaks to him in his dream:

> *. . . But Michael, I was well;*
> My mind was well;
> I wanted to be loved—to thaw, to change,
> To *April!* Now our mountains, seventeen
> Bald Brothers, green
> Below the timberline, must change
> Their skullcaps for the green of Sherwood Forest;
> Mount Leather-Jacket leads the season. Outlaws,
> We enter a world of children, perched on gaunt
> Crows-nests in hemlocks over flat-iron torrents;
> And freely serve our term
> In prison. I will serve you, Love. Affirm
> The promise, move the mountains, while they lean,
> As dry as dust for want
> Of trusting . . .

Lowell does not quite break the meter here; the footwork is recognizably iambic, although the lines are highly irregular in length and run-over with absolute freedom. The later poems in *Life Studies* (1959) fragment the dominant iambic meter. We hear the clear rhythms of Lowell's speaking voice unhampered by the exigencies of precise line length and exactly patterned stresses.

A willful, self-conscious craftsman, Lowell explains how he effected a major change in his prosodic style. In a fascinating interview, published in *The Paris Review,* Lowell tells us

> . . . I began to have a certain disrespect for the tight forms. If you could make it easier by adding syllables, why not? And then when I was writing *Life Studies,* a good number of the poems were started in very strict meter, and I found that, more than the rhymes, the regular beat was what I didn't want. I have a long poem in there about my father, called 'Commander Lowell,' which actually is largely in couplets, but I originally wrote perfectly strict four-foot couplets. Well, with that form it's hard not to have echoes of Marvell. The regularity just seemed to ruin the honesty of sentiment, and became rhetorical; it said, 'I'm a poem'—though it was a great help when I was revising having this original skeleton. I could keep the couplets where I wanted them and drop them where I didn't; there'd be a form to come back to.[32]

Examining "Commander Lowell," we get no clue to Lowell's methods of composition; its texture and syntax show no stitching. Only the rhymes remain from its original couplet form—and these are absorbed into the taut prose phrasing:

> There were no undesirables or girls in my set,
> when I was a boy at Mattapoisett—
> only Mother, still her Father's daughter.
> Her voice was still electric
> with a hysterical, unmarried panic,
> when she read to me from the Napoleon book.

Heartbreaking in their absolute "honesty of sentiment" are the lines addressed to Lowell's infant daughter in "Home after Three Months Away." The metric, moving "between fixity and flux," is strict enough to keep the emotions in order, supple enough to prevent artificiality:

> Three months, three months!
> Is Richard now himself again?
> Dimpled with exaltation,
> my daughter holds her levee in the tub.

Our noses rub,
each of us pats a stringy lock of hair—
they tell me nothing's gone.
Though I am forty-one,
not forty now, the time I put away
was child's-play. After thirteen weeks
my child still dabs her cheeks
to start me shaving. When
we dress her in her sky-blue corduroy,
she changes to a boy,
and floats my shaving brush
and washcloth in the flush . . .

Dearest, I cannot loiter here
in lather like a polar bear.

These lines are not unmetered; the meter is concealed by running over the lines, breaking the syntax with numerous heavy pauses, and abruptly shifting the tempo:

my daughter holds her levee in the tub.
Our noses rub . . .

we dress her in her sky-blue corduroy,
she changes to a boy . . .

Perhaps the most shattering poem in *Life Studies* is the last one in the volume, "Skunk Hour." The idiom is so personal that we cannot separate technical means from Lowell's anguish. Rhythm touches raw nerves moved by hysteria held barely in check by minimal prosodic means: the six-line stanza and the rhyme:

One dark night,
my Tudor Ford climbed the hill's skull;
I watched for love-cars. Lights turned down,
they lay together, hull to hull,
where the graveyard shelves on the town . . .
My mind's not right.

A car radio bleats,
'Love, O careless Love. . . .' I hear
my ill-spirit sob in each blood cell,
as if my hand were at its throat . . .

I myself am hell;
nobody's here—

only skunks, that search
in the moonlight for a bite to eat.
They march on their soles up Main Street:
white stripes, moonstruck eyes' red fire
under the chalk-dry and spar spire
of the Trinitarian Church.

Lowell crowds together, in an unmetered line, as many as six strong stresses:

my íll-spirít sób in éach blóod céll . . .
whíte strípes, móonstruck éyes' réd fíre . . .

The effect is explosive: a rendering of absolute emotion which stops just this side of spluttering incoherence. The strained rhythm marks the limits to which agonized personal experience can be pushed. Lowell himself has expressed doubts about this kind of confessional poetry:

> I don't think that a personal history can go on forever, unless you're Walt Whitman and have a way with you. I feel I've done enough personal poetry. That doesn't mean I won't do more of it, but I don't want to do more now. . . . other things being equal it's better to get your emotions out in a Macbeth than in a confession.[33]

Lowell's most recent work has sought greater objectivity in subjects partially removed from the suffering intimacies of *Life Studies*. Two new poems, published in *Partisan Review* (Spring, 1964), look back toward the earlier monologues and further exploit the stylistic advances of *Life Studies*. The first poem, "Caligula," is a dramatic apostrophe to the mad Roman emperor. Lowell addresses Caligula as "My namesake, Little Boots . . ." (Lowell's nickname is "Cal") and discovers in the Roman emperor an appalling *alter ego:* where he sees his "lowest depth of possibility." "Caligula" is composed in Lowell's familiar enjambed pentameter couplets, but the form is camouflaged by omitting the initial capitals and breaking the meter with harshly sprung lines:

Your true face sneers at me, mean, thin, agonized . . .

The second poem, "The Mouth of the Hudson," shows no trace of either syllable-stress meter or strong-stressing. It moves with an almost deathly stillness, sustained by a quiet activity of verbs and a tragic inwardness. The poem describes a romantically sentient urban landscape—a landscape which is a state of mind and a state of culture. Rhythm in this poem is "the poet himself": he observes and at the same time inhabits his subject,

> in the sulphur-yellow sun
> of the unforgiveable landscape.

Epilogue: The Footsteps of the Muse

I

Near the conclusion of his *History,* Saintsbury summarizes the progress of English prosody—from Chaucer to "Mr. Swinburne." He sees it dialectically, a fruitful struggle between the "exultation of freedom" and the tyranny of "severe restriction."[1] Against the historically determined prosodic "given" of our language—what Saintsbury calls "foot-arrangement," what we have called syllable-stress meter—freedom and restriction have operated. Early in English poetic history, Chaucer's practice laid the groundwork for syllable-stress meter. The Tudor lyricists recovered the principles of syllable-stress meter; Sidney and Spenser confirmed them, once and for all. Shakespeare and Milton, in their handling of blank verse, showed what "miraculous powers" inhered in traditional meter. After their prosodic triumphs, the slack blank verse of the Jacobean and Caroline dramatists signaled the dangers of excessive freedom; the rigid neoclassic couplet was the needed reaction to "the second doggerel of broken-down blank verse."[2]

The first fifty years of modern prosody have shown a similar dialectical movement. The most typically "modern" poetry was conceived in an exultation of freedom; by 1930 it began to settle back into the prosodic norm. Early experimenters (including Whitman and Hopkins) attempted the overthrow of syllable-stress meter and devised prosodies based on units of linguistic segmentation larger than the common iambic or trisyllabic meters. The best poets of the forties and fifties have been controlled prosodists who only occasionally work open rhythms and seem happy conservatives in the traditional meters. The sixties, as I have previously conjectured, seem again turning away from the norm toward the less rigidly metrical prosodies.

Does the dialectic of freedom and restriction define the period style of modern prosody? Do any of the techniques we have examined—*vers libre,* sprung rhythm, quasi-metrical prosody—derive from some basic rhythm which flows out of modern consciousness? I do not intend to turn amateur sociologist or cocktail party psychiatrist and investigate how the internal combustion engine has affected, or the neurotic personality of our time has afflicted, the rhythms of modern poetry. A period style does not radiate from the local disorders of culture and personality; it represents an apotheosis of individual techniques and methods into spiritual fact, "the sublimation of technique into aesthetic results."[3]

If, however, we think of prosody only as technique, it becomes impossible to locate period style. We are then forced to a process of atomization and reduction: this poet writes free verse, that poet is a syllabist; this poet follows the school of Pound, that poet the school of Auden. We must relate a particular technique, or group of techniques, to major forms of thought and feeling in order to approach a definition of larger style. Certain stylistic characterizations of previous literary eras do not strain critical good sense. The powerful blank verse of the early Elizabethan dramatists expresses the hope and exuberance of the 1580's and 1590's; the marvelously flexible and perhaps decadent verse of later Shakespeare and Webster reflects the *Weltschmerz* of the Jacobean age and the new philosophy which put all in doubt. To the critics of the eighteenth century, the "perfected" couplet of Waller, Dryden, and Pope represented the triumph of Reason and Nature in audible metric.

There is danger in pushing such close formulations for our age. Mirrored in the shrinking glass of history, the style of a remote literary period seems closely appropriate to its inner spirit and outward stance. (And arguments for period style are often circular: we deduce the spirit of the age from a stylistic analysis of the literature and discover that the spirit suits the style. An over-enthusiastic historicism will always find in the past exactly what it seeks.) Our own age seems a tangle of combatting styles; what can we name as characteristic?

The matter depends on our philosophy of history: does it comprehend, like the hedgehog, "one large thing," or like the fox, "many things."[4] Hedgehogs see profound unity in the cultural and artistic expressions of each age and will name and even eulogize period styles. The foxes see accident or occasional resemblance and generally discredit the notion that period styles exist; or, if they do admit their reality, doubt that living men can assess the style of their own age. A pessimistic fox like Denis de Rougement sees little hope of discovering period style in modern art:

> No epoch, perhaps, has known less unity than our own. In any case, none has shown so deliberate a desire to shun every appearance of unity, not only in style and technique, but even in its animating beliefs. And if some day, nevertheless, after all these negotiations and ruptures, all these refusals to continue anything else or resemble anything else, some profound relationship between the principal works of our century becomes apparent, in spite of all the efforts of their authors, it is not our generation which will see it.[5]

Looking at the same historical landscape, Ortega Y Gasset sees exciting unity; all the arts are animated by the fateful power of a determining *Zeitgeist:*

> It is amazing how compact a unity every historical epoch presents throughout its various manifestations. One and the same inspiration, one and the same biological style are recognizable in the several branches of art. The young musician—himself unaware of it—strives to realize in his medium the same aesthetic values as his contemporary colleagues—the poet, the painter, the playwright—in theirs.[6]

My own temperament inclines toward hedgehogism—though I do not insist that every vagary of experiment and trick of technique, every fad and fashion of the poetic movements must be regarded as an emanation of the World-Soul. Many changes in technique never are absorbed into style; mere idiosyncrasy of technique does not make a style. When we are reading well and fully responding to a poem, our actual awareness of technique *qua* technique is subliminal; we are conscious of the aesthetic result. In Eliot's line,

> I no longer strive to strive towards such things . . .

the springing of the fourth foot will be felt as a kinaesthetic flexing of muscles, an inner gesture that the reader motionlessly acts out.

Few readers will say to themselves, "Ah, that fourth foot is beautifully sprung," as few listeners will say, responding to the tense, ominous second statement of the opening theme of the *Appassionata Sonata,* "Ah, Beethoven repeats that phrase in the flat super-tonic!"

A poet's individual style is more than the techniques he uses; it is neither sprung rhythm nor Websterian blank verse that distinguish Hopkins and Eliot as poets who have achieved individual style. It is these techniques channeling the deep and turbulent sources of feeling that create significant style; these prosodic devices help subdue the "messy imprecision" of language to artistic vision. In the hands of imitators—or when these poets are not operating efficiently—sprung rhythm and Websterian verse can degenerate into mannerism, stale technique; we then have something less than authentic style. An imitator can learn to parrot a technique; he cannot counterfeit the emotion the technique discovers. A genuine prosodic style, "the poet himself," as Robert Lowell suggests, is the submergence of personal history and cultural experience in those symbolic structures most capable of controlling feeling—the multiple forms of rhythm.

The period style in contemporary prosody transcends all particular techniques; it originates in the work of those men who first caught the modern temper in their verse. It shows analogies with the other "modern" styles: in music and in painting. The style does not emerge out of precisely identifiable historical or social circumstances but rather reflects an aesthetic mood; as we have previously argued, rhythms are only superficially imitative. The "modern rhythm" felt in twentieth-century poetry is not primarily the throb of machines and the steadily increasing pace of life. Our apprehension of modern rhythm goes deeper than our physical reactions: it lies in fundamental matters of coherence, perception, and how we conceive the structure of space and time.

2

The shift from nineteenth-century style to modern style occurred simultaneously and suddenly. In a very brief period before World War I, a group of poets, painters, and musicians broke with traditional idioms and initiated a period of experimentation. Schönberg published his first compositions without key signatures, the *Three Piano Pieces,* in 1910. Eliot began *Prufrock* in 1910 and finished it in 1911. Picasso painted his Cubist "Man with Violin" in 1911. Stravinsky produced *Petrushka* in the same year, *The Rite of Spring* two years later. In that moment before World War I, many other artists were enlarging and shattering forms.

Modern poetry and its expanded, complex rhythms emerged with the first appearances of atonality and bitonality in music and the fragmentation of natural forms in painting. This coincidence of innovation need not be regarded as the inexorable working out of mysterious aesthetic destiny; however, it was hardly accidental. These excursions into new methods were well prepared for. Schönberg enlarged harmonic resources developed by Liszt, Wagner, and Mahler. The distortion of space and form practiced by the Cubists was preceded by the work of Cézanne. We have already seen how the work of Whitman and Hopkins and the French *vers libres* poets foreshadowed the prosodies of the twentieth century. All beginnings are ends: what burgeoned as "modern style" circa 1910 was also the culmination of nineteenth-century developments.

Common to all the arts in this initial outbreak of modernism was the challenge to older ideas of coherence, continuity, and point of view. The structural unity of a musical composition no longer relied on the expected return to an established tonality; its unity rested on a complex relationship of harmonic and rhythmic constants and melodic development. Painting distorted spatial relationships and manipulated point of view. Picasso could see, in his "Girl Before a Mirror," profile and full-face simultaneously. Similarly, the visual prosody of E. E. Cummings, through typographical line work, allows us to receive two verbal messages at once:

l(a

le
af
fa

ll

s)
one
l

iness

I, from *95 Poems*

This period of experimentation and its orientation toward a new style in the arts reflected fundamental revisions in western thinking about space and time. The older mechanistic and chronological approaches to the temporal flux had been replaced by relativistic and psychologic theories. Earlier we said prosody images human process as it moves through time; a poet's rhythm reveals his feelings about temporal relationship and movement. Modern prosodic style, whether flatly conversational or flashily rhetorical, has interpreted "Time present and time past." I intend no elucidation of Einstein's influence on Schönberg and Eliot; they were, in all probability, unaware of Einstein's existence in 1910. However, Eliot had listened to Bergson lecture at the Sorbonne; Symbolist theory and practice had long recognized that the deepest and most significant part of human consciousness functioned in a realm outside of measurable space and time.

Two passages, the first from James Thomson's *The City of Dreadful Night,* the second from *The Waste Land,* interpret the time-sense of their respective periods; their rhythmic styles point to a profound difference in Victorian and modern responses to temporal process. A theme of both poems is urban despair; the subject of each passage is the river:

A river girds the city west and south,
  The main north channel of a broad lagoon,
Regurging with the salt tides from the mouth;
  Waste marshes shine and glister to the moon
For leagues, then moorland black, then stony ridges;
Great piers and causeways, many noble bridges,
  Connect the town and islet suburbs strewn.

Upon an easy slope it lies at large,
  And scarcely overlaps the long curved crest
Which swells out two leagues from the river marge.
  A trackless wilderness rolls north and west,
Savannahs, savage woods, enormous mountains,
Bleak uplands, black ravines with torrent fountains;
  And eastward rolls the shipless sea's unrest.

———

The river's tent is broken; the last fingers of leaf
Clutch and sink into the wet bank. The wind
Crosses the brown land, unheard. The nymphs are departed.

> Sweet Thames, run softly, till I end my song.
> The river bears no empty bottles, sandwich papers,
> Silk handkerchiefs, cardboard boxes, cigarette ends
> Or other testimony of summer nights. The nymphs are
> departed . . .
> But at my back in a cold blast I hear
> The rattle of the bones, and chuckle spread from ear to ear.

We note the tempo of each passage. Thomson's steady meter and extended syntax are carefully locked in by rhyme and stanza. Time flows at an even pace: one thing follows another in chronologic order. Eliot's nervous syntax comes out in short gasps; no sentence runs for much more than two lines. Instead of temporal sequence, the intrusions of Spenser and Marvell create montage effects—where time is shattered into sudden historical glimpses. Again we have the illusion of simultaneity. Spenser and Marvell join the twentieth-century narrator in his mordant comments on the pollution of cities and human relationships.

The rhythms of each passage image a different kind of temporal experience. Thomson's age still felt time as forward action, a movement both teleological and mechanical. His phantasmagoric vision of London is oppressed by mutability which destroys but also releases; history moves toward its destined goal in the inevitable future. Eliot's age is also oppressed by time: not because it regrets the snows of yesteryear or fears the tread of History, but because past, present, and future seem a jumble of unrelated events. Instead of Time's awesome chariot, Eliot's narrator hears meaningless city noises,

> The sound of horns and motors, which shall bring
> Sweeney to Mrs. Porter in the spring.

The intricate rhythms of *The Waste Land* are not imitative of chaos, disorderly symbols of disorder; they allow us to feel a world in which time and history have been abruptly suspended.

Prosodic style, as it coalesces in *The Waste Land,* depends on the techniques we have examined in Chapter VII; it also grows out of rhythmic meaning living in the most harmonious relationship with the poem's ideas and feelings. We could no more imagine *The Waste Land* composed in the blank verse of *The Prelude* than we could imagine *The Rite of Spring* composed in the harmonic idiom of Mozart. These examples are not as absurd as they sound; poets do indeed make bad choices in technique. Crane, as we have argued, had no facility with nonmetrical prosody; Lowell seemed muscle-bound in his "brazen metric" and has done better work in looser rhythms. More importantly, that poets do err in their choice of prosody is strong evidence for period style. Crane developed under the domination of Pound and Eliot; Lowell started in the generation of Auden. Their own temperaments led them away from the prevailing conventions. Crane died before leaving his impress on the style of the twenties, but Lowell shows every sign of setting his prosodic mark on the most contemporary verse.[7]

3

The long poem testifies reliably for period style. In Elizabethan poetic drama, Miltonic epic, and the satirical and didactic poetry of neoclassicism, we discover the prosodic style of previous eras. The long poems written by the first generation of modern poets—the *Cantos, The Waste Land, The Bridge, Paterson*—possess common stylistic features. An associative and anachronistic compositional method plunges these works into "creative incoherence." None of these poems is sustained by a carrying metric in the way that *The Rape of the Lock* and *The Prelude* are sustained by the closed couplet and blank verse. They all, more or less, forsake rational prosody for absolute rhythm, organic metric, or the speaking voice in its raw inarticulation.

The "speaking voice" has been often noted as a distinguishing aspect of modern style; the language of English poetry was energized by the American dialect:

> The clean
> Conversational voice of the American
> Once and for all outlawed the late-Victorian
> Lilt. Tennyson, Swinburne and the like
> Went down . . .[8]

At the outset of their careers, Pound and Eliot saw themselves repeating Wordsworth's attempt "to imitate and, as far as possible, to adopt the very language of men." Such language would be purified of obvious poeticisms and Victorian diction: "There must be no book words, no periphrases, no inversions . . . no cliches, set phrases stereotyped journalese . . . nothing that you couldn't, in some circumstance, in the stress of some emotion, actually say."[9]

And this language would move to different rhythms—not the rhythms of the dominantly iambic meters but the flow of conversation.

However, actual practice diverged, often widely, from the theory. Just as we now see that Wordsworth's language was hardly rustic speech, and that it has demonstrable relationships to the forcefully repudiated poetic diction of the eighteenth century, so we are aware that Pound was considerably influenced by late-Victorian diction and Eliot by late-Victorian meter. The so-called conversational idiom of modern poetry is as much the child of Browning as it is of twentieth-century poetic practice. And long before either Pound or Browning there was Donne's example of impassioned talk directing the rhythms of verse.

Often what superficially sounds like the very language of men may be structured on artificial rhythms:

When Lil's husband got demobbed, I said—
I didn't mince my words, I said to her myself,
HURRY UP PLEASE ITS TIME
Now Albert's coming back, make yourself a bit smart.
He'll want to know what you done with that money he gave you
To get yourself some teeth. He did, I was there.

Eliot allows us to think that we are overhearing a conversation between two charwomen. The passage as much resembles the speech of London charwomen as the antiphonal wisecracking of Al and Max, in Hemingway's *The Killers,* resembles the speech of real Chicago hoodlums. In *Sweeney Agonistes* Eliot set the conversation of his lower-class characters to the beat of a jazz tom-tom: an effect far removed from the very language of men.

There is a theoretic muddle about the question of "the real language of men" and its relevance to the "conversational mode" of modern verse. It might be well to make a few distinctions useful to prosodic inquiry. A great deal of modern verse is written to the syntactical rhythm of prose; this verse may be either metrical or nonmetrical. Prose rhythm directs the poems of Marianne Moore or more sharply stressed lines like these of William Carlos Williams:

> But when I got here I soon found out that I
> was a pretty small frog in a mighty big pool. So

I went to work all over again. I suppose
I was born with a gift for that sort of thing.

Paterson, Book Two

In these lines Williams is rendering dramatically the talk of a character; the prose rhythm approaches speech rhythm. (It might do well to remember that we do *not,* under normal circumstances, speak prose; most real talk has a rhythm considerably looser and more dissociated than the hard syntactical rhythm of the written language.) A poet may choose to mimic the speech of another class or group,

'Ain' committed no federal crime,
jes a slaight misdemeanor . . .'

Pound, *Canto LXXX*

and this is certainly the very language of some men—but not of all men living in our time.

Speech rhythm can also be rendered in close metrical structure:

The wind dies in our canvas; we were running dead
Before the wind, but now our sail is part
Of death. O Brother, a New England town is death
And incest—and I saw it whole. I said,
Life is a thing I own. Brother, my heart
Races for sea-room—we are out of breath.

Robert Lowell, "Her Dead Brother"

Because the dramatic monologue has been a leading genre, perhaps *the* leading genre since the examples of Pound and Eliot, the question of verse-as-speech has assumed particular importance. In the *Cantos, The Waste Land,* and *The Bridge*—which might be described as poetic dramas without scenarios—a great many characters speak to a variety of rhythms. The same poem may offer the rhythms of lower-class speech,

'Bring 'em to the main shack,' said Baldy,
And the peons brought 'em;
'to the main shack brought 'em,'
As Henry would have said.

Canto XII

and the grand rhetoric of Homeric hexameter,

> 'But thou, O King, I bid remember me, unwept, unburied,
> 'Heap up mine arms, be tomb by sea-bord, and inscribed:
> '*A man of no fortune, and with a name to come.*'
>
> *Canto I*

Pound's *Cantos* present a striking instance of a modern work in which high literary style and a controlled prosody consort with the babble of unpremeditated and unpurified speech.

The distinctions may be now more carefully drawn. We have verse written to prose cadence, verse structured on speech rhythms, and direct dramatic representation of common language. The period style cannot be subsumed under any one of these—conversational idiom and prose song are properly stylizations, not styles. However speech and prose modified the prosody of the 'teens and the twenties, modern rhythmic style must be sought in some larger formulation—one which includes the poet's voice and what it says. Eliot talks like Madame Sosostris or Tiresias in *The Waste Land;* his voice in *Four Quartets* is not distinct from what the words, in all their permutations and interpenetrations, mean. The rhythms, inseparable from the words, are primary elements of meaning.

Our definition of rhythmic style returns to the idea of rhythmic cognition. We have searched the historical ground and discovered the large alternation of nonmetrical and metrical prosodies; we have seen the revolution against nineteenth-century metered regularity and the reaction, in Auden's generation, against that revolution. And now we seem to be witnessing a reaction to the reaction. We have examined the technical procedures of many individual poets and analyzed differences and similarities. But the rhythm of poetry is an image of "vital process." It conveys an awareness of the movements which actuate all physical life: the rhythm of the cell and the pulse of the modern physicist's perpetually self-renewing universe, so like the cosmos of Heraclitus, "that has ever been and is and will be eternal Fire, kindled by measure and quenched by measure." The rhythmic style of our age has blazed up and died away and blazed up again—showing its own pulse and measure. We identify it, finally, as an on-going process that carries the unmistakeable sense of "how feelings go" in a time of political disasters and human reorientation.

4

Aeneas knew Mother Venus by the grace of her walk:

> pedes vestis defluxit ad imos,
> et vera incessu patuit dea . . .

Measuring the footsteps of the Muse has afforded many glimpses of the divine presence. The elucidation of technical problems has reached down to matters that go beyond technique: to the sources of aesthetic effect. Tennyson once excoriated a critic as "a fool and a brute" for mentioning the word *anapest* in a review. Alas! we have mentioned *anapest* and *amphimacer* and *catalectic* and many other hard words here. We have scanned and dissected and exposed the quivering surface of the poet's language. But I have assumed neither that rhythm is a mere physical fact of language nor that the poem ceases its effect with our audible perception of it. The physical facts of significant rhythm subserve imaginative ends. It is toward fathoming these ends that we have directed this inquiry.

We pose one final question: how great a measure of poetic value is the prosodic test? The question is answered on every page of this book, but let Coleridge substantiate our implicit assumption that " 'The man that hath not music in his soul' can indeed never be a genuine poet":

> But the sense of musical delight, with the power of producing it, is a gift of imagination; and this together with the power of reducing multitude into unity of effect, and modifying a series of thoughts by some one predominant thought or feeling, may be cultivated and improved, but can never be learned. It is in these that 'poeta nascitur non fit.'[10]

Coleridge argues from the evidence of Shakespeare's *Venus and Adonis* and "the perfect sweetness of the versification. . . ." Sweetness or smoothness, of course, are not the only measures of prosodic value; strength, sureness of direction, and sinuosity are equally important in effecting rhythmic interest and vitality. The muscular cross-rhythms of Yeats give his lines great thrust and power; the polished textures of Wallace Stevens have their own expressive relevance to his meditations on imaginative process and aesthetic reality. The "music of poetry" need not be all perfect consonance; dissonance and rhythmic displacement may also give proof of a good ear.

The judgment of prosody remains, perhaps, the most highly subjective of critical acts. Critics hurl the terms "good ear" and "bad ear" with little understanding of the prosodic nature of the verse they criticize; often "a good ear" means no more than that the poet writes conventionally mellifluous verse. Ears are strange and highly selective instruments; like other organs of sense, their perceptions often filter through prejudice and preconception. A colleague, a dogmatic denouncer of Eliot, denied to me that Eliot possessed any "ear." When I offered, as an example of Eliot's astonishing lyric gifts, "Time and the bell have buried the day," he dismissed it as "an obvious jingle." Some hear exactly what they want to hear. My own judgments have undoubtedly been biased by what I hear as "good rhythm"; my neural structure responds unfavorably to lines like these:

> Never met you in the lyric arsenical meadows
> When children call and your heart goes stone in the bosom;
> At the orchard anguish never, nor ovoid horror . . .

The temptation is strong to dismiss "orchard anguish" and "ovoid horror" as the poetry of a "bad ear."

Earlier I characterized Empson's verse as metrically awkward, Roethke's as metrically provocative and beautiful. I still stick by these judgments—although I hesitate to label Empson a poet with a poor ear; rather, I would say his verse often succeeds in spite of its metrical harshness. A little odious comparison makes this abundantly clear:

> And now she cleans her teeth into the lake:
> Gives it (God's grace) for her own bounty's sake
> What morning's pale and the crisp mist debars . . .
>
> Empson, "Camping Out"

> By swoops of bird, by leaps of fish, I live.
> My shadow steadies in a shifting stream;
> I live in air; the long light is my home . . . .
>
> Roethke, "Meditations of an Old Woman"

No poet striving for melody would write "crisp mist debars"—an almost unpronounceable mouthful of labials and sibilants; the phrase clogs the rhythm. But Empson strives for "character"; his gritty lines move along an adequate, if not melodious, prosody. I *prefer* Roethke and the felt life which sings and animates his lines. His rhythms touch deeper and more delicate feelings; "the sense of musical delight" allows him the greater reach of imagination.

Prosodic analysis takes the measure of poetry's innermost life; I have examined this life with some care and, I hope, a great deal of love. Modern poetry has had more than fifty vigorous years busy with novelty and loud with self-advertisement. We must not, however, mistake noise and excitement for achievement. Turning to the major figures, we discover that their prosodic practice clearly isolates them from the small fry who swam in schools and practiced arhythmical *vers libres,* or "absolute rhythm," or composed, without demonstrable musical talent, "in the sequence of the musical phrase." The poetry which survives the wreckage of experiment and the parochialism of the movements emerges with qualities typical of all great poetry: urgency of subject, variety and resonance of language, and a prosody consonant with the ideas and evocative of the feelings.

Notes

NOTES TO THE PROLOGUE: IN THE DARK WOOD

1 Yvor Winters, *The Function of Criticism* (Denver, 1957), p. 99.

2 Robert Hillyer, *In Pursuit of Poetry* (New York, 1960), p. 31

3 Herbert J. C. Grierson, *Metaphysical Lyrics & Poems* (New York, 1959), p. xxiv.

4 Sidney Lanier, *The Science of English Verse,* Vol. II, Centennial Edition, *Works* (Baltimore, 1945), p. 135.

5 George Saintsbury, *A History of English Prosody,* I (London, 1906), 74.

6 C. S. Lewis, "Metre," *A Review of English Literature* I, 1 (January 1960), 46.

7 W. K. Wimsatt, Jr., and Monroe C. Beardsley, "The Concept of Meter: An Exercise in Abstraction," *PMLA,* LXXIV, 5 (December 1959), 588.

NOTES TO CHAPTER I: PROSODY AS RHYTHMIC COGNITION

I am indebted, in this chapter, to the work of Susanne Langer, and I have drawn on her *Feeling and Form* (New York, 1953) and the earlier *Philosophy in a New Key* (Cambridge, Massachusetts, 1942). Readers of these works will recognize that I not only use her ideas, but that I adapt some of her terminology to my own (I hope not inappropriate) uses. Rather than resort to the clumsy expediency of noting every obligation, I here make general acknowledgement to Mrs. Langer's theories.

1 Victor Zuckerkandl, *Sound and Symbol* (New York, 1956), p. 200.

2 Yvor Winters, *In Defense of Reason* (Denver, 1957), p. 546.

3 Donald Davie, *Articulate Energy* (New York, 1955), p. 31.

4 This is not a scansion of the line, but an attempt to analyze an important musical element, rate, or tempo.

5 Seymour Chatman, in *Style in Language,* ed. Thomas A. Sebeok (Cambridge, Mass., & New York, 1960), p. 151.

6 That horses can dance to music and dogs "count," notwithstanding. Human symbolic activity involves both physical response to the symbol and the ability to communicate the symbol's complex meanings. A horse can dance to music; he cannot tell us whether he prefers Beethoven to rock-and-roll.

7 The term belongs to D. W. Prall; see his *Aesthetic Analysis* (New York, 1936) and Susanne Langer's *Feeling and Form,* especially pp. 54–58.

8 Story has it that the young men at Oxford paraded around the quad to the meter of *Atalanta in Calydon.*

9 See Susanne Langer's *Philosophy in a New Key,* pp. 93–95; 201.

10 T. S. Eliot, *On Poetry and Poets* (New York, 1957), p. 32.

NOTES TO CHAPTER II: THE SCANSION OF THE ENGLISH METERS

1 Poems of Gerard Manley Hopkins (2d ed.; London, 1930), p. 5.

2 See Otto Jespersen's "Notes on Metre," in his *Linguistica* (Copenhagen, 1933), pp. 249–74. This article appeared originally in 1900.

3 Ronald Sutherland, "Structural Linguistics and English Prosody," *College English,* XX, 1 (October 1958), 14.

4 René Wellek and Austin Warren, *Theory of Literature* (New York, 1949), p. 159.

5 *Poetical Works of Robert Bridges* (2d ed.; London, 1953), p. 408.

6 Rhythmic movement here recalls Meredith's prosodic curiosity, "Love in the Valley."

7 T. S. Eliot, *Selected Essays, New Edition* (New York, 1950), p. 286.

8 Robert Bridges, *Milton's Prosody* (Oxford, 1921), p. 87.

9 Coventry Patmore, quoted by Saintsbury, *A History of English Prosody,* III (London, 1910), 440.

NOTES TO CHAPTER III: MODERN POETRY IN THE METRICAL TRADITION

1 Uncommon, that is, to first-rate poetry. We have curiosities tender or tedious, such as Hood's "Bridge of Sighs" and "The Charge of the Light Brigade."

2 W. B. Yeats, *Essays and Introductions* (New York, 1961), p. 163.

3 Susanne Langer, *Philosophy in a New Key* (New York: Mentor Books, 1948), p. 198.

4 In his *Practical Criticism* (New York: Harvest Books, n. d.), pp. 214 ff.

5 Robert Bridges, "Humdrum & Harum Scarum/A Lecture on Free Verse," *Collected Essays Papers* &c II, (London, 1928), 54–55.

6 Albert Guérard, *Robert Bridges* (Cambridge, Mass., 1942), p. 269.

7 *Ibid.,* Appendix A, 269–84.

8 Robert Bridges, *Milton's Prosody* (Oxford, 1921), pp. 92–105.

9 Guérard, *op. cit.,* pp. 276–77.

10 *Collected Essays Papers* &c. XV (London, 1933), 70–71. n.

11 *Ibid.,* pp. 87–91.

12 *Ibid.,* p. 91.

13 *Ibid.,* p. 90.

14 *The Testament of Beauty,* II, 204–10. I have added the initial capitals and regularized Bridges' purified spelling.

15 "Wintry Delights," pp. 405–8.

16 See W. J. Stone's "Classical Metres in English Verse." Bridges includes Stone's treatise as an appendix to the first edition of *Milton's Prosody* (Oxford, 1901), pp. 113–64. Stone formulates a system of rules for quantitative verse: like all such systems it is based on very personal and very queer ways of pronouncing English vowels. Stone's "quantities" must be accepted on religious faith; they are quite undemonstrable.

17 *Collected Poems of Edwin Muir* (New York, 1957), p. 13.

18 John Crowe Ransom, "The Strange Music of English Verse," *Kenyon Review,* XVIII, 3 (Summer 1956), 474.

19 "Criticism as Pure Speculation," in *The Intent of the Critic,* ed. Donald A. Stauffer (Princeton, 1941), pp. 110–11.

20. *Ibid.,* p. 122.

21 *The New Criticism* (Norfolk, Conn., 1941), p. 259.

22 "Criticism as Pure Speculation," p. 104.

23 John Crowe Ransom, "The Inorganic Muses," *Kenyon Review,* V, 2 (Spring 1943), 287–90.

24 *The New Criticism,* p. 234.

25 See Ransom's draft of the "metrical code" in "The Strange Music of English Verse," p. 471.

26 "The Strange Music of English Verse," p. 470.

27 *Ibid.*

28 *Ibid.*

29 *Ibid.,* p. 466.

30 Arnold Stein, "A Note on Meter," *Kenyon Review* (Summer 1956), 451–60.

31 "The Strange Music of English Verse," p. 473.

NOTES TO CHAPTER IV: NINETEENTH-CENTURY PRECURSORS

1 Wylie Sypher, *Rococo to Cubism in Art and Literature* (New York, 1960), p. 150.

2 George Saintsbury, *A History of English Prosody,* III, 513.

3 See Eliot's Introduction to Pound's *Selected Poems* (London, 1928 and 1933), pp. 6 ff.

4 Robert Graves, *The Crowning Privilege* (New York, 1956), p. 135.

5 We find good descriptive treatment in Gay Wilson Allen's *American Prosody* (New York, 1935); however, Professor Allen makes no attempt to search theoretical grounds.

6 See Donald Davie's *Articulate Energy,* pp. 85–91.

7 *Ibid.,* p. 129.

8 Saintsbury, *op. cit.,* p. 391.

9 Paull F. Baum, "Sprung Rhythm," *PMLA,* LXXIV, 4 (Sept. 1959), 424.

10 Yvor Winters, *In Defense of Reason,* p. 110.

11 *The Letters of Gerard Manley Hopkins to Robert Bridges,* ed. C. C. Abbott (London, 1935), p. 246.

12 James Joyce, *Finnegans Wake* (New York, 1939), pp. 215–16.

NOTES TO CHAPTER V: IMAGISM AND VISUAL PROSODY

1 *Literary Essays of Ezra Pound,* ed. T. S. Eliot (London, 1954), p. 3.

2 T. E. Hulme, "A Lecture on Modern Poetry," reprinted in Michael Roberts' *T. E. Hulme* (London, 1938), pp. 269–70.

3 *Ibid.,* p. 267.

4 *Ibid.,* p. 270.

5 *Ibid.,* p. 215, n. 2.

6 *Ibid.,* p. 262.

7 See the Preface to *Some Imagist Poets* (London, Boston, & New York, 1915), pp. vii–viii; also, *Literary Essays of Ezra Pound,* pp. 7, 13, 288, 385, and 401; and *The Letters of Ezra Pound,* ed. D. D. Paige (New York, 1950), p. 23.

8 *Notes sur la technique poétique,* pp. 3, 15. All quotations are from the second edition (Paris, 1925).

9 *Ibid.,* pp. 25–26.

10 *Literary Essays of Ezra Pound,* p. 4.

11 Stanley K. Coffman, Jr., *Imagism* (Norman, Oklahoma, 1951), p. 182.

12 H. D., *Helen in Egypt* (New York, 1961), p. 1.

13 *Literary Essays of Ezra Pound,* p. 4.

14 See Harold Whitehall's *Structural Essentials of English* (New York, 1956), especially pp. 16–18.

15 We find this version in Williams' *Collected Earlier Poems* (Norfolk, Conn., 1951), pp. 429–30. Some of these lines appear in a different context in *Paterson, Book Two* (New Classics Edition, 1948), p. 66.

16 *The Autobiography of William Carlos Williams* (New York, 1951), pp. 174–75.

17 See Williams' remarks on page 217 of *The Autobiography.*

18 *The Autobiography,* p. 264.

19 *Ibid.,* p. 256.

20 Joseph H. Summers, *George Herbert, His Religion and Art* (London, 1954), p. 123.

21 See R. P. Blackmur's *Form and Value in Modern Poetry* (New York: Doubleday Anchor Books; 1957), pp. 374–75.

22 Karl Shapiro, *Essay on Rime,* p. 23.

NOTES TO CHAPTER VI: "THE CELEBRATED METRIC" OF EZRA POUND

1 Paul Elmer More, *Shelburne Essays on American Literature,* ed. Daniel Aaron (New York, 1963), p. 230.

2 John Berryman, "The Poetry of Ezra Pound," *Partisan Review,* XVI, 4 (April 1949), 389.

3 *Ibid.,* p. 378.

4 *The Cantos of Ezra Pound: Some Testimonies* (New York, 1933), p. 16.

5 [T. S. Eliot], *Ezra Pound / His Metric and Poetry* (New York, 1917), p. 15.

6 See Introduction to Pound's *Selected Poems* (London, 1928), pp. 5, 18.

7 It was Gertrude Stein who called Pound "a village explainer: alright if you're a village."

8 Ezra Pound, *ABC of Reading* (New Directions Paperback, 1960), p. 206.

9 *Literary Essays of Ezra Pound,* ed. T. S. Eliot (London, 1954), p. 6.

10 *Ezra Pound / His Metric and Poetry,* p. 15.

11 Charles Norman, *Ezra Pound* (New York, 1960), p. 282.

12 *Autobiography of William Carlos Williams* (New York, 1951), p. 225.

13 According to Charles Norman, the Hungarian composer Tibor Serly "arranged" the sonata from a single voice line. Tibor added development, harmony, and sectioning.

14 *Antheil and the Treatise on Harmony* (Chicago, 1927).

15 *Literary Essays of Ezra Pound,* p. 6.

16 *ABC of Reading,* pp. 198–99.

17 Pound is distantly related, on his mother's side, to Longfellow—a fact Robert Graves mentions with malevolent relish. See *The Crowning Privilege* (New York, 1956), p. 128.

18 *Literary Essays of Ezra Pound,* pp. 12–13.

19 *Ibid.,* p. 93.

20 *Ezra Pound / His Metric and Poetry,* p. 12.

21 *Literary Essays of Ezra Pound,* p. 375.

22 Ezra Pound, "Harold Monro," *Criterion,* XI, 45 (July 1932), 590.

23 John Espey, *Ezra Pound's Mauberley* (Berkeley and Los Angeles, 1955), p. 42.

24 Letter to Felix E. Schelling, July 9, 1922; *The Letters of Ezra Pound,* p. 180.

25 *Ibid.,* p. 181.

26 See Pound's *The Spirit of Romance* (Norfolk, Conn., 1952), p. 8.

27 Hugh Kenner, *The Poetry of Ezra Pound* (Norfolk, Conn., 1951), p. 262.

28 So highly stylized, indeed, that I offer the following analogy. A Chinese reading the ideogram for man no more "sees" a *man* than we see in our letter *A* the Semitic *aleph* or ox.

29 Ernst Cassirer, *An Essay on Man* (Garden City, 1953), p. 219.

30 With *Section: Rock Drill* Pound changes to Arabic numerals for the *Cantos.*

As it now stands, it goes *Canto I* to *Canto LXXXIV;* then *Canto 85* to *Canto 116.*

31 *The Paris Review,* 28 (Summer-Fall 1962), 47–49.

32 Caedmon Record, TC 1122.

NOTES TO CHAPTER VII: T. S. ELIOT AND THE MUSIC OF POETRY

1 Stéphane Mallarmé, *Selected Prose Poems, Essays, and Letters,* tr. Bradford Cook (Baltimoré, 1956), p. 42.

2 Susanne K. Langer, *Philosophy in a New Key* (Cambridge, Mass., 1942), p. 261.

3 T. S. Eliot, *On Poetry and Poets* (New York, 1957), pp. 24–25.

4 Susanne K. Langer, *op. cit.,* p. 261.

5 My notation of the rhythms may be compared with Eliot's reading on H.M.V. Record C. 3598. Any attempt to note precisely a particular reading is necessarily mechanical. What I wish to show is the changes in tempo and movement. This can be done only by musical notation.

6 For example, see Bonamy Dobrée, *The Lamp and The Lute,* and E. M. Stephenson, *T. S. Eliot and the Lay Reader.*

7 *On Poetry and Poets,* p. 18.

8 T. S. Eliot, "Reflections on *Vers Libre,*" *The New Statesman,* VIII, 204 (March 3, 1917), 518–19.

9 Sister M. Martin Barry, *An Analysis of the Prosodic Structure of Selected Poems of T. S. Eliot* (Washington, D.C., 1948), p. 105.

10 ". . . the meter of *The Waste Land* . . . is a broken blank verse interspersed with bad free verse and rimed doggerel." In "T. S. Eliot or The Illusion of Reaction," *In Defense of Reason* (Denver, 1947), p. 500.

11 "Reflections on *Vers Libre.*"

12 Grover Smith, Jr., *T. S. Eliot's Poetry and Plays* (Chicago, 1956), p. 28.

13 Quoted in Helen Gardner, *The Art of T. S. Eliot* (London, 1949), p. 107.

14 Ezra Pound, *Literary Essays,* p. 421.

15 Winters remarks: "Mr. Eliot never got beyond Websterian verse, a bastard variety, although in *Gerontion,* he handled it with great skill—with far greater skill than Webster usually expends upon it." *In Defense of Reason,* p. 124.

16 "Reflections on *Vers Libre.*"

17 Yvor Winters, *In Defense of Reason* (Denver, 1947), p. 143.

18 Eliot owes to Tourneur and Middleton these passages worked into the texture of "Gerontion":

> Now to my tragic business, Look you, brother,
> I have not fashioned this only for show
> And useless property; no, it shall bear a part
> E'en in its own revenge. . . .

Tourneur, *The Revenger's Tragedy,* III, iv.

I am that of your blood was taken from you
For your better health; look no more upon't,
But cast it to the ground regardlessly,
Let the common sewer take it from distinction . . .

Middleton, *The Changeling,* V, iii

Grover Smith, Jr., makes a full accounting of Eliot's debts to the Jacobean dramatists; see *T. S. Eliot's Poetry and Plays,* p. 305, n. 1.

19 *Ibid.,* pp. 50–54.

20 In Lawrence Durrell's *Key to Modern British Poetry,* we find a fascinating arrangement of the opening section of *The Waste Land* as a radio play. Mr. Durrell separates out the characters and adds stage directions and sound effects.

21 It is also the stanza of Dryden's *Annus Mirabilis* and John Davies' *Nosce Teipsum.* Eliot comments (*On Poetry and Poets,* p. 159): "No one, not even Gray, has surpassed Davies in the use of the quatrain which he employed for *Nosce Teipsum . . .*"

22 On Harvard Vocarium record H. F. S. 3122 / 3124.

23 The italics in the last line are my own and correspond to Eliot's reading. He syncopates the line by stressing the off-beats.

24 "Poetry and Drama," in *On Poetry and Poets,* p. 88.

25 Edmund Wilson, *A Piece of My Mind* (Garden City, N.Y.: Doubleday), p. 138.

26 In the Senecan tragedies we find iambic trimeter in the dialogue; the choruses are set to a variety of lyric meters.

27 In *Memoirs of Hecate County* (Garden City, N.Y., 1946), p. 275.

28 "Poetry and Drama," in *On Poetry and Poets,* p. 92.

29 *Ibid.,* p. 91.

30 *Ibid.,* p. 92.

31 Donald Tovey, *The Main Stream of Music* (New York: Meridian Books, 1959), pp. 222–23.

32 See *T. S. Eliot's Poems and Plays,* p. 151.

33 On *Caedmon* record TC1045.

34 Donald Davie describes these lines as "syntax like music"—which is perhaps another way of saying Eliot is using his syntax as prosody. See *Articulate Energy,* pp. 90–91.

35 From a lecture given at New Haven and reported by F. O. Matthiessen. See *The Achievement of T. S. Eliot* (3rd ed.; New York, 1959), pp. 89–90, and the note, p. 96.

36 Herbert Howarth, "Eliot, Beethoven, and J. W. N. Sullivan," *Comparative Literature* IX (Summer 1957), 322–32.

37 J. W. N. Sullivan, *Beethoven, His Spiritual Development* (New York: Mentor Books, 1949), pp. 127–28.

38 See Howarth, *op. cit.* But also see my article, "Music and the Analogue of Feeling: Notes on Eliot and Beethoven," *The Centennial Review,* III (Summer 1959), 269–88.

39 I follow here a suggestion made by Helen Gardner: "I suspect that the element which prosodists will concentrate on in the future is the use [Eliot] makes of quantity to counterpoint his stress," *The Art of T. S. Eliot.*

40 "Reflections on *Vers Libre.*"

41 See Grover Smith, Jr., p. 286.

42 Donald Davie, "T. S. Eliot: The End of an Era," in *T. S. Eliot / A Collection of Critical Essays,* ed. Hugh Kenner (New Jersey, 1962), p. 195.

NOTES TO CHAPTER VIII: HART CRANE AND WALLACE STEVENS

1 Letter to Allen Tate, June 12, 1922. *The Letters of Hart Crane,* ed. Brom Weber (New York, 1952), p. 90.

2 Letter to Gorham Munson, January 5, 1923, *The Letters of Hart Crane,* pp. 114–15.

3 "Marlowe," *Selected Essays* (1950), p. 100.

4 *Conversations on the Craft of Poetry,* ed. Cleanth Brooks and R. P. Warren (New York, 1961), p. 59.

5 In *The Achievement of Wallace Stevens,* ed. Ashley Brown and Robert S. Haller (Philadelphia, 1962), p. 35.

6 *Ibid.,* p. 37.

7 *Ibid.,* pp. 41–45.

8 Marianne Moore early recognized the similarity of "Le Monocle" and "Prufrock." See her *Predilections* (New York, 1955), pp. 33–34.

9 Wallace Stevens, *The Necessary Angel* (New York, 1951), p. vii.

10 *Ibid.,* p. 81.

11 *Ibid.,* p. 73.

12 *Ibid.,* p. 78.

13 Marianne Moore, *Predilections,* p. 33.

14 Yvor Winters, *In Defense of Reason,* p. 448.

15 A line by line count of the first part, "It must be Abstract," may interest the statistically minded:

90 lines with 10 syllables
83 lines with 11 syllables
28 lines with 12 syllables
7 lines with 13 syllables
2 lines with 14 syllables

16 See F. O. Matthiessen, *The Achievement of T. S. Eliot* (3rd ed.; New York, 1959), pp. 89–90.

17 *Ibid.*

18 Thomas Mann, *Dr. Faustus* (New York, 1948), p. 54.

NOTES TO CHAPTER IX: THE GENERATION OF AUDEN

1 A. Alvarez, *The Shaping Spirit* (London, 1958), p. 87.

2 W. H. Auden, *The Dyer's Hand* (New York, 1962), p. 47.

3 See Eliot's "In Memoriam," *Selected Essays* (1950), p. 286.

4 These lines show Owen's experimentation with *pararhyme:*

> Leaves
> Murmuring by myriads in the shimmering trees.
> Lives
> Wakening with wonder in the Pyrenees.
> Birds
> Cheerily chirping in the early day.
> Bards
> Singing of summer scything thro' the hay.
>
> *From My Diary, July 1914*

5 The order of end words in the original Provençal form was:

123456, 615243, 364125, 532614, 451362, 246531,

the envoy, of three lines, was:

25, 43, 61.

6 This is Sebastian's monologue (*Collected Poetry* [New York, 1945], pp. 370–71); the order of end-words is 123456, 364125, 615243, 532614, 246531, 451362, 13, 54, 26.

7 Aristotle, *Poetics,* 1, 9.

8 Austin Warren, *Rage for Order* (Chicago, 1948), p. 33.

9 William York Tindall, *A Reader's Guide to Dylan Thomas* (New York, 1962), p. 133.

10 *Ibid.,* p. 11.

11 This does not seem one of the traditional forms of *cynghanedd croes,* but it is certainly as ingeniously effective as any specified by the Welsh Court Poets.

12 I am indebted to G. S. Fraser for calling this to my attention. See his *Vision and Rhetoric* (London, 1959), pp. 233–34.

13 *Ibid.,* pp. 234–35.

14 Remarks at a public reading. Recorded on Caedmon Record, TC1043.

15 *Encounter,* XI, 4 (October 1958), 49–55. My friend Mr. William B. Goodman brought this poem to my attention.

16 Untermeyer's *Combined Mid-Century Edition* (1950) of his *Modern American Poetry* omits both Roethke and Kunitz. The *New and Enlarged* Untermeyer (Eighth Edition, 1962) includes a selection from both poets. They have "arrived."

17 *Conversations on the Craft of Poetry,* ed. Cleanth Brooks and Robert Penn Warren (New York, 1961), pp. 48–62. This essay appeared earlier as "Some Remarks on Rhythm," *Poetry* 97, 1 (October 1960), 35–46.

18 *Ibid.,* p. 48.

19 *Ibid.,* p. 50.

20 *Ibid.,* p. 60.

21 *Ibid.,* pp. 61–62.

22 With important qualifications by Ralph J. Mills, Jr., in *Poets In Progress* (Northwestern, 1962), pp. 20–22.

23 *Conversations on the Craft of Poetry,* p. 62.

24 *Ibid.,* p. 59. Roethke is repeating, nearly verbatim, Eliot's remarks in "Reflections on *Vers Libre.*"

25 The phrase is Lowell's own; *ibid.,* p. 35.

26 *Ibid.,* p. 33.

27 *Land of Unlikeness* appeared in a limited edition of only 250 copies (Cummington Press, 1944).

28 A full exposition of the Miltonic resemblances is given by Hugh B. Staples in his *Robert Lowell, The First Twenty Years* (New York, 1962), p. 45.

29 *Conversations on the Craft of Poetry,* p. 38.

30 Lowell speaking in an interview published in *The Paris Review,* 25 (Winter-Spring 1961), p. 66.

31 *Ibid.,* p. 66.

32 *Ibid.,* p. 67.

33 *Ibid.,* pp. 70–71.

NOTES TO THE EPILOGUE: THE FOOTSTEPS OF THE MUSE

A remark of Paul Valéry suggested the title of the Epilogue: "Even if we measure the footsteps of the goddess, note their frequency and *average* length, we are still far from the secret of her instantaneous grace," from *The Art of Poetry* (New York: Vintage Books, 1961), p. 88.

1 *A History of English Prosody,* III, 512–13.

2 *Ibid.*

3 Donald Francis Tovey, *The Main Stream of Music* (New York: Meridian Books, 1959), p. 165. "The fact is that every technical problem connected with a work of art has its aesthetic result. The process misnamed by Horace the concealment of art is the sublimation of technique into aesthetic results."

4 See Isaiah Berlin's *The Hedgehog and the Fox* (New York, 1953), pp. 1–4.

5 Denis de Rougemont, "There is no 'Modern Music,'" *Encounter,* III, 2 (August 1954), 50.

6 Ortega Y Gasset, *The Dehumanization of Art* (New York: Anchor Books, 1956), p. 4.

7 A recent poem of Stanley Kunitz, "The Mound-Builders" (*Partisan Review* 1963), is written in a free meter very close to Lowell's. This is a departure for Kunitz who has always maintained iambic discipline.

8 Karl Shapiro, *Essay on Rime,* p. 17.

9 Ezra Pound to Harriet Monroe, January 1915. *The Letters of Ezra Pound,* ed. D. D. Paige (New York, 1950), p. 49.

10 *Biographia Literaria,* 11, Chap. XV, ed. J. Shawcross (London, 1907), p. 14.

Index